GOD'S MISSION IN THE CITIES

OF THE BIBLE

Jude Tiersma-Watson

Christina T. Accornero

Charles E. Van Engen

Editors

Stephen Burris, General Editor

Urban Loft Publishers | Skyforest, CA

God's Mission in the Cities of the Bible

Urban Loft Publishers
P.O. Box 6
Skyforest, CA 92385
www.urbanloftpublishers.com

Senior Editors: Stephen Burris & Kendi Howells Douglas
Graphics: Brittnay Parsons
Cover Design: Elisabeth Arnold

ISBN-13: 978-1-949625-13-4

Made in the U.S

Table of Contents

Acknowledgements

For a number of years, Jude and Chuck talked about creating a sequel to their earlier book about mission in the city: *God So Loves the City* (MARC, 1994; reprinted in 2009 by Wipf & Stock). But every attempt to envision a sequel did not seem to work. They created three or four draft tables of contents but were not happy with any of them.

Then Stephen Burris invited them to lunch in Pasadena. He broached the subject of doing a new book about mission in the city. During that conversation, an idea began to emerge. What would it look like to study the histories and cultures of cities mentioned in the Bible and ask, What might God's mission in those cities look like?

Thank you to Stephen Burris and Urban Loft for being willing to publish this work, despite the length of time it has taken for us to create it.

We are also deeply grateful to the authors of the chapters. Every person whom we invited to participate in this project accepted our invitation. All did original research on the history and culture of the city we assigned them. Their enthusiasm about the concept and commitment to the project were deeply encouraging to us. This has been very much a shared endeavor.

Thank you to Jean Van Engen for copy-editing and formatting the chapters, as we received them from the authors. You set us up to be able to work constructively as editors on each chapter.

We hope the readers of this work will increase in their love for the cities of our Twenty-first Century world and gain new insights and deeper understanding of God's unique contextualized mission in the city.

The Editors
October 30, 2020

Introduction

by Jude Tiersma-Watson[1]

The seed for this book emerged during a dinner conversation with Steve Burris, Chuck Van Engen, and me in a family restaurant in Pasadena. Steve had just acquired Urban Loft Publishing and was eager to see more urban mission books published. During our conversation, we were surprised to realize that no resource existed that examined the various cities in the Bible, their contexts, and histories. We began asking what we might learn from these cities for urban mission in our world and brainstorming how such a volume might look, what cities should be included, and who we might invite to write about these biblical cities.

Each author was invited to research the history and context of the city they had been assigned, study the scripture texts related to that city, and then draw missiological themes or metaphors relevant to our times. In many cases, it proved to be a challenging assignment. Some cities like Athens are hardly mentioned at all in scripture while references to others like Babylon and Jerusalem are so extensive it is daunting. We are grateful to each of the authors for their diligent and careful research.

---

[1] Jude Tiersma-Watson (Ph.D. in Intercultural Studies, Fuller Theological Seminary) is Associate Professor of Urban Mission at Fuller Theological Seminary. She has lived for 30 years in central Los Angeles, sharing life with her neighbors as part of InnerChange/Novo. She co-edited *God So Loves the City* with Charles Van Engen and has written numerous chapters and articles. Jude is especially interested in the ways that our context forms and transforms our life and faith.

The move toward urbanization is now well documented. Mission in and with cities continues to be one of the great missiological challenges of our times. But one cannot simply move to a city and know what is needed. To develop a contextually appropriate and biblically grounded mission theology in the city, missional workers need to take history, context, and biblical text seriously.[2] There is no shortcut for the hard work of exegeting context, listening to the city and to the biblical texts. Our hope is that this edited volume will add fresh perspectives of biblical approaches to mission in the cities of our world.[3]

In addition to history, context, biblical material, and missiological themes, we were also looking for metaphors that might contribute to our understanding of the various cities. What is the ethos of the city? What drives a city to become what it is? What metaphor describes it? Some of the cities lent themselves more to metaphors than others. Metaphors help us structure our world, or in this case, our city. A metaphor can be central to how we understand a city, both in the biblical cities as well as the cities in which we find ourselves. Metaphors integrate knowledge, creating an interface of the numerous factors and variables that make up the life of a city.

Metaphors powerfully shape perceptions and can cast a vision of reality. We live into metaphors and cities can live into their metaphors. These can be either positive or negative or a bit of both and need to be evaluated as situations change over time. For example, for years, the United States described itself as a melting pot. This metaphor was intended to help the various European cultures that might have been at war in Europe live together in this country. But we realize now that this is an assimilationist metaphor

---

[2] For a method of listening to city stories, exegeting the context and applying biblical truths in an integrative approach to urban mission, see Charles Van Engen and Jude Tiersma, edits. *God So Loves the City: Seeking a Theology for Urban Mission;* reprinted by Wipf & Stock Publ., Eugene, OR, 2009, particularly pages 241-285.

[3] Note: As editors, we have chosen to use nondiscriminatory language where possible. Women have always lived in cities but often without access to the systems of power in the city. This was not God's intent but due to the patriarchy of the times. By using nondiscriminatory language, we seek to affirm the full participation of women in God's mission in our cities.

that strengthens the hegemony of the dominant culture and contributes to erasing other cultures present in a city. As one of my young African American friends used to say, "In the melting pot some of us just melted away." Some have suggested a salad bowl as an alternative, but that too has its limits. One important question is who has the power to set the metaphor? Is it an inclusive metaphor or does it exclude groups of people?

In my city, Los Angeles, as we have struggled to describe our multicultural city, the metaphor we use has been a point of discussion. One mayor used mosaic as a metaphor. But in a mosaic, there are clear borders delineating the different parts of the mosaic, they make a beautiful image but there is no interface between the parts. Is that our reality, our vision? What describes our multicultural, multiracial, multifaith city? A salad? Patchwork? Kaleidoscope? These metaphors are descriptive but also cast a vision for where we are headed. Pondering the metaphor of a particular city has benefits for the future of that city. Our authors wrestle with a metaphor for their biblical city.

The book has a simple organization. After this introduction, except for Jerusalem, the chapters are listed in alphabetical order according to city name. A short bio for the authors is embedded in the first footnote of each chapter.

We chose to place Jerusalem last in this collection for several reasons. First, it is unique in the way the Bible deals with this "city of God", sometimes called "Mount Zion". Secondly, it is associated with the eschatological hope of Israel and the Church for a new and transformed future. Thirdly, to mention a few of the metaphors, in the new Jerusalem the Lamb will one day sit on the throne and reign over a new heaven and new earth. And the "river of the water of life" flows from the throne, through the streets of the new Jerusalem, flanked on either side by the tree of life "whose leaves are for the healing of the nations." So, to signal Jerusalem's special place in the biblical narrative, we chose to place it last. Following are brief summaries of each chapter.

1. Antioch – God's mission amid multicultural networks. Miriam Adeney describes the flavor of this region and shows us that like the diverse, flavorful foods of the region, so the peoples are diverse. The church and leadership in Antioch were multicultural from the start. We are reminded that in our current world, this is true for our churches as well as the leadership of our churches.

2. Athens – God's mission among contending worldviews. Nathan Hieb describes the philosophies and resulting worldviews that compete with each other in Athens, as well as Paul's approach to them. Paul did not back away from these philosophies but was able to engage the Athenians in the space of competing worldviews while faithfully proclaiming the truth of Jesus Christ. How might this approach be missiologically important for our cities today?

3. Babylon – God's mission related to judgment and redemption in the city. Jerusalem and Babylon are both mentioned many times in scripture, as metaphors for a city of peace or a city of human ambition. Both serve as metaphors beyond the physical city in scripture. Jorge Barro challenges urban Christians – that we are not to live in a Babylon as passive people. Rather we live as God's people, called to stand up to the injustices of Babylon. Amidst a world filled with injustice, this message is so needed in 21st Century cities.

4. Capernaum – God's mission on the borders. Sarita Gallagher Edwards raises the question of why Jesus chose a remote border town to center his ministry and asks what this means for 21st Century missiology. Instead of placing his ministry in a center of power, Jesus chose a small, insignificant village on the edges of power, reminding us that the ways of Jesus are not located at the center of empires but in the borderlands.

5. Corinth – God's mission of rediscovering wisdom. Jayakumar Christian shares his wisdom and reminds the church of the call to be a prophetic community living out the foolishness of the gospel in

God's space in the city. God's people must refuse to be co-opted by abusive systems that damage the souls of those on the margins.

6. Egypt – God's mission among displaced peoples. Daniel Rodriquez, with the region of Egypt functioning as a city, sees the mission of God as a framework to view the entire scripture. He describes the Exodus narrative as a model for redemptive mission with diaspora peoples, very relevant in our cities that are filled with diaspora peoples.

7. Ephesus – God's mission of peace and reconciliation amidst beauty, myth, and poetry. Mary Motte highlights (in a delightful right-brain approach) the role of imagery and beauty in the ancient city of Ephesus. The message of Ephesus that opens a space for peacemaking and the reconciliation made possible in Christ is so needed in a world hungering for peace and reconciliation.

8. Nineveh – God's mission of love and the enemy. Mary Glenn contrasts the differing ways that Jonah and God see the city of Nineveh. Jonah could not get past Nineveh as the enemy, yet God saw much more. God looked at Nineveh through the lens of God's missional and compassionate heart. This question of how we see our cities continues to be foundational to the ways we approach our own cities.

9. Philippi – God's mission of hope amid distress and suffering. Enoch Kim takes us through Philippi and draws out the theme of Christ's sufferings, especially relevant in cities where Christians are the minority. The message of Philippi reminds us of the believers' purposeful suffering for Christ, the value of relationships and the hope of Christ in the midst of despair.

10. Rome – God's mission that the wolf and the Lamb live and eat together. Rob Gallagher describes the metaphor of the oppressive power of the wolf, long a metaphor for Rome. How are we to live as God's people surrounded by the oppression of Rome? We are to take

the humble posture of the Lamb, knowing the final vision is that the lamb and the wolf will live and eat together.

11. Jerusalem – God's mission of longing for the City of God. Jerusalem is the final chapter, despite starting with a "J." The Bible begins in a garden but ends in a city, the City of God, Jerusalem. David Leong goes beyond the externals of the city to the metaphorical symbolism of Jerusalem as the fulfillment of what we live for on this earth and beyond, what we have longed for whether we knew it or not.

Chuck Van Engen concludes with some thoughts as to how the various metaphors of cities in the Bible that we have considered in this volume may together offer us a vision of the *Missio Dei* in our cities today.

Part of our process was a video call once a week to edit and discuss together each chapter. During the calls, we often remarked how much we had not known and now learned about these cities and what they mean for us today. Our hope is that the reader will also be inspired and encouraged to look deeper into the cities mentioned in the Bible and learn from them, as we did, for a wider and more robust understanding of God's mission in the ever-expanding cities of our world today.

Chapter 1: Antioch

by Miriam Adeney[4]

God's Mission Amid Multicultural Networks

Long before its confirmation in the Jerusalem Council, the call to transcend boundaries resonated with the multicultural church in Antioch. This seems to have been the first congregation to recognize that if God's grace truly extends universally, we should share that good news intentionally, beyond ethnic and national borders. So, under the leading of the Spirit, the believers in Antioch anointed Paul and Barnabas and sent them out as missionaries. The result was a necklace of churches in various cities, countries and language groups spread across the Greek world and eventually across the Roman empire. Here the great movement of Christian mission began. If you or I were sent as cross-cultural missionaries to Syria today, what would we want to learn from the story of the multicultural church in multicultural Antioch to help us understand that context today?

Introduction

Breakfast on the Mediterranean coast of the Levantine means warm fresh pita bread, soft goat cheese, local apricot jam, big homegrown olives,

---

4 Miriam Adeney (Ph.D. in anthropology from Washington State University) is an anthropologist and missiologist at Seattle Pacific University in Seattle, Washington. With a focus on Southeast Asia and Latin America, her passions include global Christianity, world religions, gender, oral art genres, economic community development, multiethnic ministry, diasporas, training writers for publication, and preparing workers for cross-cultural living, An award-winning author and writing coach, her many books include *Kingdom Without Borders The Untold Story of Global Christianity, Daughters of Islam: Building Bridges with Muslim Women,* and *God's Foreign Policy: Practical Ways to Help the World's Poor.*

tomatoes, mint, cucumbers, and robust coffee. With a similar richness, the church in Antioch in biblical times displayed a mélange of flavors from different sources that complemented each other, so that the delectable whole was more than the sum of the parts.

This was the church where Gentiles were full members along with Jews almost from the beginning. That raised issues that in turn precipitated some of the key events in the early church. Antioch was where Jewish believers began witnessing actively to Gentiles, resulting in a truly multicultural congregation (Acts 11:19-21). Antioch was the destination to which the Jerusalem elders sent their conclusions when they had decided what the gospel required of Gentiles (15:23-33). Antioch was the base for many of the apostle Paul's transnational missionary journeys (13-14, 15:35-20). Interestingly, Antioch also was the place where Jesus' followers were first called Christians (11:26).

Antioch Before Rome

Syria, the region where Antioch is located, boasts the oldest continuously inhabited cities in the world: Damascus and Aleppo. The Ugaritic alphabet of the area may be the world's oldest alphabet. By 3500 BCE, the Ebla civilization flourished there. By 1200 BCE the Phoenician culture had developed on the shore of the Mediterranean not far from Antioch, planting colonies as far away as Malta, Sicily, Spain, and North Africa. Around 900 BCE, Assyrian power moved in. They introduced the Aramaic language, which held sway until Arabic–speaking Muslims arrived around 650 CE. Babylonians and Egyptians battled over this ground periodically.

In 539 BCE, a leader named Cyrus took Syria from Babylonia and founded the Achaemenid or Persian empire. In 330 BCE, Alexander the Greek conquered the Persians. However, Alexander died young, without an adult heir, and without sufficiently consolidating his governance over the conquered territory. The administration of his empire was divided between four of his generals. One of these was Seleucus I Nicator. This was the man who founded the city of Antioch.

In the division of the empire, Seleucus was awarded the region of Babylonia. He was ambitious, and in time expanded his rule enormously, absorbing central Anatolia, Lebanon, Persia, Mesopotamia, and parts of Afghanistan, Pakistan, and Turkmenistan. The Seleucid Empire was second only to Alexander's in its extent. When he turned to the region of Antioch, Seleucus first established the port city of Seleucia on the Mediterranean, expanding a trading post named Pieria. Then, twenty miles inland, he laid the foundations of Antioch, naming it for his son. The river Orontes runs through Antioch, and Mount Silpius stands at its back. Seleucus planted cypress trees in a watered and woodsy area known as Daphne.[5] Unfortunately, since Antioch was on the northern edge of the Dead Sea Rift, its location was marred by earthquakes, which caused destruction throughout its history.

Recognized as the capital of the western region of the Seleucid Empire, the city grew. Successive rulers developed more sections until, under Antiochus IV Epiphanes, Antioch had become a tetrapolis in which four quarters were circled by an outside wall, as well as being separated by interior walls. One district took shape on an island in the river. During the succeeding centuries, this island disappeared from sight as the channel of the Orontes silted up. However, recent excavations have uncovered the ruins, including two ancient cemeteries and a wall constructed by Justinian in the sixth century. The Seleucid empire lasted from 312 to 63 BCE. Around 83 BCE Antioch was taken by Tigranes of Armenia. Twenty years later the city was in turn taken from Armenia by the Romans.

Roman Antioch

One of the largest cities in the Roman empire, Antioch was surpassed only by Rome in Italy and Alexandria in Egypt. The three cities comprised a

---

[5] Matthew Spinka. *Chronicle of John Malalas, Books VIII-XVIII, translated from the Church Slavonic*. Princeton, N.J.: Department of Art and Archeology of Princeton University, 1940, pp. 13-15.

triangle, with Rome on the north shore of the Mediterranean, Alexandria on the south, and Antioch on the east, located north of Palestine in southern Turkey. Estimates of Antioch's population during the Roman period range between 100,000 and 600,000 people.

Besides its key location at the eastern end of the Mediterranean, Antioch was a nexus for international communication. From the west came seafaring ships. To the east stretched the Silk Road and other key trade routes. North were the Turkic peoples, and to the south were the Jews and Arabs. All met and mingled in Antioch, in a rather free-thinking environment. Nomads, travelers, and traders from diverse cultures who had survived sea storms and desert sand–exchanged goods and ideas in Antioch. This city was a key network node.

Under the Romans, Antioch was classified as a free city, which meant it enjoyed a fair amount of self–government. Capital of the Roman province of Syria, it also served as headquarters for a Roman legion in Syria. Emperor Julius Caesar visited in 47 BCE. Other emperors like Augustus and Tiberius contributed to the city's development and beautification. Later emperors Trajan and Julian also spent time there.

Antioch was known as "The Beautiful." The area named Daphne lay on a plateau which rose more than 300 feet above the city. From the springs on Daphne's plateau at Antioch, aqueducts carried water down to the heart of the city. Hadrian built one of the aqueducts, and several are named for Caesars. Daphne was also the site of large pleasure villas. A theater was built there in a natural bowl formed by the hills, where patrons could look down the slope and enjoy the view of the valley of the Orontes.

Among the notable constructions in Antioch was a temple to Apollo, an even larger temple to Jupiter, and shrines to other gods, including those associated with mystery cults. There was a palace and a forum and many public baths. Large streets were laid out in an orderly pattern. Herod the Great paved a broad avenue through the city and erected colonnades along its route. At least one street was paved with granite. The apex of all of these achievements, the outstanding edifice in Antioch, was the circus, modeled on the Circus Maximus in Rome, and one of the largest in the empire. Its length was 1,610 feet (nearly five times the length of a modern football field) and its width 98 feet. It could seat 80,000 spectators who came mainly to watch chariot racing.

Today, we can see the remnants of spectacular floor mosaics throughout the city. These beautifully crafted works have been dated from 100 to 500 CE. Their subjects include a drinking contest between Heracles and Dionysus, various gods swimming amid the fishes of the ocean, hunting scenes, landscapes, and "an illustrated calendar in which the months of the year are personified as little figures carrying fruits and other symbols of the months."[6]

Amid materialism, paganism, and Roman power, there was also a thriving Jewish community of perhaps 20,000 people, possibly ten per cent of the city's population.[7] These Jewish men and women enjoyed the freedom to worship Jehovah and live according to the Mosaic law. In Antioch, they were accorded the right of citizenship and "privileges equal to those of the Macedonians and Greeks who were the inhabitants."[8] They were much less segregated than the Jews of Alexandria, for example. During the persecution which took place throughout the region in 66-70 CE, Antioch's Jews were spared in contrast to those in other Gentile cities. Quite a few proselytes and uncircumcised sympathizers attended the synagogues in Antioch.

Despite its beauty, power, free speech, tolerance, and respect for foreigners, Antioch had a reputation for immorality. Complaining about superstition and licentiousness spreading into Rome from the East, Juvenal described it as flowing from the Orontes into the Tiber.[9] Roman power,

---

[6] Jack Finegan. *Light from the Ancient Past: The Archeological Background of Judaism and Christianity*. Princeton, NJ: Princeton University Press, 1959, p. 340.

[7] Craig Keener. *The IVP Biblical Background Commentary for the New Testament*. Downers Grove, IL: InterVarsity Press, 2014, p. 354.

[8] Josephus, *Antiquities of the Jews*, XII: iii.

[9] Juvenal, *The Satires of Juvenal*. Translation by G. G. Ramsay. New York: G. P. Putnam's Sons, 1918, p. 37.

material competition, pagan gods, and freethinking did not foster righteousness. Something more was needed.

The Multicultural Church in Antioch

A church that knows its historical and multicultural roots is a beautiful thing. Each culture arranges life a little differently, with particular emphasis, priorities, and nuances. In each culture, elders have stories. Musicians have songs. Language shapes thought. Food smells like home and family and occasionally like a grand celebration. Each culture has its own patterns for generating income, training the next generation, resolving conflict, giving to those in need. Christians in each culture differ as they interpret scripture, teach, preach, witness, counsel, and theologize. It is a beautiful thing when a church is aware of its heritage, values it, and draws from it.

Due to the persecution of Christians (both Jewish and Greek) in Jerusalem, many of the followers of Jesus, as followers of "The Way", ended up in multicultural Antioch. In Antioch, due to exuberant witnessing and the sovereign blessing of the Holy Spirit, the church was flooded by non-Jewish Greeks who worshipped Jesus but knew nothing of the Mosaic law. According to Acts 11:22-24, when "news of this reached the ears of the church at Jerusalem...they sent Barnabas to Antioch. When he arrived and saw the evidence of the grace of God, he was glad and encouraged them to remain true to the Lord with all their hearts. He was a good man, full of the Holy Spirit and faith, and a great number of people were brought to the Lord."

Coming from a Jewish-Cypriot priestly family, Barnabas was an early member of the church in Jerusalem. Throughout his lifetime, Barnabas would play the role of peacemaker, resolving conflicts, and helping others make wise decisions. When the Gentiles in Antioch came to faith in Jesus, and Barnabas arrived and saw the wonderful new things that God was doing, he realized that it would be wise to have an experienced Christian teacher among these young believers. Ideally, the teacher would feel at home with non-Jewish life and worldviews yet would also understand the Jewish Scriptures thoroughly, and would be able to testify to a robust experience with Jesus. Which Christian leader would fit those requirements? And who would be free to come? Barnabas could have traveled 300 miles south to Jerusalem to find a teacher. Instead, Barnabas remembered Paul and traveled 100 miles northwest to Tarsus to invite that former tormentor to join him in Antioch.

As the followers of Jesus in Antioch grew in understanding and faith, they received a new vision. Abraham had been blessed to be a blessing to all the families of the earth. Isaiah had envisioned God's people as a light to the nations. Jesus had come for all and had commissioned his disciples to witness to all peoples.

> You will be my witnesses in Jerusalem, and in all Judea and Samaria, and to the ends of the earth (Acts 1:8).
> Go, therefore, and make disciples of all nations (Matthew 28:19).

Paul in particular had a sense of call to the peoples of many cultures who had never heard the gospel. He reiterates this often throughout his writings. In the book of Romans, for example, he begins by acknowledging his "debt" to share the gospel with both Jews and Greeks (1:14-16). He wraps up the book of Romans by stating his intention to evangelize in Spain, the outer edge of the known world. "It has always been my ambition to preach the gospel where Christ was not known" (15:20-24). Paul and Barnabas would consult the elders in Jerusalem "in response to a revelation" about "the gospel that I preach among the Gentiles." The elders, Paul says, "saw that I had been entrusted with the task of preaching the gospel to the Gentiles, just as Peter had been to the Jews....They recognized the grace given to me and agreed that we should go to the Gentiles" (Gal. 2:2, 7-9).

So, as the believers in Antioch worshipped, they heard the Holy Spirit say, "Set apart for me Barnabas and Saul for the work to which I have called them" (Acts 13:2). After confirming this through fasting and prayer, the church members placed their hands on the two men and sent them off. Sent on their way by the Holy Spirit, the pair went down to Seleucia and sailed from there to Cyprus, where Barnabas had kin and connections.

After planting the church in numerous places and cultures, the pair headed home. To Jerusalem? Or Tarsus? No, they headed to Antioch. That was their sending church and home base. The church in Antioch had prayed for them and now waited with great anticipation for their face-to-face reports.

> They sailed back to Antioch, where they had been committed to the grace of God for the work they had now completed. On arriving there, they gathered the church together and reported all that God had done through them and how he had opened the door of faith to the Gentiles. And they stayed there a long time with the disciples (Acts 14:26-28).

How Much Can We Contextualize?

Meanwhile, in the larger church of Paul's day disputes simmered. Plenty of believers felt nervous about setting up Gentile-dominated worship groups, omitting so much of the law that had marked and guided God's people down through the centuries. Moses had received the law and warned the people never to let it go. Josiah had rediscovered the law after centuries of dissipation and dissolution and led the community in a new start in righteousness. Ezra commanded the reading of the law to all the people, and its explanation in Aramaic so that they would be sure to understand it. Jesus himself said that not one jot or tittle of the law would be erased (Matt.5:17-19). How then could these missionaries from Antioch treat it so casually? And circumcision! God personally mandated that through Abraham. It was the key distinctive.

> Some men came down from Judea to Antioch and were teaching the brothers, "Unless you are circumcised, according to the custom taught by Moses, you cannot be saved." This brought Paul and Barnabas into sharp dispute and debate with them (Acts 15:1-2).

The famous gathering of the Jerusalem Council was the result. Paul and Barnabas were sent by the Antioch church as delegates to that meeting. On the way, passing through Phoenicia and Samaria, they shared with believers "how the Gentiles had been converted. This made all the brothers very glad" (15:3). Once in Jerusalem, they were welcomed by the apostles and elders, "to whom they reported everything God had done through them" (15:4).

Then the formal dispute began. Must the Gentiles be circumcised and obey the law of Moses? There was much discussion. Finally, Peter stood up. He had experienced a personal and complex encounter with this issue. Even before the church at Antioch had begun, Peter had been summoned by a vision to the home of a Roman centurion who feared God. Under the Spirit's direction, Peter shared the gospel there, and the household believed! The Spirit directed Peter to baptize them (without circumcision) and to eat with them foods that the Mosaic law had banned (Acts 10). Later, at the Council of Jerusalem, he was asked to justify this to Christian leaders. This he did, simply recounting the story and the obvious presence of the Holy Spirit in the new disciples.

Eventually, James, the brother of Jesus, and the recognized leader of the Council spoke up. Would James require obedience to the Old Testament laws from the new believers? In actuality, a plain reading of James' words shows that he commended deeds of charity rather than legal or ritual acts. James outlined a compromise. He quoted the Jewish prophets, especially Amos, about the Gentiles coming to God. He recommended simple standards. "The few requirements James suggests they impose may derive from requirements of Gentiles living among Israelites in Leviticus 17-18, and are representative of the handful of laws that Jewish tradition came to believe that God gave Noah."[10] Nowhere on James' list is circumcision.

The multicultural church in Antioch was the pivot of this famous decision. After the decision was reached, it was expressed in an elegantly written letter that was sent to Antioch. Of course, it would be circulated elsewhere, but its first destination was the multicultural congregation with its glowing international outreach. Like at Antioch, an issue that arises in multicultural contexts and churches around the world has to do with the

---

[10] Keener, *op. cit.*, 366.

relationship of the Gospel to multiple cultures. This issue continues to vibrate today. On one hand, we want to express the Gospel in local terms, connected to local values. On the other hand, we want to stay true to the meaning of the gospel. That was the Jerusalem Council's concern. Inevitably, it is also ours. Christians in every culture must wrestle with it. Antioch faced that challenge first.

Luke, the man who recorded and wrote this narrative is thought to have been a Gentile born in Antioch. Trained as a physician, he was also a careful researcher and writer (Luke 1:1-4). He became a close companion of Paul and may have written the books of Luke and Acts during Paul's imprisonments. Luke gave special attention to women and the sick and the poor. Luke had a well—educated literary style and a scientific mind, and today is considered one of the best historians of his time. Like Paul, Luke may have spoken three languages: Aramaic, Greek, and Latin. Free—thinking, multicultural Antioch may have helped to shape him.

Antioch Christianity Through the Centuries

The story of God's mission and the church's life in Antioch does not end with the first Christian century. A brief historical summary may be helpful. Around 650 CE Islam arrived. Damascus, immediately to the east of Antioch, became the center of Umayyad Islamic civilization. However, the Umayyads could not conquer the Anatolian plateau, and Antioch was pressured from both sides for 300 years. In 969 CE the Byzantine empire recaptured the area, conquered in turn in 1078 CE by Seljuk Turks.

Twenty years later, the First Crusade swept in. The Siege of Antioch resulted in a three-day massacre of both Muslim and Christian citizens. Overall, the Crusaders brought great shame to the name of Christ. Later a Muslim invader named Baibar would raze the city and kill or enslave nearly all the people. Meanwhile, further to the east, as Mongols swept across the continent, trade routes moved north. Antioch's economy declined significantly. The region experienced repeated earthquakes and cholera epidemics. Ottoman power flourished intermittently from 1350 to World War I, after which the French controlled the area. Syria became independent in 1946. Through it all, the church has been there. Theologians and martyrs, ecclesiastical administrators and writers, evangelists, and peacemakers all have emerged out of the church in Antioch.

One of the most renowned sons of the Antioch church was John Chrysostom (347-407 CE). He rose from that local congregation to become Patriarch or Archbishop of Constantinople. During his lifetime and still today, Chrysostom is honored for the fine craftsmanship of his writings and talks, his attention to the biblical text, his care for the poor, his passion for missions, and his emphasis on a pure and holy life. Because of his eloquence, Chrysostom was known as "golden-tongued." He was also prolific. Only Augustine composed more writings that have survived to the present time. Of the hundreds of exegetical homilies that Chrysostom produced, 67 are on Genesis, 59 on Psalms, 90 on Matthew, 88 on John, and 55 on Acts. His liturgical compositions also are valued. Even today, the Roman Catholic catechism cites him in eighteen sections, particularly on prayer.

Chrysostom's heritage involved multiple cultures. He grew up in Antioch with a father who was a Roman general and a mother who was reputedly a Christian. He studied under a local rhetorician and developed a love for language, literature, and oratory. Then he moved on to study theology, after which he spent two years as a hermit. Extreme asceticism damaged his kidneys and stomach, and he was forced to return to regular life.

When he was ordained, a schism was nearly splitting the church in Antioch. Chrysostom managed to keep clear of the feud, and later mediated a reconciliation on a larger scale between church leaders of Alexandria, Rome, and Antioch, achieving a unity which had not existed for seventy years.

Meanwhile, his sermons attracted people. Just before he began his ministry, local citizens had gone on a rampage in which they defaced statues of the emperor. Imperial retaliation loomed. Chrysostom preached 20 sermons urging people to stop their rioting. These caught the attention of the populace.[11] Many converted to the Christian faith. Chrysostom championed foreign missions, an appropriate Antiochian heritage. As Patriarch, he commissioned evangelists to pagan peoples, including the Goths. However, one set of his writings does sound somewhat racist. These are eight talks titled *Against the Jews,* delivered during his first years of ministry in Antioch. Yet, notwithstanding the title, these are not anti-Semitic. They were addressed to Christians who had become too preoccupied with Jewish rituals and legalities. As a man from Antioch, John Chrysostom drew on the rich multicultural experience of his birthplace to serve his generation with wisdom and skill and heart. He is honored as a saint in the Catholic, Eastern Orthodox, and Anglican churches.

Sadly, in the eras that followed, schisms plagued Antiochian churches. The bishop of Antioch in the fourth century governed an area extending from Turkey to Iran, serving the largest number of Christians in the known world. By the next century, however, the Council of Ephesus (431 CE) and the Council of Chalcedon (451 CE) precipitated massive church splits. These were rooted in different interpretations of the nature of Christ. A further disagreement, the Schism of 1054 CE, broke communion between Catholic and Eastern Orthodox churches. The Muslim-dominated society allowed Christians some freedoms with limitations. The Crusader heritage continued to contaminate the church. A variety of churches developed, including Syriac Catholic, Syriac Orthodox, Maronite, Melkite, and Greek Orthodox.

In 1823 Pliny Fiske of the American Board of Mission arrived in Beirut. This is thought to be the beginning of Western Protestant work there. Unfortunately, local Roman Catholic and Orthodox leaders opposed Protestants even more strongly than did the Muslims. The patriarch of the Maronite Church warned his flock against them:

---

[11] Regarding Chrysostom's preaching, see J. H. Liebeschuetz. *Barbarians and Bishops: Army, Church, and State in the Age of Arcadius and Crysostom.* Oxford: Clarendon Press, 1990, p. 176 and Robert Wilken. "John Crysostom," in Everett Ferguson, ed., *Encyclopedia of Early Christianity.* New York: Garland Publishers, 1997, p. 30.

> They are accursed, cut off from all Christian communion....We permit no one to visit them, or employ them, or do them a favor, or give them a salutation, or converse with them in any form or manner, but let them be avoided as a putrid member and as hellish dragons.[12]

In 1870 the American Board turned over their work to the United Presbyterian Church in the USA. Thereafter the Presbyterians maintained a large mission in Syria and Iran, with a special focus on educational and medical work. Eventually, this grew into the autonomous National Evangelical Synod of Syria and Lebanon. A century ago, Christians made up 20% of the Middle East population. Syrians were 13% Christian as recently as 1970. Historically Syrian Christians enjoyed significant religious freedom, except for the freedom to convert Muslims, and that limitation was social more than it was legal. The country developed many fine Christian institutions such as Aleppo College, which was supported cooperatively by four Christian bodies, including the Armenian Evangelical Union, the Arab Protestant Synod, and the United Presbyterian Church USA.

Now, however, Christians constitute only about 4% of the population in the Middle East. Many have had to flee from Syria. Yet amid this tragedy new people are encountering the gospel, and some are affirming Jesus as Lord. Lebanese churches help Syrian refugees with food, schooling for children, health care through mobile clinics, and job connections. This is remarkable given that refugees comprise one-third of the Lebanese population, placing great demands on water, electricity, schooling, and other resources.

As the gospel is lived and shared in these new encounters, the Syrian church grows in surprising ways. Many Syrians are hearing the gospel for the first time and experiencing the transformation of life. Egyptian and Jordanian churches are helping refugees, as are European churches. Today it is estimated that there are 800 Arabic-speaking churches spread across Europe,

---

[12] William Strong. *The Story of the American Board*. Boston: The Pilgrim Press, 1910, p. 99.

many born out of the refugee crisis. The Syrian church today is a transnational body, vibrant with new life. There are some Syrian Christians who have not fled. They have stayed in their homeland. Some are intentionally determined to maintain a Christian presence where the apostle Paul saw the light and where Jesus' people were first called Christians.

The city of Antioch itself has slipped under a new national boundary. Just inside the border of Turkey, it goes by the name of Antakya. The food of the city remains Levantine, and both Arabic and Turkish are spoken. The multicultural ethos remains. Though much smaller than in its heyday, the city is peaceful, with functioning community institutions and even a university. Sunnis, Alawites, and a few Christians live together harmoniously. Regrettably, the Christians in Antakya are few. Turkey is a nation of 75 million people yet has fewer than 200,000 Christians of all kinds, probably around 4,000 evangelicals.[13] While for centuries Turkey was the seat of the Ottoman Empire and the guardian of Islam's holy places, a sweeping reform in the 1920s turned it into a secular state. In practice, however, Islamists remain strong and are increasingly powerful under the current head of state. Persecution of Christians continues.

Conclusion

Today there are Antioch churches and missions all over the world. Brazil's Antioch Mission in the 1970s began to send Brazilians internationally. Its mission statement says,

> Antioch Mission is an evangelical, interdenominational association...with the purpose of announcing the glory of God among the nations and of making disciples of our Lord and Savior Jesus Christ, inspired by the work of the Holy Spirit in the New Testament church in Antioch, which, having been born through missionary effort, became a missionary church.[14]

---

[13] Jason Mandryk. "Syria" and "Turkey" in Patrick J. Johnstone, ed., *Operation World*. Colorado Springs, CO: Biblical Publishing, 2010, p. 831.
[14] Barbara Burns. "Brazilian Antioch Community, Spirituality, and Mission," in William Taylor, ed., *Global Missiology for the 21st Century: The Iguassu Dialogue*. Grand Rapids, MI: Baker Academic, 2000, p. 516.

As our communities become radically multicultural, with global diasporas spreading everywhere. the church of Antioch offers us a relevant paradigm. Like Antioch, the local churches, like a local breakfast in the cities of our world today, combine diverse flavors resulting in a wholesome nourishment. The delectable whole is more than the sum of its parts.

Long before its confirmation in the Jerusalem Council, the call to transcend boundaries resonated with the multicultural church in Antioch. This seems to have been the first congregation to recognize that if God's grace truly extends universally, we should share that good news beyond ethnic and national borders in an intentional way. Under the leading of the Holy Spirit, the believers in Antioch anointed Paul and Barnabas and sent them out as missionaries. The result was a necklace of churches in various cities and countries and language groups spread across the Greek world and eventually across the Roman empire. Here the great movement of Christian mission began.

Chapter 2: Athens

by Nathan D. Hieb[15]

God's Mission Among Contending Worldviews

In Athens, Paul enters the arena of contending worldviews and presents the message of Jesus Christ before the philosophers of his age. He listens for the worldview gaps that the Athenians themselves acknowledge, for local narratives that may serve as metaphors of the truth, and for local claims that become true when reframed and re-centered in Jesus Christ. He then boldly calls for worldview transformation, relying on the power of God. When local worldviews and the message of Jesus Christ diverge irreconcilably, as they do regarding resurrection, Paul looks for common ground while uncompromisingly proclaiming Christ's resurrection and calling his hearers to consider possibilities beyond their worldviews. By doing so, Paul shows us the path that we too must walk along – one of careful, well-reasoned engagement with the worldviews of our day, and faithful proclamation of the message of Jesus Christ.

Introduction

---

[15] Nathan D. Hieb (M.A. Intercultural Studies and M.Div., Fuller Theological Seminary; Ph.D. Princeton Theological Seminary) has ministered for twenty years among immigrant congregations, the urban poor, and youth countercultures in New Jersey, Los Angeles, and Minneapolis. He has served on ministry projects in Asia, Europe, and Latin America. He is the Pastor of the English Congregation of Monmouth Chinese Christian Church (NJ), Partnering Adjunct Professor of Theology at Alliance Theological Seminary (New York City), and Adjunct Assistant Professor of Mission Theology and Urban Studies at Fuller Theological Seminary. Nathan's publications include *Christ Crucified in a Suffering World: The Unity of Atonement and Liberation. Minn.: Augsburg Fortress*, 2013.

Athens barely appears in Scripture, where it serves simply as an unexpected rest along Paul's emergency evacuation route away from persecution elsewhere.[16] The Bible's reticence toward this influential philosophical center is striking and underscores the vast theological and cultural distance between Athens and Jerusalem.[17] The answers formulated in these cities to ultimate questions regarding human life, community, and divine reality differed to such a degree that neither seems to have regarded the other as providing helpful proposals. While some early Christian theologians eventually began to draw upon Greek philosophy, others continued along the biblical trajectory by either ignoring the arguments of the Athenian schools or by engaging them as sources of heresy that required refutation. Tertullian, an example of the latter, declared in the early third century: "What indeed has Athens to do with Jerusalem? What concord is there between the Academy [of Plato] and the Church? What between heretics and Christians?"[18]

Athens and Jerusalem, the Academy and the church, would never entirely part ways, however, after Paul opened the door between the two. In Paul's conversations with Epicureans and Stoics in the marketplace, and his address before the Areopagus, we find the first serious engagement between Christianity and the philosophies of Athens. This engagement would continue in various forms during subsequent centuries and would culminate in the church's eventual adoption of Greek philosophical notions of "substance" (*ousia*, οὐσία) to clarify and re-affirm Scripture's teaching concerning the full divinity of Jesus Christ at the Councils of Nicaea (325 CE) and Constantinople (380 CE).

---

[16] The only references to Athens in the Old or New Testaments are Acts 17:15-18:1 and I Thessalonians 3:1.

[17] Greek philosophy in the first century seems to have exerted greater influence upon Jewish thinkers in the diaspora, such as Philo of Alexandria.

[18] Tertullian, *The Prescription Against the Heretics*, Trans. Peter Holmes, in Philip Schaff, ed. *Ante-Nicene Fathers, Vol 3: Latin Christianity*, Grand Rapids: Christian Classics Ethereal Library [online], 1885, 510. For the dating of this statement, see E.A. Judge. *Jerusalem and Athens: Cultural Transformation in Late Antiquity*, ed. Alanna Nobbs, Tübingen: Mohr Siebeck, 2010, 109.

For urban ministry today, Athens serves not as a fountainhead of helpful philosophical categories but as an archetype of an intellectual milieu. We find this in our cities wherever people gather to question accepted norms, experiment with new ways of thinking, and search for fresh perspectives on questions of ultimate meaning. Athens represents the settings where community members compare, contrast, and debate differing understandings of human flourishing, social justice, and spirituality.[19] Seen in this light, the spirit of Athens may be found in university towns, such as Princeton, New Jersey, where I currently live. The spirit of Athens may also be recognized in impoverished, crime-ridden inner-city neighborhoods, such as Cedar-Riverside in Minneapolis, where I also lived and ministered. What connects Princeton and Cedar-Riverside to ancient Athens is that each is shaped by a struggle to evaluate, debate, and challenge competing interpretations of human significance, ethical values, and ultimate meaning. Athens may be found in each of our cities today, in the coffee shops and bars, on street corners and barber shops, in taxicabs and university hallways. Athens is the arena of contending worldviews.

Historical Athens in Paul's Day

Legend cloaks the earliest days of Athens, where traces of human settlement date to 5,000 BCE. Although Athens at times exerted regional influence in Attica and beyond at the point of a sword, the city's greatest and most lasting contributions were intellectual, in the areas of philosophy and democratic political theory. Socrates, Plato, and Aristotle deeply shaped this legacy, and in so doing established an enduring foundation for Western philosophy. The influential contributions of Socrates, Plato, and Aristotle

---

[19] In ancient Athens, these debates often considered topics such as human flourishing (*eudaimonia*, εὐδαιμονία), virtue (*arete*, ἀρετή), practical wisdom (*phronesis*, φρόνησῐς), politics (*politica*, πολιτικά), and the composition of the natural world (*physike*, φυσική).

established Athens as the intellectual center of the Mediterranean region long before Paul entered the city.[20]

Within the city of Athens, intellectual debate thrived particularly in the Agora and the Areopagus. By Paul's day, the Agora, a popular marketplace, and commercial center, served a political function as a site for debate among responsible citizens.[21] Paul's strategic choice to engage those in the Agora, and the presence there of Epicureans and Stoics eager for philosophical discussion, tells us of the lively intellectual exchanges that must have filled the air (Acts 17:17-18).[22] In addition, the council of the Areopagus met on the "Hill of Ares,"[23] located near the Acropolis in Athens. The Areopagus at one point possessed the power to veto the decisions of the Athenian Assembly.[24] After 462 BCE it could decide only the outcomes of various criminal trials.[25] Some believe that the Areopagus may have served as the court that tried and condemned Socrates to death in 399 BCE.[26] In Paul's day, however, the members of the Areopagus would no longer have treated a philosopher so harshly, though their interest in Paul's "new teaching" (17:19) about "foreign divinities" (17:18) evokes the concern over the teaching about "new gods" for which Socrates was condemned.[27] Both the Agora and the Areopagus functioned as arenas where differing worldviews competed for adherents and contended for influence in Athens and beyond.

---

[20] For this reason, Athens may be viewed as "the heart and captial of classical [Western] culture." Thomas F. Torrance. *"Phusikos Kai Theologikos Logos*, St Paul and Athenagoras at Athens," in *Scottish Journal of Theology*, 41 (1988): 14.

[21] Jonathan Hall points out that the term *agora* is derived from the Greek "verb *ageirein*" which means "to gather together." See Jonathan M. Hall. "Polis, Community, and Ethnic Identity," in H.A. Shapiro, ed. *The Cambridge Companion to Archaic Greece*, Cambridge: Cambridge University, 2007, 46-47.

[22] All Scripture quotations in this chapter are taken from the NRSV.

[23] This hill is also called the Areopagus, and it is from the hill that the council took its name. Throughout this chapter, the term "Areopagus" refers to the council.

[24] Victor Parker. "Tyrants and Lawgivers," in Shapiro, H.A., ed. *The Cambridge Companion to Archaic Greece*, Cambridge: Cambridge University, 2007, 26.

[25] This change "eliminate[d] [the Areopagus council's] role in reviewing (and possibly setting aside) legislation passed by the assembly." Josiah Ober. *The Rise and Fall of Classical Greece*, Princeton: Princeton University, 2015, 197.

[26] Andrew D. Irvine. "Introduction," *Socrates on Trial*, Toronto: University of Toronto, 2008, 13-14.

[27] Anthony Kaldellis. *The Christian Parthenon: Classicism and Pilgrimage in Byzantine Athens*, Cambridge: Cambridge University, 2009, 55.

Scripture discusses Athens only in Acts 17, when Paul stopped there during his second missionary journey. Paul's arrival in the city seems unplanned and accidental, an emergency measure taken by the church to whisk him away from threats and dangers elsewhere. Rather than taking a break from his missionary work because of this unexpected turn of events, however, Paul chose to encounter and engage the city of Athens.

In the Agora

Paul began to immerse himself in his new and perhaps unexpected missional context by walking through the streets of Athens. In other words, he first saw the city; he encountered and studied the urban landscape. He then responded to the reality he observed. We read that he was "deeply distressed" (*paroxunomai*, παροξύνομαι; 17:16), which in Greek carries the sense of being provoked to the point of anger. In other words, Paul's response to the urban, missional context of Athens was deep, visceral, and negative. The idolatry of the city profoundly troubled him. Rather than stepping back, however, Paul stepped further into the Athenian urban context in order to engage it more deeply. He moved beyond the familiar confines of the synagogue into the public square, the Agora, a marketplace filled with hagglers of both goods and ideas. Luke, the author of Acts, at this point uses the same word to describe Paul's reasoning with the Athenians (*dialegomai*, διαλέγομαι; 17:17) that Plato had earlier used to describe Socrates' arguing with his opponents.[28] Paul entered the arena of contending worldviews.

In the Agora, "some Epicurean and Stoic philosophers debated with [Paul]" (17:18). Luke shares the initial Athenian response to Paul, which was less than flattering: "Some said, 'What does this babbler want to say?'" (17:18). They depicted him as an empty talker, literally a "seed-picker" (*spermologos*, σπερμολόγος) who played with tiny scraps of knowledge the way a bird might play with a seed, and who "want[ed]" to say something but failed to

---

[28] Allen R. Hilton. *Illiterate Apostles: Uneducated Early Christians and the Literates Who Loved Them*, London: T&T Clark, 2018, 144, 154 fn 68.

communicate sensibly. Clearly, they were unimpressed. Others, though, attempted to understand Paul and concluded: "He seems to be a proclaimer of foreign divinities" (17:18). Luke tells us that Paul was actually proclaiming "the good news about Jesus and the resurrection" (17:18), which we may interpret as a "compressed," shorthand description of the message that Paul proclaimed everywhere he traveled.[29] Yet, Paul's words were so strange to the Athenians that he seemed barely intelligible. Surrounded by their pantheon of gods and goddesses, the Athenian philosophers seemed to miss entirely the monotheism at the heart of Paul's theology, which would have appeared far more "foreign" to them than the names of unfamiliar gods.[30]

The specific views of the Epicureans and Stoics were less relevant to this scene than Paul's presence on terrain where differing philosophical worldviews clashed and contended. The Epicureans[31] and Stoics[32] advocated vastly different worldviews and disagreed profoundly with each other. Yet, in this moment at least, they united in their mocking and misunderstanding of Paul, to whom they responded either with condescending ridicule or an attempt at understanding that nevertheless failed. Yet, God was working, even

---

[29] N.B. Stonehouse. *The Areopagus Address,* London: Tyndale, 1949, 46-48. I thank F.F. Bruce for alerting me of this source. F.F. Bruce. *Commentary on the Book of Acts,* in F.F. Bruce, ed. *The New International Commentary on the New Testament,* Grand Rapids: Eerdmans, 1980, 365, fn 68.

[30] To the Athenian ear, the Greek words for "Jesus" (Ἰησοῦς) and the "resurrection" (ἀνάστασις) would have sounded like the names of deities that could easily be incorporated within the Greek pantheon of gods. Chase writes, "The name Ἰησοῦς ... would be naturally connected by the Athenians with ἴασις ... and Ἰασώ ..., the goddess of healing and health." The term "resurrection" (ἀνάστασις) would have sounded like the personification and veneration of a ritual sacrifice offered after healing. F.H. Chase. *The Credibility of Acts,* London: Macmillan, 1902, 205-206, fn 3. I thank F.F. Bruce for alerting me to this source. Bruce, *op.cit.* 351, fn 21.

[31] Epicureans followed Epicurus (341-270 BCE) and devoted themselves to the pursuit of pleasure, of which the highest form is a "life of tranquility [sic], free from pain, disturbing passions, and superstitious fears (including particularly the fear of death)." They believed the gods remained unconcerned with, and uninvolved in, human life. Bruce, *op.cit.,* 351.

[32] Stoics followed Zeno (340-265 BCE), who taught in a covered walkway, or Stoa, in Athens. Stoics attempted to live rationally, self-reliantly, harmoniously with nature, and with "great moral earnestness and a high sense of duty." They affirmed a pantheistic, deterministic view of reality, as well as a "world-state, in which all truly free souls had equal citizen-rights." *Ibid.,* 349-350.

through this apparent failure, to open the door for Paul to speak before a much more influential audience: the Areopagus.

Before the Areopagus

At this point, the philosophers invited Paul to explain his views before the esteemed council of the Areopagus. "May we know what this new teaching is that you are presenting? It sounds rather strange to us, so we would like to know what it means" (17:19b-20). Paul began his address before the Areopagus by offering a compliment: "Athenians, I see how extremely religious you are in every way" (17:22b). As evidence of their piety, Paul mentioned that when he walked through the city and "looked carefully at the objects of [their] worship," he saw an altar thus inscribed: "To an unknown god."[33] Paul identified a gap in the Athenian worldviews, acknowledged by the Athenians themselves, that provided an opening for his proclamation of the one true God. Paul seemed to regard this gap as an implicit question to which the message of Jesus Christ supplied the answer: "What therefore you worship as unknown, this I proclaim to you" (17:23).[34] Despite the idolatry that distressed Paul (17:16), he told the Athenians that they already worshipped the God whom Paul would proclaim to them. His negative assessment of Athenian idolatry did not prevent him from seeing and using this opening, however small it may have been, to present the Christian God as One whom the Athenians already perceived in imperfect, limited ways. John Calvin wrote of the *sensus divinitatis* (sense of the divine) within humanity that causes even those ignorant of scripture to believe that God exists and to devise ways to worship God.[35] To this Athenian sense of the divine, Paul now

[33] Various commentators, going at least as far back as Jerome, have thought that Paul may have modified the inscription in his address from the plural "gods" to the singular "god." However, Kaldellis argues that this distinction would have been irrelevant to the Athenians: "[F]ew ancient readers would have made much of the difference, 'God' being a generic term in Greek for all the gods (cf. 'man' in English), and there were almost certainly many altars with different inscriptions anyway." Kaldellis, *op.cit.*, 56 fn 94.

[34] "It was, quite possibly, to honor such foreign gods as the one Paul was about to proclaim that the ancestors of the Athenians had established the Altar in the first place." *Ibid.*, 56.

[35] John Calvin. *Institutes of the Christian Religion*, Vol. I: 1.3.1, Henry Beveridge, trans., G.R.: Eerdmans, 1973, 43-45.

appealed; the One whom this sense vaguely perceived, Paul now proclaimed.[36]

Paul began his address by speaking of the one God who created the world, rules heaven and earth, and transcends the confines of physical temples (17:24).[37] Rather than needing human service or offerings, this God is the source of "life and breath and all things" (17:25). Immediately, Paul pushed against two core features of Athenian religion, specifically polytheism and anthropomorphism, by asserting that only one God "made the world and everything in it," and by arguing that a clear ontological divide separates God as the Creator and the source of all life from all creatures who depend upon God's gracious provision (17:24-25). After finding an opening by way of the altar to the unknown god through which he might engage Athenian worldviews from within, Paul thus underscored the differences between the God he proclaimed and the Greek pantheon of gods.

Paul then emphasized the common origin of all humanity in God's act of creation, and God's sovereignty in placing people in specific times and places (17:26), "so that they would search for God and perhaps grope for him and find him – though indeed he is not far from each one of us" (17:27). Paul's declaration that God is near to even the idolatrous Athenians provided implicit theological support for the way he was about to use pagan authors. No matter how distant Athenian worldviews may be from the God revealed in Jesus Christ, this distance is always bridgeable from God's end. God is near to "each one," and is able to speak even through dim lights that imperfectly reflect God's truth. These dim lights, in this moment, take the form of philosophical scraps that Paul gathered from Athenian philosophers. In a sense, Paul was now living up to the charge leveled against him in the Agora – that of being a "seed-picker" – as he pulled quotations from Greek authors

---

[36] Kaldellis regards the Athenian altar to the unknown god as evidence of God's grace at work. Kaldellis, *op.cit.*, 56.

[37] Anthony Kaldellis writes, "Paul's surprisingly generic God does not dwell in handmade temples, which his audience of Epicureans and Stoics would have accepted, as Paul probably knew in advance." Kaldellis, *op.cit.*, 56.

and employed them beyond their original, philosophical context. He seed-picked metaphors from the worldviews of his hearers that might provide an opening for the message of Jesus Christ.

Local Metaphors

Let's take a closer look at the scraps of Greek literature that Paul quoted in 17:28: "For 'In him we live and move and have our being'; as even some of your own poets have said, 'For we too are his offspring.'" The first quotation is believed to have been written by Epimenides,[38] an important figure in Athens' early history, and the second is from Aratus, a Stoic philosopher.[39] By quoting Epimenides ("In him we live and move and have our being"), Paul revealed his missional strategy: he used a local legend as a metaphor for the work of Jesus Christ. By quoting Aratus ("For we too are his offspring"), Paul showed how certain Athenian claims became true when reframed and recentered within a Christian theological framework.

Originally from the island of Crete, Epimenides lived in the sixth century BCE and is remembered as a "prophet, poet, and religious lawgiver"[40] who relied on reason in order "to reform the thought and conduct of Athens."[41] Other luminaries of the ancient world, including Plato, Aristotle, and Plutarch pay respectful tribute to Epimenides. However, it is from the *Lives of Eminent Philosophers*, written by the historian Diogenes Laertius in the third century CE, that we gain the most complete picture of the legends surrounding this man, and of the two legends in particular to which Paul alluded in his speech before the Areopagus.

---

[38] I follow Clare K. Rothschild who argues in support of attributing this quotation to Epimenides, drawing upon evidence from Clement of Alexandria, Theodore of Mopsuestia, Isho'dad, and others. Clare K. Rothschild. *Paul in Athens: The Popular Religious Context of Acts 17*, Tübingen: Mohr Siebeck, 2014, 7-24, 71. Others who support the attribution of this quote to Epimenides include Bruce, (See footnote 29.) and Johannes Munck. *The Acts of the Apostles*, rev. William F. Albright, C.S. Mann, Garden City, NY: Doubleday, 1967, 171. Those who contest this attribution include Joseph A. Fitzmyer. *The Acts of the Apostles*, New York: Doubleday, 1998, 610; and C.K. Barrett. *The Acts of the Apostles*, Edinburgh: T&T Clark, 1998, 847.

[39] For example, see Stonehouse, *op.cit.*, 34.

[40] William M. Ramsay. *Asianic Elements in Greek Civilization*, 20-21. Quoted in Rothschild, *op.cit.*, 39. Epimenides is considered "one of the Seven Sages of Greece." Munck, *op.cit.*, 171.

[41] Ramsay, *op.cit.*, 28. Quoted in Rothschild, *op.cit.*, 39.

One of the earliest recorded events in Athens' history is a rebellion led by Cylon, who attempted to seize control of the city in 632 BCE.[42] He and his followers captured the acropolis but were then surrounded and trapped by their enemies. Shortly before their dwindling provisions forced them to surrender, they appealed to the goddess Athena for protection and were promised safe conduct by their enemies. As Cylon's men left the acropolis, though, their opponents brutally killed them, violating their promise and disregarding the appeal to Athena; a crime regarded as both dishonorable and sacrilegious.[43] Soon afterward, a plague ravaged the city, which the Athenians viewed as a curse because of their unjust attack upon Cylon's followers. The Athenians appealed to their gods and received instructions through an oracle to bring Epimenides to the city from his home on the island of Crete. When he arrived, Epimenides told the Athenians to perform a unique ritual sacrifice: they were to follow the various sheep that wandered on the Areopagus and to slaughter each animal as a sacrifice at the spot where it chose to lie down.[44] The plague ended and the Athenians passed a law preserving the altars built on the Areopagus under Epimenides' guidance. The historian Diogenes Laertius writes: "Hence even to this day altars may be found in different parts of Attica with no name inscribed upon them, which are memorials of this atonement."[45] Paul's mention of an altar to an unknown god would have reminded his hearers of Epimenides' nameless altars on the Areopagus and of the sacrifice of the sheep to end the deadly plague.[46] Paul seemed to evoke this legend as a metaphor of Christ's sacrificial death as the Lamb of God who frees humanity from the curse of sin and death.

A second episode in Epimenides' life provided leverage for Paul's proclamation of Jesus' resurrection. Most Greeks at this time affirmed the

---

[42] *Ibid.*, 42.
[43] Victor Parker. *A History of Greece, 1300 to 30 BC*, Oxford: Wiley Blackwell, 2014, 122-123. Historians believe that Cylon eluded his enemies and escaped unscathed.
[44] Rothschild, *op.cit.*, 42.
[45] Laertius Diogenes. 1.110. Quoted by Rothschild, *op.cit.*, 42.
[46] Paul's hearers would have been deeply familiar with the history of Epimenides because he is believed to be the friend of Solon, who is credited with founding the Areopagus as an institution. *Ibid.*, 53-54.

immortality of the human soul but believed that a person's physical body could never be revived after death.[47] Yet, in spite of this cultural headwind, Paul seemed to evoke a second Epimenidean legend as a metaphor for Christ's resurrection, in order to challenge the Athenians to consider resurrection as a real possibility. Diogenes Laertius mentioned that when Epimenides was a young man in Crete, his father sent him to look for a lost sheep and that as he searched he wandered into a cave, fell asleep, and awoke fifty-seven years later. Locals believed that Zeus would sometimes meet humans in the caves of Crete, and so Epimenides' long sleep in one of these grottos was viewed as evidence of divine blessing and as the source of his prophetic insight.[48] Furthermore, because of his sudden reappearance after an absence of nearly six decades, Epimenides' emergence from the cave was viewed as a type of resurrection.[49] Perhaps Paul purposely called to mind the Epimenidean legends in order to present himself to the Athenians as a figure like Epimenides, who could explain what was left unexplained by Epimenides (i.e., who the unknown God actually is), and who functioned like Epimenides by bringing spiritual reform through the cleansing of a curse (this time, of sin) and news of resurrection (this time, of Jesus Christ).[50]

Paul's second quotation in Acts 17:28 ("For we too are his offspring"), attributed to the poet Aratus who wrote in the 3rd century BCE, has caused significant theological hand-wringing. Was this an example of appropriate missional contextualization by using non-Christian literature to support a Christian argument? Or, was this an example of inappropriate syncretism, in which connections made to the local religious context distort the message proclaimed? John Chrysostom, the "golden mouthed" fourth-century preacher, felt deep unease concerning the Apostle's rhetorical strategy at this point. The difficulty lay in the fact that Aratus was referring to Zeus in his

---

[47] Aeschylus, in *Eumenides*, records Apollo's speech at the founding of the Areopagus: "Once a man dies and the earth drinks up his blood, there is no resurrection." Quoted by Bruce, op.cit. 363-364. See also Rothschild, *op.cit.*, 77, fn 125.
[48] *Ibid.*, 7-8, 41-42.
[49] *Ibid.*, 54.
[50] See, for example, *Ibid.*, 72-73.

statement, but Paul used the same statement to describe the one true God, the Creator of heaven and earth. Paul, Chrysostom exclaims, "was not referring to the same god as was the other, heaven forbid!"[51] As Paul redirected the Athenians from an unknown god, whom they placed among their pantheon of deities, to the only living God, whom they did not yet know, Chrysostom argued that Paul was redirecting the object of Aratus' statement away from its original referent (Zeus) to the only referent to whom this description accurately applies.[52] Paul did not validate the religious belief behind Aratus' statement, that all are the offspring of Zeus, nor did he equate Zeus with the Triune God. Rather, Paul took a line of poetry familiar to the Athenians and declared that it becomes true when reframed within a Christian theological framework.

The Call to Repentance

Paul then used this point of agreement (humanity's shared origin in God) as the springboard for returning with increased emphasis to the topic with which he had begun: "Since we are God's offspring, we ought not to think that the deity is like gold, or silver, or stone, an image formed by the art and imagination of mortals" (17:29). He used the small piece of common ground between himself and his hearers, the cultural scraps he had 'seed-picked' from their worldviews, the tenuous connections he had established between their philosophers and poets on one side and Christ on the other, to confront the idolatry at the center of the Athenian worldviews. Though not condemning visual art in itself, Paul rejected any notion that the living God could be reduced to a finite, material image.[53] He then declared, "While God has overlooked the times of human ignorance, now he commands all people

---

[51] Chrysostom, John. *Homily 38 on Acts*, quoted by Kaldellis, *op.cit.*, 57. Kaldellis explains that Chrysostom "was concerned here with religious contamination.... His anxiety stemmed from the possibility that future readers of Acts might be encouraged to adopt a stance of religious syncretism," *Ibid.*, 57.

[52] Chrysostom, *op.cit.*

[53] Hans Conzelmann sees "two motifs intersect[ing] here: (1) the Greek, that the living can be represented only by something that is living ... (2) the Jewish, that the Creator is not to be represented by the created .... But the obvious synthesis, that humanity in the image of the living God, is not spelled out." Hans Conzelmann. *Acts of the Apostles*, 145. Quoted in Rothschild, *op.cit.*, 74, fn 109.

everywhere to repent" (17:30). Paul connected the worship of the "unknown god" in 17:23 (*agnosto theo*; Ἀγνώστῳ θεῷ) to the "times of ignorance" (*kronous tes agnoias*; χρόνους τῆς ἀγνοίας) that God mercifully overlooks. Only repentance (*metanoia*, μετάνοια) overcomes Athenian ignorance through "mind reversal"[54] and worldview transformation.

Finally, Paul explained the urgency behind his appeal: God will judge the world in righteousness (17:31). Paul's abrupt transition from noting common ground to bluntly declaring judgment may appear jarring, but in ancient Athens the meetings of the Areopagus often culminated in a declaration of "righteous judgment by an individual with a divine call."[55] As a guarantee of the coming judgment, God has raised Jesus Christ from the dead and appointed him to judge the world in righteousness (17:31). Rothschild notes that "For those picking up on allusions to *Epimenidea* [i.e., the writings attributed to Epimenides]" in Paul's address, "resurrection is precisely that proof they would have anticipated since it was the hallmark trait of the prophet (i.e. Epimenides)" that Paul had quoted and alluded to throughout his speech.[56] Paul knew his audience, and he engaged their familiar legends as metaphors as he proclaimed the one living God, Jesus Christ's resurrection from the dead, repentance, and the coming judgment.

At this point, the uncompromising character of Paul's proclamation before the Areopagus emerged fully into view. Although he quoted Greek poets and employed Athenian legends, he did not soften the radicality of his message in order to make it more palatable to the Athenians. He did not fit Christian claims into their worldviews, but rather connected Christian claims to the legends interwoven within their worldviews, in order to draw them beyond their worldviews toward faith in Jesus Christ.

---

[54] *Ibid.*, 75.
[55] *Ibid.*, 76; cf. 80.
[56] *Ibid.*, 76.

The response of the Areopagus was mixed: "When they heard of the resurrection of the dead, some scoffed;[57] but others said, 'We will hear you again about this,'" (17:32). In spite of Paul's effort to contextualize his proclamation of Christ's resurrection by referring to local religious practice and drawing upon relevant legends, most of those present remained unwilling to consider his challenge to their established worldviews. Yet, a handful believed Paul's message, including a member of the Areopagus named Dionysius.[58]

Reliance on God's Power

One final aspect of Paul's encounter with the Athenians may be gleaned from Paul's later description of his mindset as he left Athens and arrived in the city of Corinth. Although some view Paul's words in 1 Corinthians 2:1-5[59] as indicating a shift in Paul's evangelistic strategy after he debates with the Athenian philosophers, compelling reasons suggest that this is not the case.[60] Throughout Acts, including in the account of Paul's preaching in Athens, "Luke gives every impression of presenting Paul as a masterful orator who knew exactly how to suit his message to a distinctive and challenging situation."[61] To regard Paul's address in Athens as "a failure," or an example of "how the gospel was not to be preached," would require "the

---

[57] The harshly negative response by those who reject Paul's message is underscored by Luke's use of a word that occurs nowhere else in Scripture (*chleuazo*, χλευάζω), which means "to joke, jest, scoff, jeer" and "ridicule." Henry George Liddell and Robert Scott, *An Intermediate Greek-English Lexicon*, Oxford: Clarendon, 1889, online: www.perseus.tufts.edu. Kaldellis, *op.cit.* 57.

[58] Acts 17:34. "It is … no surprise that someone with the name Dionysius ('son of Zeus'), namesake of the god known to regularly die and return to life, was quick to trust the message …" Rothschild, *op.cit.*, 80. Kaldellis remarks, "Athens offered stony ground in which to sow the Gospel, which explains why Paul did not tarry long." Kaldellis, *op.cit.*, 57.

[59] I Corinthians 2:1-5: "When I came to you, brothers and sisters, I did not come proclaiming the mystery of God to you in lofty words or wisdom. For I decided to know nothing among you except Jesus Christ, and him crucified. And I came to you in weakness and in fear and in much trembling. My speech and my proclamation were not with plausible words of wisdom, but with a demonstration of the Spirit and of power, so that your faith might rest not on human wisdom but on the power of God."

[60] F.F. Bruce believes that the "popular idea" that I Cor. 2:1-5 indicates a change in Paul's evangelistic strategy "has little to commend it." Bruce, *op.cit.*, 365.

[61] Stonehouse, *op.cit.*, 41.

most decisive proofs," which are lacking from both Acts and I Corinthians.[62] Furthermore, we should not assume that the small number of converts in Athens, as compared to the larger number in Corinth, suggests that Paul's message in Athens was somehow deficient. To do so would be to "precarious[ly]" reason "from the number of converts to the correctness of the message."[63] When we read that Paul preached Christ's resurrection in Athens (Acts 17:18, 32), but in Corinth preached "Jesus Christ, and him crucified" (I Corinthians 2:2), we should understand both as "compressed" shorthand descriptions that refer to full presentations of the good news of Jesus Christ.[64] In both Athens and Corinth, Paul preached "Christ Jesus, who died, yes, who was raised." (Romans 8:34).[65] Paul clearly understood, and his preaching proclaimed, that Christ's crucifixion and resurrection are two aspects of Christ's one reconciling work that cannot be separated.

Missiological Insights from Athens

Although Paul cleverly engages Athenian worldviews and draws upon Athenian history and legends, his boldness in proclaiming the one true God and Jesus' resurrection before polytheists and pantheists who rejected bodily reanimation reveals the One upon whom he depends. In the Agora and before the Areopagus of Athens, Paul did not stand upon his wisdom and his persuasiveness did not spring from the relevance of his speech. Rather, he stood in vulnerability, perhaps even "in weakness and in fear and in much trembling" (I Corinthians 2:3), and depended upon the power of God. Later, Paul would write in Romans 1:16, "For I am not ashamed of the gospel; it is the power of God for salvation to everyone who has faith, to the Jew first and also to the Greek" – even to the Greek in Athens.

---

62 *Ibid.*, 41.
63 *Ibid.*, 42.
64 *Ibid.*, 46-48.
65 Stonehouse quotes an older translation of this verse. *Ibid.*, 48.

Engaging Narratives as Metaphors of the Truth

Paul engaged local legends about Epimenides to encourage the Athenians to consider possibilities beyond their local worldviews, such as Jesus' sacrifice as the Lamb of God and his resurrection from the dead. In Paul's sermon, the Epimenidean legends functioned as metaphors[66] of the truth of Jesus Christ, or as "parables of the kingdom."[67] These legends were able to function in this way because they partially resembled while remaining distinct from, the message Paul proclaimed. The resemblance enabled the Epimenidean legends to evoke concepts that were asserted with greater clarity and precision by Christians, such as the claim that resurrection is not only possible, but that Jesus Christ rose from the dead, and that through his death and resurrection he breaks the curse of sin, making a way for believers to share in his resurrection life. The dissimilarity, however, meant that the Epimenidean legends remain as distant metaphors of the content Paul proclaims and cannot, in themselves, communicate God's truth.[68] Jesus Christ's resurrection bestows significance upon the Epimenidean legends as relevant parables of the truth, but the legends do not establish Jesus Christ's significance.[69] This unidirectionality means that, apart from God's revelation in Jesus Christ, the Athenians could never reason from the Epimenidean legends to an accurate understanding of Jesus Christ's death or resurrection. The interpretive key of Paul's sermon is Jesus Christ, and the Epimenidean legends maintain significance as parabolic sermon illustrations only to the degree that they resemble, and may be pointed toward, the truth of Jesus Christ.

---

[66] Metaphors are, by definition, both similar to and different from the objects they describe.

[67] Karl Barth. *Church Dogmatics* IV/3.1. Trans. Geoffrey W. Bromiley. G. W. Bromiley and T. F. Torrance, eds., Edinburgh: T&T Clark, 1961, 117; cf. 112-143. George Hunsinger, referring to Barth's view, uses the term "secular parables of the truth." George Hunsinger. *How to Read Karl Barth: The Shape of His Theology*, New York: Oxford University Press, 1991, 234; cf. 234-280.

[68] The distance in this case between the metaphors (legends of Epimenides) and the reality (Jesus Christ) precludes the possibility of these "parables of the kingdom" becoming a basis for natural theology.

[69] George Hunsinger interprets Karl Barth along these lines: "In circumstances where Jesus Christ himself does not set the context, but where the context is set instead by some other word, his life cannot and does not speak for itself." Ibid., 252.

Karl Barth wrote about "parables of the kingdom" that may be found in non-Christian cultural sources.[70] In God's "free revelation of grace," God is free to speak through any human words God chooses, even when these words arise "outside the sphere of the Bible and the Church."[71] The points at which non-Christian worldviews align to the truth of Jesus Christ constitute points of grace at which God speaks through "secondary forms" that serve to "accompany and attest the one Word of God."[72] Barth believed that Christ's parables model how this is done. George Hunsinger explains: "This transformation and elevation of form by content, and the every day by the new [in Christ's parables], is taken as the prototype for the transformation and elevation of human words by the Word."[73] All truth, no matter its source, relates to the truth of Jesus Christ as a series of concentric spheres. The truth of scripture forms the inner sphere. Truth proclaimed by sources influenced by Christianity forms a second sphere surrounding the first. Truth arising apart from any discernible Christian influence occupies the third, outermost sphere. Yet, wherever truth is found, its center is Jesus Christ. "[T]his means that in the world reconciled by God in Jesus Christ there is no secular sphere abandoned by him or withdrawn from his control, even where ... it seems to approximate dangerously to the pure and absolute form of utter godlessness."[74]

As we enter the arena of contending worldviews, we will encounter legends and narratives that shape the cultural self-understandings and perspectives of the people we engage. As Barth wrote, "We may quietly listen to others. We may hear what is said by the whole history of religion, poetry, mythology and philosophy. We shall certainly meet there with many things which might be claimed as elements of the Word spoken by Jesus Christ."[75] As we listen to the narratives operating in the background of our urban

---

[70] Barth, *op. cit.*, 117; cf. 112-143. Hunsinger, *op.cit.*, 234; cf. 234-280.
[71] Barth, *op. cit.*, 101.
[72] *Ibid.*, 112-113. Also quoted in part by Hunsinger, *op.cit.*, 254.
[73] *Ibid.*, 254.
[74] Barth quoted in Hunsinger, *op.cit.*, 257-258. See Barth, *op.cit.*, 119.
[75] Barth, *op.cit.*, 108; see also Hunsinger, *op.cit.*, 252.

contexts, we will likely discover truth claims that align to the truth of Jesus Christ and that may function as parables of the kingdom. These parables may only distantly resemble our message, as Epimenides' waking from a long nap only vaguely evokes Christ's resurrection. Yet, by appealing to local narratives as metaphors of the truth, our witness will display conceptual similarity to aspects of local worldviews, while also calling our hearers beyond their worldviews to the truth of Jesus Christ.

Guiding Toward Worldview Transformation

Even though Paul engages Athenian history and philosophy, he refuses to play by Athenian rules or to follow the methods typical of Greek philosophy. If he had, he would have begun with "first principles," or self-evident assertions, and then reasoned from these to his particular view of reality. Instead, "[Paul's] argument is firmly based upon the biblical revelation of God, echoing throughout the thought, and at times the very language, of the OT Scriptures."[76] Paul's method reveals his goal. He is not attempting to win the admiration or respect of his hearers, as other visiting teachers from the edges of the Greek-speaking world might have done. Nor is he hoping that his views will achieve acceptance as simply another viable philosophical system to be placed alongside the others and debated among those who gather throughout Athens to discuss "something new" (17:21). Rather than promoting himself or his ideas, Paul speaks of "Jesus and the resurrection," a message that sharply contrasts with prevailing Athenian views. To entrenched polytheists, Paul proclaims monotheism; to those who venerate capricious, self-absorbed gods, Paul proclaims God's Son who gave his life for the salvation of the world; and to those who view physical reanimation after death as logically impossible, Paul proclaims the resurrection of Jesus Christ.

---

[76] Bruce, op.cit., 355. See also Karl Barth. The Church Dogmatics, II/1, Bromiley G.W. & T.F. Torrance. eds., trans. W.B. Johnston, T.H.L. Parker, Harold Knight, J.L.M. Haire, New York: T&T Clark, 1957, 123.

Paul then sharpens his point by arguing that this logical impossibility is the peg upon which his entire argument hangs, for Christ's resurrection provides "assurance to all" that God "has fixed a day on which he will have the world judged in righteousness by a man [i.e. Jesus Christ] whom he has appointed." (17:31). Of all in Athens, the philosophers listening to Paul would have been the least likely to accept an argument that depends not only upon a logical impossibility but also upon an event disavowed by Apollo in the founding myth of the Areopagus![77] Yet, Paul cannot diminish the radicality of his message or its irreconcilability to Athenian views. Rather, he is calling the Athenians beyond their philosophies and into the truth of Jesus Christ, a call that entails the deep worldview transformation of repentance (*metanoia*, μετάνοια; 17:30). Repentance requires the alteration of our philosophical commitments, our most basic assumptions, and our interpretations of reality.[78] Scripture, then, reframes and re-centers the true elements of our prior worldviews in Jesus Christ.[79] We see this process at work in Paul's use of Aratus' statement ("we too are his offspring"). The One to whom Aratus' statement applies is not Zeus, but rather the God revealed in Jesus Christ. Aratus' statement is reframed and re-centered in Jesus Christ and as this occurs, its truth is illumined, expanded, and deepened beyond measure. We are not simply God's "offspring"; rather, in Jesus Christ, we are now God's "children" and "heirs" (e.g. Romans 8:16-17). C.S. Lewis wrote that God "always gives back to [us] with his right hand what he has taken away with his left."[80] When Jesus Christ reframes and re-centers the true elements of our worldviews, he gives back much more than he takes away.

---

77 Bruce, *op.cit.*, 363-364. Rothschild, *op.cit.*, 77, fn 125.
78 As we have seen, Rothschild refers to repentance in the Athenian context as "mind reversal." Rothschild, *op.cit.*, 75.
79 Karl Barth argues that, in Acts 17:28, "Paul made use of heathen wisdom, but he immediately gave it a Christian sense and thus in a sense baptized it." Karl Barth. *The Church Dogmatics*, III/2, Geoffrey W. Bromiley & Thomas F. Torrance, eds. trans. Geoffrey W. Bromiley Harold Knight, J.K.S. Reid, R.H. Fuller, Edinburgh: T&T Clark, 1960, 347.
80 C.S. Lewis. *The Screwtape Letters*, New York: HarperOne, 2000, 72.

Relying on God's Power

Despite his clever allusions to Greek authors and Athenian legends, Paul knows the One upon whom he relies, and his reliance is not upon his wisdom, rhetoric, or philosophical skill. Paul knows that he cannot transform a person's worldview from Greek polytheism or Stoic pantheism to Trinitarian monotheism. Only God can open blinded eyes and illumine darkened minds to see and accept the truth of Jesus Christ. In the arena of contending worldviews today, we too must know the One upon whom we rely, for our proclamation of the truth of Jesus Christ will contain within it a call to "all people everywhere to [the] repent[ance]" that entails worldview transformation (17:30). As in Paul's day, this call may at times be heard by others as unsettling and the object of this call is logically impossible. Proclaiming such a difficult but necessary call requires that we, like Paul, rely not on our own "lofty words or wisdom," but rather "on the power of God" (I Cor. 2:1—5). In the arena of contending worldviews, as we discern worldview gaps that provide openings for dialogue, as we engage local legends as "secular parables of the truth," and as we call others toward the worldview transformation entailed by Christ's death and resurrection, we too must depend entirely upon God's work through the Holy Spirit to convince minds, to change hearts, and to draw people to Jesus Christ.

Conclusion

In Athens, Paul entered the arena of contending worldviews and presented the message of Jesus Christ before the philosophers of his age. He listened for local narratives that might serve as metaphors of the truth and for local claims that became true when reframed and re-centered in Jesus Christ. He then boldly called for worldview transformation, relying on the power of God. For the Athens of today, the settings in which ultimate questions are proposed and debated in our cities, Paul instructed us not only through his specific actions but also through the attitude his actions signify: his posture of openness to conversation with views vastly different from his own and of humble determination to present to Athens the same good news he presented elsewhere. When local worldviews and the message of Jesus Christ diverged irreconcilably, as they did regarding resurrection, Paul looked for common ground while uncompromisingly proclaiming Christ's resurrection and calling his hearers to consider possibilities beyond their worldviews. By doing so, Paul showed us the path that we too must walk along – one of careful, well-reasoned engagement with the worldviews of our day, and of faithful proclamation of the message of Jesus Christ. Neither the difficulty of this task nor the conceptual distance between our message and the messages around us, ought to prevent us from studying and engaging the philosophies of our age as we also enter the arena of contending worldviews and therein proclaim the unknown God as One made known in Jesus Christ.

Chapter 3: Babylon

by Jorge Henrique Barro[81]

God's Mission Related to Judgment and Redemption in the City

The city of Babylon is mentioned 255 times in the biblical narrative. There are two central cities in the Bible: Jerusalem and Babylon. Jerusalem is portrayed as the city of God, the city of peace. Babylon is portrayed as the city of human ambition and as the city of Satan. It was described by the Apostle John as being "a dwelling place for demons, a haunt for every unclean spirit" (Rev 18:2). In the first part of this chapter, I will offer a description of Babylon in history. The second part is dedicated to the summary of the biblical material on Babylon. This research shines a light on the missiological issues of God's mission in Babylon.

Introduction

The story of Babylon as a great civilization and as a city-state challenges us to reflect deeply concerning our presence in and interaction with the city. We are not called to live in the city as passive Christians, accepting all the injustices and consequences of the abuse of an oppressive

---

[81] Jorge Henrique Barro (PhD in Intercultural Studies at Fuller Theological Seminary) is the co-founder and Academic Dean of South American Theological Seminary (*Faculdade Teológica Sul Americana*) in Londrina, Brazil. Jorge is a former president of Latin American Theological Fellowship (FTL); evaluator of ministry education of Brazil for Theology; and Presbyterian pastor. His numerous publications in urban missiology and pastoral ministry include *De Cidade em Cidade* (Descoberta, 2002, 2013, 2020); *O Pastor Urbano* (Descoberta, 2012); *Missão para la Cidade* (Descoberta, 2013); *Missão integral* (Descoberta, 2014); and *Discipulado Missional* (Descoberta, 2016). Personal webpage: www.missaourbana.com.br

system that conspires against life and God's *imago Dei*. Jesus said that our priority is to "seek first the kingdom of God and God's justice" (Matt 6:33). Justice is the high value of God's kingdom. Here is the challenge. "We really can turn Babylon into the New Jerusalem by means of radical reform."[82] This is the radical reformation proposed by God in which the Church is called to participate. Is there redemption for cities like Babylon? How are Christians supposed to live in exile, even in their own country?

Babylon's Unique History

Some familiarity with Babylon's extensive history will help us better understand its phenomenal influence over the entire Fertile Crescent area, including Israel and Judah. Paul-Alain Beaulieu, Canadian Assyriologist at the University of Toronto, tells us that, "The subject of the history of Babylon cannot be studied without first considering the context of the rise of civilization in that part of the world."[83] Beaulieu tells us that it is essential to observe Babylon's unique context, history, and personality, as well as some of the metaphors that have been applied to it and some cultural aspects that made this city and its civilization unique.

The city-state of Babylon – Babylonia was located in central Mesopotamia (meaning between two rivers: the Tigris and the Euphrates). This area was located "to the eastern part of the 'Fertile Crescent' that stretches from Palestine through Syria and Northern Mesopotamia to Southeast Iran. It was here in the north that the first farming villages in Mesopotamia emerged around 8000 BCE."[84]

The story of Babylon as a city dates back to 2700 BCE when Kish, Akkad, Ur, and Babylon were conquered in the Old Elamite period, for trade and commercial reasons. The city of Elam lay to the north of the Persian Gulf

---

[82] Richard John Neuhaus. *American Babylon: notes of a Christian exile*. Philadelphia: Basic Books, 2009, 13.

[83] Paul-Alain Beaulieu. *A history of Babylon 2200 BC–AD 75*. Hoboken, NJ: John Wiley & Sons Ltd, 2018, 24.

[84] Hannes D. Galter. "Looking down the rivers: the interrelations between Assyria and Babylonia," in Gwendolyn Leick, edit. *The Babylon World*. New York: Routledge 2007, 527.

and the Tigris River, east of Sumer and Acadia, equivalent to the region called Khuzestan in what is now southwestern Iran and Iraq. The area is bounded to the north by the Zagros Mountains. Later, the city of Susa became the capital of the Elamites.

Babylon emerged as the hegemonic power in a politically unstable world where alliances between competing dynasties shifted constantly and cities changed hands several times within one generation.[85] In the first half of the second millennium, Babylon rose in status from being a provincial center to becoming the political capitol of Sumer and Akkad.[86] Genesis 10:10 mentions a list of some cities like the Sumerian city of *Uruk (Erech)*. The Sumerian age is also called Presargonic, because it preceded the dynasty of Sargón of Akkad. Under Sargón of Akkad an empire was built beginning in 2457 BCE that ended only when king Hammurabi entered the scene.

During the Amorite dynasty in Babylon, Hammurabi became the sixth king of Babylon, taking the throne of his father (king Sin-Muballit) in 1792 BCE and reigned until 1750 BCE. His reign brought economic, political, cultural, and legal growth, making Babylon the center of that world at the time. "Hammurabi transformed Babylon from a kingdom of moderate size into an empire."[87] Hammurabi promulgated a document called the Hammurabi Code around 1700 BCE to establish and regulate the common law codes for the kingdom. Also known as the Talion Law, it was composed of 282 articles. According to Beaulieu, the influence of Hammurabi's Law Code can be seen in the book of Deuteronomy.[88] During the reign of Hammurabi, one of the most powerful gods called Marduk became the patron of the city of Babylon. Marduk was referred to as "Lord" and became the most prestigious god of the Mesopotamian pantheon. Besides Marduk, the Mesopotamians worshipped other gods such as Assur and Ninhursag (a feminine deity). One of the greatest conquests of Hammurabi was the city of Uruk with its famous

---

[85] Beaulieu. *op cit, 60.*
[86] *Ibid., 60.*
[87] *Ibid., 76.*
[88] *Ibid., 24.*

king called Gilgamesh. The city of Uruk became an important cultural and economic center, a kind of trade hub.

The Hammurabi dynasty was wiped out by the invasion of the Kassites, a small military aristocracy.[89] They controlled Babylonia after the Hittite sack of the city in 1595 BCE until 1225 BCE. This ushered in a time known as the dark age that culminated in the control by the Assyrians in 1220 BCE. The Assyrian Empire would become a showcase of human motivations and appetites to conquer other nations. They were greedy, ambitious, insatiable, and voracious when it came to conquering peoples, their possessions, culture, knowledge, raw materials, and riches. The list of Assyrian kings and their conquests is impressive.[90] For example, Sennacherib, king of Assyria, conquered Israel and went home to live at Nineveh (II Kings 19:36). By the beginning of the 600s BCE, Assyria was crumbling and Babylon was reemerging, as the prophet Nahum noted in his oracle concerning Nineveh (Nah 3:18-19).

In 605 BCE, Nebuchadnezzar II (605-562 BCE), son of king Nabopolassar (626-605 BCE), came to the throne in the period known as the Neo-Babylonian Empire (626-539 BCE). Earlier, Nabopolassar had defeated the Assyrians and established the foundation so that his son Nebuchadnezzar II could continue to expand and strengthen the kingdom. Nebuchadnezzar II conquered Judah in 586 BCE. One of his acts was the destruction of Jerusalem and the temple of Solomon (II Kings 25:1, 8-9).

In 485 BCE, Xerxes, King of Persia destroyed Babylon. Then in 331 BCE, the area became part of the Greek empire under Alexander the Great. Alexander died only eight years after conquering Babylon in 323 BCE. In 312

---

[89] Andre Parrot. *Mundos sepultados*. Barcelona: Ediciones Garriga, 1961, 98.
[90]
- Tiglatpilesar I (1115-1093) reached the Mediterranean.
- Asurbanipal II (884-860), established Nimrud (the capital).
- Tiglatpilesar III (745-727), advanced to Gaza (2 Kings 15, 19).
- Salmanasar V (727-722) besieged Samaria, the capital of Israel.
- Sargon II (722-705), conquered the south of Israel.
- Sennacherib (701) conquered Jerusalem.
- The soldiers of Asarhaddón (680-669) crossed the "torrent of Egypt" and penetrated for the first time in history the Nile Delta and sacked Memphis.

BCE, the Seleucids conquered Babylon as part of the Seleucid Empire. The Seleucids "restored the famous temples of Sagili and Zida."[91] The domination of Phoenicia and Syria by the Seleucids accelerated the Hellenization process.

After three wars against Carthage from 264 BCE to 146 BCE,[92] Rome put an end to the Seleucid control of the region. A final shift in power came under the Parthian Empire (247 BCE to 224 BCE). Once considered the center of civilization, Babylon suffered so many sacks and so much destruction that it eventually became a forgotten city. Today, Babylon is an important archaeological site located 55 miles south of Baghdad in Iraq. With this historical background, we can turn to the biblical narrative concerning Babylon.

Babylon in the Bible

The city of Babylon is prominent, though often seen negatively, in the biblical narrative. The Bible presents two cities, with various symbolic and metaphorical implications, representing two significant images: Jerusalem as the city of peace, the prototype of what God intends for God's city. On the other hand, Babylon is portrayed as an evil city, the prototype of what God does not want to see in the city. A good city versus an evil city. It is impossible to understand either of these two cities without contrasting one to the other. Studying one separate from the other would be like assembling a puzzle without seeing the picture. Keep in mind that this chapter is about Babylon, not Jerusalem.

The name of the city of Babylon comes from the Hebrew word *Babel* (בָּבֶל). The Greek word is *Babyloñ* (Βαβυλων). The word Babylon appears 255 times in the Bible, 244 times in the Old Testament, and 11 times in the New Testament. See Appendix A, at the end of this chapter, regarding these references that show how visible Babylon is in the Bible, especially in three books: I Kings (28 times), Jeremiah (150 times), and Revelation (6 times).

---

[91] E.A. Wallis Budge. *Babylonian life and history.* Piccadilly: The Religious Tract Society, 1981, 97.
[92] They are known as the Punic Wars. *Punicus* means Carthaginian.

The biblical references seem to represent *three moments* in the life and history of Babylon.

1. The first moment shows Babylon as an actual city, with its historical facts and events registered in the narrative of the book of Kings. Here are the situations, realities, and occurrences that happened in history related to the city of Babylon. It has to do with what happened (the history that cannot be changed, only studied, and understood).

2. The second moment shows the critique of the prophets (196 times) about the lifestyle of the city of Babylon. Every city has its personality, character, culture, and manner as if it were like a person with a life of its own. No wonder many cities have names of people. The prophets denounced the lifestyle of Babylon contrasting what it was with what it should be in God's perspectives.

3. The third moment, in a future tense, is about what was going to happen to Babylon in the eschatological perspective of the book of Revelation. The future of Babylon is predicted and revealed as the "Fallen, fallen is Babylon the great! (It) has made all nations drink the wine of the passion of (its) sexual immorality" (Rev 14:8).

Just as the book of Jeremiah dominates the portrayal of Babylon in the Old Testament, so the book of Revelation dominates in the New Testament. Between them, past and future, continuity and discontinuity are in tension.

Babylon in the Old Testament

From Genesis to I Kings, the word Babylon appears only once. It is accepted by many scholars that Babel refers to Babylon, as it appears in Genesis 10:10: "The beginning of his [Nimrod] kingdom was Babel, Erech, Accad, and Calneh, in the land of Shinar."

Babylon or Babilum (in Assyrian) means, then, "the gate of God." It has been generally stated that Babylon means "confusion," but the inscriptions prove this to be incorrect; the history of the matter is that the Semites made a pun upon the name of the city. There is a root in Hebrew, *bâlal,* which means "to confuse, to mix," and from this word they derived the name Babylon, because the confusion of tongues took place there. It will be remembered that in a Talmudic discussion the question, "Why is Babylon so-called?" was asked. Rabbi Johanan replied, "Because it is confused in Scripture, in Mishnah, and in Talmud." And the Rabbi explained the words "dark places" in the verse "He hath set me in dark places," by saying that it meant the doctrine of Babel.93

Commenting on Genesis 10:10, Kvanvig says,

What the text describes is the foundation of the Babylonian and Assyrian empires, assigned to the legendary king Nimrod, of whom we know nothing except the notice in Mic 5:3 where Assyria is called the land of Nimrod. Most of the cities are, however, recognizable as great Mesopotamian cities: Babel, Erech, Akkad, Nineveh, and Calah. The confusion lies in the idea that the origin of the Mesopotamian empires should have anything to do with Cush (Nubia). 94

Nimrod belonged to the Hamite clan, people who were cursed by Noah for his son Ham's attitude, revealing to his brother the nudity of his father, caused by overconsumption of wine (Gen 9:21-22). Ham begat Cush, who begat Nimrod. Two words clarify the personality of Nimrod: powerful as a land conqueror, and brave hunter. He was "the first mighty man of the earth" (Gen 10: 8). He was an aggressive and bloodthirsty man, a cruel conqueror who gradually grew stronger in his crusades at the price of much bloodshed. If Cain built a city to protect himself and his family from his enemies, the cities of Nimrod had another perspective: to become centers of military might, a base for his assaults to dominate and subdue territories. If the city of Cain represents security, those of Nimrod represent domination. Both are symbols

93 Budge, *op cit.,* 19.
94 Helge S. Kvanvig. *Primeval history: Babylonian, Biblical, and Enochic - an intertextual reading.* Boston: Brill, 2011, 418.

of human ambition that drives the creation of cities. The city of Babel is an example of the ambition of its builders.

The problem is not that cities are centers of power in their countries. The problem resides in the way that power is used. In this case, the person is Nimrod, the founder, and architect of Babylon. Nimrod's name as the "mighty warrior on the earth" (Gen 10:8, נִמְרוֹד – Nimrôḏ) also implied rebellion.[95] Some argue that,

> The meaning…is "The Rebel." Thus "Nimrod" may not be the character's name at all. It is more likely a derisive term of a type, a representative, of a system that is epitomized in rebellion against the Creator, the one true God. Rebellion began soon after the flood as civilizations were restored. At that time, this person became very prominent.[96]

The ancient historian Josephus said this about Nimrod.

> Now it was Nimrod who excited them to such an affront and contempt of God. He was the grandson of Ham, the son of Noah, a bold man, and of great strength of hand. He persuaded them not to ascribe it to God, as if it were through his means they were happy, but to believe that it was their own courage which procured that happiness. He also gradually changed the government into tyranny, seeing no other way of turning men from the fear of God, but to bring them into a constant dependence upon his own power…. He also said he would be revenged on God, if he should have a mind to drown the world again; for that, he would build a tower too high for the waters to be able to reach! and that he would avenge himself on God for destroying their forefathers![97]

It seems that the personality of Nimrod, a tyrannical opponent to God, permeated the lifestyle of Babylon.

---

95 C. F. Keil and P, Delitzch. *Commentary on the Old Testament.* Vol. 1. Grand Rapids: Eerdmans, 1975, 165.

96 David P. Livingston. *Associates for biblical research.* Originally published in ABR's *Bible and Spade* 14.3, 2001, pp. 67-72. Viewed 02 Jun 2018, <http://www.biblearchaeology.org/post/2006/10/Who-Was-Nimrod.aspx>.Livingston, 2001.

97 Flavius Josephus. *Jewish antiquities.* Cambridge: Harvard University Press, Loeb Classics, 1998, 2.

The city of Babel, as the beginning of Babylon, was characterized by its arrogance, a desire for superiority, ambition to be a superpower, and independence from God. Instead of submitting to God, Babel's beginning shows the intentionality of building a city, a tower, a name for themselves, and creating their own gods like Succoth-benoth.

Babylon in the Historical Books of the Bible

Babylon is mentioned for the first time in the Historical books in II Kings 17:24. Hoshea began to reign in Samaria over Israel for nine years (II Kings 17:1). But Shalmaneser, the king of Assyria, invaded Israel. Hoshea became his vassal, paying tribute to Shalmaneser. According to the view of the narrator, "this occurred because the people of Israel had sinned against the Lord their God" (II Kings 17:7). As a result,

> The king of Assyria brought people from Babylon, Cuthah, Avva, Hamath, and Sepharvaim, and placed them in the cities of Samaria instead of the people of Israel. And they took possession of Samaria and lived in its cities. And at the beginning of their dwelling there, they did not fear the Lord (II Kings 17:24).

Because "they did not fear the Lord" (II Kings 17:25), God "sent lions among them, which killed some of them" (II Kings 17:25). The king Shalmaneser, understanding that this was an action from God, took this decision:

> Send there one of the priests whom you carried away from there and let him go and dwell there and teach them the law of the god of the land. So, one of the priests whom they had carried away from Samaria came and lived in Bethel and taught them how they should fear the Lord (II Kings 17:27-28).

To accommodate the situation, they tried to please God and worship other gods: (II Kings 17: 25, 32-33). The people of the city carved a god image and called it Succoth-benoth. This god may have been associated with either the worship of astrological constellations (see Amos 5:26) or a metaphor of a hen and her chicks. According to Klein,[98] only a hen cares for her chicks by covering them with her wings. In the case of other birds, the male helps the female protect their young. This symbolism may explain why the "men of Babylon" brought this god to Samaria. As a hen gathers and protects her chicks, so this god would also gather and protect Babylon and, by extension, Samaria. (II Kings 17:38-40).

Later, when King Hezekiah became sick, the Babylonian king Merodach-baladan (the son of Baladan) sent messengers with a letter and gifts to the people of Samaria. "They have come from a far country, from Babylon" (II Kings 20:14). In this context, Isaiah prophesied the future of Judah, saying:

> Hear the word of the Lord: Behold, the days are coming, when all that is in your house, and that which your fathers have stored up until this day, shall be carried to Babylon. Nothing shall be left, says the Lord. And some of your own sounds, who will come from you, who will you father, shall be taken away, and shall they be eunuchs in the palace of the king of Babylon (II Kings 20:16-18).

Nebuchadnezzar, king of Babylon, came up against Judah, and Jehoiakim became his servant for three years. Eventually, Jehoiakim rebelled against him. But Babylon was expanding its empire. "The king of Babylon had taken all that belonged to the king of Egypt from the Brook of Egypt to the river Euphrates" (II Kings 24:7). Then the prophecy that Isaiah had pronounced to king Hezekiah in II Kings 20:16-18 was fulfilled when "Nebuchadnezzar king of Babylon came up to Jerusalem, and the city was besieged" (II Kings 24:10).

> The king of Babylon conquered Jerusalem and carried off all the treasures of the house of the Lord and the treasures of the king's house, and cut in pieces all the vessels of gold in the temple of the Lord, which Solomon king of Israel had made, as the Lord had foretold. He carried away all Jerusalem and all the officials and all the mighty men of value, 10,000 captives, and all the craftsmen and the smiths. None remained except the poorest people of the land, and he

---

[98] Reuven Chaim Klein. *God versus gods: Judaism in the age of idolatry.* Mosaica Press, 2018, 355.

carried away Jehoiachin to Babylon. The king's mother, the king's wives, his officials, and the chief men of the land he took into captivity from Jerusalem to Babylon. And the king of Babylon brought captivity to Babylon all the men of valor, 7,000, and the craftsmen and the metal workers, 1,000, all of them strong, fit for war. (II Kings 24:13-16).

II Kings 25 shows in great detail the sacking of Jerusalem by Nebuchadnezzar, leading to the Babylonian captivity, and burning down the House of the Lord (II Kings 25:9). The reason for that is obvious to the writer of Chronicles. "And Judah was taken into exile in Babylon because of their breach of faith...to fulfill seventy years" (II Chron 36:21).

In the process of the Israelite return from Babylonian captivity, the role of Babylonian kings like king Darius and king Cyrus was fundamental. "Darius...made a decree, and search was made in Babylonia, in the house of the archives where the documents were stored" (Ezra 6:1). A scroll was found on which was written the records of the first year of Cyrus who decreed:

Concerning the house of God at Jerusalem, let the house be rebuilt, the place where sacrifices were offered, and let its foundations be retained. Its height shall be sixty cubits and its breadth sixty cubits, with three layers of great stones and one layer of timber. Let the cost be paid from the royal treasury. And also let the gold and silver vessels of the house of God, which Nebuchadnezzar took out of the temple that is in Jerusalem and brought to Babylon, be restored and brought back to the temple that is in Jerusalem, each to its place. You shall put them in the house of God. (Ezra 6:3-5)

Darius ultimately observed Cyrus' decree: "I Darius make a decree; let it be done with all diligence" (Ezra 6:12). And Nehemiah lists those who returned from the exiles:

These were the people of the province who came up out of the captivity of those exiles whom Nebuchadnezzar the king of Babylon had carried into exile. They returned to Jerusalem and Judah, each to his town. They came with Zerubbabel, Jeshua, Nehemiah, Azariah, Raamiah, Nahamani, Mordecai, Bilshan, Mispereth, Bigvai, Nehum, Baanah. (Neh 7:6-7).

The last mention of Babylon in the historical books is associated with Mordecai, "a Benjaminite, who had been carried away from Jerusalem among the captives...whom Nebuchadnezzar king of Babylon had carried away" (Est 2:6).

Babylon in the Poetic Books

Babylon is mentioned in the poetic books only in two Psalms, 87 and 137. In Psalm 87, the contrast between Jerusalem and Babylon is strong. On the one hand, the sons of Korah sing about the holy mount that stands in the city God founded, the dwelling place of Jacob, which is the glorious "city of God" (v. 3). On the other hand, "among those who know me, I mention Rahab and Babylon" (v. 4). Psalm 137 is a vivid melancholy record of God's people in their experience as captives who express their sorrow "by the waters of Babylon, there we sat down and wept when we remembered Zion" (v. 1). This Psalm is considered an imprecatory Psalm with the lament for God's people living in Babylonian exile for seventy years. An imprecation is a way of invoking a curse asking for misfortune to befall someone. Again, the contrast of the cities is observed in this Psalm. Jerusalem is the "highest joy" (v. 5, 6, 7) and Babylon (v. 1), is the "daughter...doomed to be destroyed."

Babylon in the Prophets

The prophet Isaiah mentions Babylon 13 times. He mentions the destruction of Babylon, "The oracle concerning Babylon" (3:1). It is an oracle "against them" (the Babylonians; 13:17), because "Babylon, the glory of kingdoms, the splendor, and pomp of the Chaldeans, will be like Sodom and Gomorrah when God overthrew them" (v. 19). Babylon "will never be inhabited or lived in for all generations" (v. 20), and "its time is close at hand and its days will not be prolonged" (v. 22).

The imprecatory Psalm 137 gives place to this triumphal hymn of Babylon's fall in Isaiah 14:3-21:

> How the oppressor has ceased, the insolent fury ceased!
> The Lord has broken the staff of the wicked, the scepter of rulers,
> that struck the peoples in wrath with unceasing blows,
> that ruled the nations in anger with unrelenting persecution.

The whole earth is at rest and quiet; they break forth into singing (Isa 14:4-8).

God is against all oppression! "'I will rise up against them,' declares the Lord of hosts, 'and will cut off from Babylon name and remnant, descendants and posterity,' declares the Lord" (Isa 14:22). And the final sentence is: "Fallen, fallen is Babylon." (Isa 21:9).

> The last mention of Babylon by the prophet Isaiah is a prophetic word of hope, saying, "Go out from Babylon, flee from Chaldea, declare this with a shout of joy, proclaim it, send it out to the end of the earth; say, 'The Lord has redeemed his servant Jacob!'" (Isa 48:20).

In contrast to Isaiah's brevity, the prophet Jeremiah mentions the word Babylon 150 times. Jeremiah is responsible for 64% of the appearances of the word Babylon in the Bible. Jeremiah dedicated most of seven chapters (from 46-52) to prophecies of judgment against Babylon. In chapters 51 and 52, Jeremiah mentions the word Babylon 62 times. The introduction of Jeremiah's oracle of judgment starts in this way.

> The word that the Lord spoke concerning Babylon, concerning the land of the Chaldeans, by Jeremiah the prophet: "Declare among the nations and proclaim, set up a banner and proclaim, conceal it not, and say: 'Babylon is taken, Bel is put to shame, Merodach is dismayed. Her images are put to shame, her idols are dismayed' (Jer 50:1-3).

The oracle begins as a proclamation, decentralizing the power of the religious system since Bel was a chief Babylonian deity and Merodach, was the chief deity of the Babylonians in the time of Nebuchadnezzar. The images and idols are put to shame and dismayed. God's people, "the portion of Jacob... Israel" are not like the Babylonians. "Not like these is he who is the portion of Jacob, for he is the one who formed all things, and Israel is the tribe of his inheritance, the Lord of hosts is his name" (Jer 51:19).

The prophet Ezekiel mentions the word Babylon 15 times. He also emphasizes the contrast between Jerusalem and Babylon when describing his prophecy of Babylonian captivity. Ezequiel says that Israel is "a rebellious house."

> In the morning, the word of the Lord came to me: "Son of man, has not the house of Israel, the rebellious house, said to you, 'What are you doing?' Say to them, 'Thus says the Lord God: This oracle concerns the prince in Jerusalem and all the house of Israel who are in it.' (Ezek 12:8-10).

As a consequence, says Ezekiel, "I will bring him to Babylon, the land of the Chaldeans" (12:13). Ezekiel uses two contrasting phrases to express God's view of God's people: (1) "a rebellious house" (12 times, to show Israel's state before God); and, (2) "then they shall know that I am the Lord their God" (60 times) to show God's intervention in their lives (Ezek 39:28).

Like Ezekiel, the prophet Daniel mentions the word Babylon 15 times. The appearance of the word Babylon in Daniel is somewhat generic, such as "the wise men of Babylon" (Dan 2:12, 14, 18), and "the province of Babylon" (Dan 3:1, 12, 30). Probably the most important passage regarding Babylon is Daniel 4:28-33. These were the words of Nebuchadnezzar when he was walking on the roof of the royal palace of Babylon. He said:

> Is not this great Babylon, which I have built by my mighty power as a royal residence and for the glory of my majesty? (Dan 4:30).

Here was a man with his great self-pride and self-glory stating that no one could withstand him. However, while the words were still in the king's mouth, there fell a voice from heaven, saying:

> O King Nebuchadnezzar, to you it is spoken: The kingdom has departed from you, and you shall be driven from among men, and your dwelling shall be with the beasts of the field. And you shall be made to eat grass like an ox, and seven periods of time shall pass over you, until you know that the Most High rules the kingdom of men and gives it to whom he will (Dan 4:31-32).

Immediately after that Nebuchadnezzar was "driven from among men and ate grass like an ox, and his body was wet with the dew of heaven till his hair grew as long as eagles' feathers, and his nails were like birds' claws" (Dan 4:33).

> Nebuchadnezzar had to recognize that only the Most High, and praised and honored him who lives forever, for his dominion is an everlasting dominion, and his kingdom endures from generation to generation; all the inhabitants of the earth are accounted as nothing, and he does according to his will among the host of heaven and among the inhabitants of the earth; and none can stay his hand or say to him, "What have you done?" (Dan 4:3).

Amazingly, Nebuchadnezzar, king of Babylon, was eventually converted to faith in YHWH, the God of Abraham, Isaac, and Jacob, creator of heaven and earth. Daniel recorded that Nebuchadnezzar declared that, "Now I, Nebuchadnezzar, praise and extol and honor the King of heaven, for all his works are right and his ways are just; and those who walk in pride he is able to humble" (4:37).

The minor prophet Micah states that the people "shall go out from the city and dwell in the open country; you shall go to Babylon" (Mic 4:10). However, the situation would not be hopeless because God would rescue them: "there the Lord will redeem you from the hand of your enemies" (Mic 4:10).

The last Old Testament reference is the prophet Zechariah who mentions God's announcing the return of God's People from the Babylonian captivity, saying:

> Up! Escape to Zion, you who dwell with the daughter of Babylon. For thus says the Lord of hosts, after his glory sent me to the nations who plundered you (Zech 2:7-8).

Babylon in the New Testament

The word Babylon appears 11 times in the New Testament. The only Gospel narrative that mentions Babylon is Matthew, who refers three times to "the deportation to Babylon" (Matt 1:11, 12, 17). In the book of Acts, Babylon is mentioned in Stephen's discourse, condemning the people for worshiping gods such as Moloch and Rephan, and, as a result, God said: "I will send you into exile beyond Babylon" (Acts 7:43).

The Apostle Peter writes to the Christians in exile, "The (church) who is at Babylon, who is likewise chosen, sends you greetings" (1 Pet 5:13). Most probably Babylon here is a metaphor for Rome because Peter probably wrote his letter from Rome. In the introduction to his letter, he wrote: "Peter, an apostle of Jesus Christ, to those who are elect exiles of the Dispersion in Pontus, Galatia, Cappadocia, Asia, and Bithynia" (1 Pet 1:1). He also mentions the exiles saying: "Beloved, I urge you as sojourners and exiles to abstain from the passions of the flesh, which wage war against your soul" (1 Pet 2:11).

Important references to Babylon appear in the book of Revelation (6 times). John's first mention on Patmos Island about Babylon is like great news from a newspaper cover: "Fallen, fallen is Babylon the great!" (Rev 14:8). Babylon fell because "God remembered who Babylon had been" (Rev 17:5). God is just. (Rev 18:2-3; 9-10). The last and final mention of Babylon in the Bible sets Babylon's future destiny. A mighty angel takes up a stone like a great millstone and throws it into the sea, saying: "So will Babylon the great city be thrown down with violence, and will be found no more" (Rev 18:17, 21). Babylon is no more. Ultimately, God judges Babylon and brings redemption in the form of a new Jerusalem.

God's Mission in the City of Babylon

A missiological reading of the Bible is interested in seeing how God works in the city. Missiology calls us to become involved in God's mission (*missio Dei*) for the sake of the world. Some eschatological views of the city may hinder rather than help. They are more concerned with an uncertain future than with the real situations and realities of cities of our day that need to be transformed by the power of the gospel. Many questions have been posed, such as whether Babylon will be rebuilt at the end of time and then permanently annihilated by God; where will be the seat of this new Babylon; who will be the political leaders. Such questions lead to speculation that paralyzes rather than setting the church in motion in transformative urban missional praxis.

Babylon can be a metaphor for a conspiratorial system against God and God's mission in the world. It is a conspiratorial system that the Apostle Paul called principalities and powers (Rom 8:38; Eph 3:10; 6:12; Col 1:16; 2:15), the world-rulers of darkness. Under the domination of the world rulers of this darkness, every city suffers the influence of a well-structured conspiratorial evil system that is unjust, corrupt, arrogant, alienating, and oppressive. This Babylonian way of acting is visible and present in our cities today. It is undeniable that people are still "following the course of this world, following the prince of the power of the air, the spirit that is now at work in the (children) of disobedience" (Eph 2:2). This is the context where we live out our missional calling in the cities of the world. In the Babylons of today, we are called to be the salt of the earth and light of the world as a response to the following five challenges of life in the city.

Arrogance and Alienation

We have considerable information on the motivations behind the building of Babel (Babylon) and God's answer to the builders. Motivated by fame and arrogance, the builders became blinded by human ambition, with no space for God. They certainly did not expect such a quick reaction from God. Many human rulers think that their initiatives are either not being observed or will not have consequences. Human arrogance and ambition results in alienation from God. "And from there the Lord dispersed them over the face of all the earth" (Gen 11:9). That is God's "no" to human ambition and arrogance. With this intervention, God reveals that God wants to be the center of every city and human gathering, as the only one to be worshiped.

The motivations of the builders of Babel were similar to those of Cain. "When he built a city, he called the name of the city after the name of his son, Enoch" (Gen 4:17). Cain attempted to make his name everlasting. The same motivations are seen in the builders of the city of Babel who wished to be famous and not scattered over the land. The first two cities of the Bible had the same ambitions and motivations: self-glory, self-protection, a demonstration that no one could defeat them. The purpose of the builders of Babel was to live a life where the center of all things was not God but themselves, wanting to make their names famous (Gen 11:4).

Exclusivity and Ethnocentricity

A second challenge to a missional life in the city has to do with exclusivity and ethnocentricity. The city of Babel is a negative symbol of the relationship between human beings and God. The intention of the builders was for Babel to become the first world power: a uniform and exclusive culture, an ethnocentric and exclusive people, and a city. Babel was the opposite of what God intended for the city. Babel was the epitome of secularization.

God knew that this was "only the beginning of what they (would) do" (Gen 11:4). That is, much more was to come because they were united as "one people" and all spoke the same language. God has always been concerned with inclusivity and stands against exclusivity. The city of Babel, with its tower, sought to be domineering, egocentric, and culturally superior. All were to speak the same language. God saw their ambitions and dispersed them. The city that God desires is inclusive, multicultural, multilingual, and multiethnic. The only one to be worshiped is God and not the powers of the city, symbolized in the tower.

The challenge of the gospel in the great cities of the world today is to be cross-cultural, even within the same city. In today's cities, the challenge is to live in unity amid a diversity of languages, cultures, and social classes. Humans today must learn to live in cross-cultural, multi-lingual, multi-racial, and multi-ethnic contexts if they want to build a healthy and balanced coexistence in the city.

The uniformity of Babel must give way to the rich diversity of the New Jerusalem. The Book of Revelation reveals that nations will march to the city, with each people and culture bringing their gifts and talents to the city. It will be a feast of nations. Peoples who have been destroyed throughout history will march into the City of God, cleansed, converted, bringing their glory into it. This is the beauty of the description of God's City with twelve gates, made of pearls, jasper walls, and twelve foundations, with different precious stones and gold-paved streets – a rich diversity united around the throne of God. To think of the development of cities today without the vision of the heavenly city is to court failure.

Religious Pluralism and Idolatry

Religious pluralism and idolatry present a third challenge for God's mission in the city.

> The name Babylon is a Greek form of the original Akkadian name Bab-Ilu, which means "the gate of god." Both literally and figuratively, Babylon has been the gate through which many gods have entered history.[99]

Religious pluralism can be understood as a parallel coexistence and often fusion of diverse religious beliefs and practices. Pluralism is the view that all religions are distinct but parallel ways of experiencing the same so-called Ultimate Reality. There were many instances of religious pluralism evident in the Mediterranean, Near Eastern, and North African cultures. By way of example, Gnosticism was prevalent during the Hellenistic period (c. 300 BCE – 300 CE) as a religious dualistic system that incorporated elements from the Oriental mystery religions, Judaism, Christianity, and Greek religious philosophical concepts.[100] Centuries earlier, the Assyrian-Babylonian religious system had involved a fusion of Sumerian and Semitic elements to form a new religious movement. Babylon is a symbol of both religious pluralism and idolatry. When king Sargon of Assyria allowed some people to relocate to Samaria "the man (or king) of Babylon" and his followers brought the Babylonian god Succoth-benoth with them.

> Marduk was already syncretised with the gods Asalluhi and Tutu (the patron deity of the city of Borsippa) in the Old Babylonian period, although in some Old Babylonian sources

---

[99] Neuhaus, *op.cit.*, 4-5.
[100] *Encyclopaedia Brittanica*, in loco; accessed at https://www.britannica.com/topic/religious-syncretism.

Asalluhi and Marduk were still understood as separate deities. The syncretism with Asalluhi is mentioned in a Sumerian literary letter to the goddess Ninisinna, in which Asalluhi is described as the 'king of Babylon.'[101]

In light of the religious pluralism and idolatry present in today's cities and the world, our challenge as Christian believers and Christian churches must be to stand faithful to the uniqueness of Jesus Christ before the "gate of god" in the Babylons of today.

A classic missiological approach to Christian conversation with people of other faiths has involved three different schemes or paradigms: pluralism, inclusivism, and exclusivism. Some years ago, Charles Van Engen described those three paradigms and stated his dissatisfaction with all three. Over against those three perspectives, Van Engen proposed a fourth paradigm that he called the "Evangelist Paradigm." In a paper presented to the Annual Conference of the Nordic Institute for Mission and Ecumenism (NIME) at the University of Aarhus, Denmark, he proposed a contextually appropriate and culturally respectful paradigm of religious encounter that could provide a way for Christians to converse with persons of other faiths while remaining firmly rooted in the uniqueness of Jesus Christ. He suggested an approach that is faith particularist (gospel-centered in Jesus Christ), culturally pluralist (distinguishing faith and culture), and ecclesiologically inclusivist (global theologizing). He affirmed that,

> When we call people of other cultures and faiths to confess "Jesus is Lord," it is not our Jesus (exclusivist), nor is it a or any Jesus (pluralist), nor is it the cosmic amorphous idea of Jesus Christ (inclusivist). Rather, it is Jesus the Lord, who calls for the conversion and transformation of ALL who confess His name. Only in humility, in personal repentance and prayer, and expectation of great cultural diversity may I invite others to join me in confessing Jesus as Lord.[102]

---

[101] Nicole Brisch. "Marduk (god)." *Ancient Mesopotamian Gods and Goddesses*, Oracc and the UK Higher Education Academy, 2016. Viewed 07 Sept 2019. http://oracc.museum.upenn.edu/amgg/listofdeities/ marduk/.

[102] Charles Van Engen, "The Religious Encounter in the New Millennium: Gospel and Culture Facing Globalization;" *Swedish Missiological Themes*, (Special Issue on "The Religious Encounter in the New Millennium"), Fall, 2000, 7. An earlier version of this

Amid religious pluralism and the multiplicity of known or unknown contemporary gods in our cities, Christian believers and Christian churches are called to proclaim the uniqueness of Jesus Christ before the "gate of god" of today's Babylons. The challenge is the same today as it was when Paul addressed the Areopagus,

> What therefore you worship as unknown, this I proclaim to you. The God who made the world and everything in it, being Lord of heaven and earth, does not live in temples made by man, nor is he served by human hands, as though he needed anything since he himself gives to all mankind life and breath and everything. And he made from one man every nation of mankind to live on all the face of the earth, having determined allotted periods and the boundaries of their dwelling place, that they should seek God, and perhaps feel their way toward him and find him. Yet he is actually not far from each one of us, for 'In him we live and move and have our being' (Acts 17:23-28).

The message was as clear to the religious men of Athens as it must also be to religious people of today. "God...commands all people everywhere to repent, because he has fixed a day on which he will judge the world in righteousness by a man whom he has appointed; and of this, he has given assurance to all by raising him from the dead" (Acts 17:30-31).

Exiles are Called to Seek the Welfare of the City

A fourth challenge facing Christians and Christian churches is the biblical call to seek the welfare of their cities even though they may find themselves in a kind of exile there. Due to global migration, thousands of people live in conditions of exile today and the challenge is to live as People of God under oppressive conditions, seeking the welfare of their city in the face of such conditions.

---

chapter was published as "The Uniqueness of Christ in Mission Theology," in Charles Van Engen. *Mission on the Way: Issues in Mission Theology*. G.R.: Baker, 1996. 169-187. See also, Charles Van Engen, "The Uniqueness of Christ" in Ralph D. Winter and Steven C. Hawthorne, eds. *Perspectives on the World Christian Movement: a Reader*, Fourth Edition, Pasadena: WCL, 2009, 176-182 and Charles Van Engen, "The Uniqueness of Christ in Mission Theology," in Robert L. Gallagher and Paul Hertig, eds. *Landmark Essays in Mission and World Christianity*. Maryknoll: Orbis, 2009, 160-178.

"Recalling the earlier Babylonian Captivity, Babylon came to be a symbol of exile in Christian thought."[103] It is evident in the biblical narratives about Babylon that God sent God's People into exile in Babylon. The prophecy of Amos, echoed centuries later by Stephen in his discourse in Acts, presents the exile as God's judgment for their worship of gods other than YAHWEH:

> Did you bring to me sacrifices and offerings during the forty years in the wilderness, O house of Israel? You shall take up Sikkuth your king, and Kiyyun your star-god, your images that you made for yourselves, and I will send you into exile beyond Damascus, says the Lord, whose name is the God of hosts. (Amos 5:25-27) (See also Acts 7:42-43.)

However, in the Bible's perspective, exile is not a place designed by God for God's people. Exile is a consequence of disobedience. But God's plan is ultimately not exile.

> For I know the plans I have for you, declares the Lord, plans for welfare and not for evil, to give you a future and a hope. Then you will call upon me and come and pray to me, and I will hear you. You will seek me and find me when you seek me with all your heart. I will be found by you, declares the Lord, and I will restore your fortunes and gather you from all the nations and all the places where I have driven you, declares the Lord, and I will bring you back to the place from which I sent you into exile (Jer 29:11-14).

Jeremiah's words echoed Israel's ancient *Shema* that was to be lived in every place, in every circumstance, even in exile.

> Hear, O Israel: The Lord our God, the Lord is one. You shall love the Lord your God with all your heart and with all your soul and with all your might (Deut 6:5); You shall not take vengeance or bear a grudge against the sons of your own people, but you shall love your neighbor as yourself: I am the Lord (Lev 19:18).

God not only promised to visit God's people during their exile and bring them back to Zion but also gave them instructions on how to live the 70

---

[103] Richard John Neuhaus. *American Babylon: notes of a Christian exile.* Philadelphia: Basic Books, 2009, 8.

years in Babylon. God's People were not authorized by the Bible and its writers to hate and destroy cities like Babylon. On the contrary, they were called by God to pray and seek the *shalom* of Babylon. This was God's expressed agenda for God's people during the exile period (See Appendix A at the end of this chapter.). Although living in exile or in conditions of exile implied loss in some areas of life, the People of God were called to seek the welfare of Babylon. The Babylonians were not wicked in their treatment of God's People.

> In analysis of this context, we observe that the Babylonians did not disperse the exiles, as did the Assyrians. A regime of bondage arises (Ezek 1:1s; Neh 7:61; Is 42:22). Thus, they were settled in agricultural communities (Ezek 3:24; 33:30). All this favored the conservation of spiritual, religious, and cultural heritage. They could speak their own language, observe their customs and religious practices. They could freely assemble, buy land, build houses, and communicate with their homeland Judah. "Build houses and settle yourselves; plant orchards and eat their fruits" (Jer 29:5). In fact, in Babylon, they even achieved some economic prosperity in a relatively short time.[104]

Centuries later, the Apostle Peter wrote to the Christians in diaspora (both Jews and Gentiles) who were spread throughout the Roman Empire and were suffering severe persecution and exile. Restating Jeremiah's challenge in a new way, Peter reminded them that God's people "are elect exiles" (I Pet 1:1) who are called to "be holy in all your conduct" (I Pet 1:15). God's people are called to "conduct yourselves with fear throughout the time of your exile, knowing that you were ransomed from the futile ways inherited from your forefathers, not with perishable things such as silver or gold, but with the precious blood of Christ, like that of a lamb without blemish or spot" (I Pet 1:17-19). This conduct, in the Christian ethical living, "as sojourners and exiles" (I Pet 2:11), was to be a way of living that "abstain from the passions of the flesh, which wage war against your soul" (I Pet 2:11). And Peter finally

---

[104] Marcelo Harrisberger. *O exílio Babilônico.* Viewed 13 Nov 2019.
<https://www.harrisberger.com.br/index.php/ 2016/12/23/o-exilio-babilonico/>.

exhorts these Christian exiles to "keep your conduct among the Gentiles honorable, so that when they speak against you as evildoers, they may see your good deeds and glorify God on the day of visitation" (I Pet 2:12).

Today we find millions of people living under conditions of exile, even within their own country. Exile is not necessarily a consequence of disobedience to God, but today it is often a consequence of injustice and persecution. According to the UNHCR (The UN Refugee Agency):

> At least 79.5 million people around the world have been forced to flee their homes. Among them are nearly 26 million refugees, around half of whom are under the age of 18. There are also millions of stateless people, who have been denied a nationality and lack access to basic rights such as education, health care, employment, and freedom of movement. At a time when 1 percent of the world's population have fled their homes as a result of conflict or persecution, our work at UNHCR is more important than ever before.[105]

Whatever the reasons for their exile, Christians are to seek the welfare of their city. (Jer 29:4-14; see Appendix A at the end of this chapter). That is the challenge: Christian ethical conduct must continue unchanged, especially in the context of exile.

Speaking Out in the Face of the Conspiratorial Evil System

A fifth missional challenge is to speak prophetically against the life-threatening situations, realities, and systems of the city. Christian conduct in conditions of exile in the Babylons of our day does not mean passive acceptance or submission to injustices, abuses, or mistreatment that conspire against the integrity of life. God did not create human beings to be subhuman. Every system that dehumanizes humankind is evil and needs to be confronted by the liberating power of the Gospel.

Many passages in the Bible show Babylon as a corrupt system that had to be confronted by God and the prophets. The most emphatic is Revelation 17 and 18, showing the complete and ultimate ruin and fall of

---

[105] UNHCR. "Figures at glance." Viewed on 23 July 2020, <https://www.unhcr.org/figures-at-a-glance.html>.

Babylon. Juan Stam, certainly one of the most significant Latin American scholars of the book of Revelation, said about chapter 17:

> From the entire passage, it is clear that the harlot is not a woman but a city (17:5, 18). It was common among the ancients, and especially the Hebrew prophets, to personify the cities as if they were people, and especially as women (Keener 2000: 404; Collins 1990: 1012). According to Is 66:7-11, Zion is a woman screaming with labor pains and breastfeeding her child. Ezekiel 16 describes Yahweh's relationship with Jerusalem as a love story from birth to puberty (16:4-7) and his eventual infidelity to the Lord (16:15-52); Ez 23 tells the sexual story of two sisters, called Oholah and Oholibah, as a parable of the spiritual adultery of Samaria and Jerusalem. That makes it clear that the harlot of the Ap 17 is not a "sex worker" and that the passage has nothing to do with her or any woman's sexual behavior, but rather describes the idolatry and corruption of a city called "Babylon."[106]

For Stam, Babylon is the Roman Empire:

> From the whole chapter, it is clear that with this phrase John refers to the city of Rome as the capital of the empire. It is typical of his style to symbolically apply details of ancient nations to the Roman Empire. Although Rome was not exactly a city "sitting on many waters", it did have all the characteristics of a new Babylon. In addition, as a city Rome was not well located for land trade, but for maritime commerce. In fact, the Mediterranean was the vital means for the expansion of its power and wealth. Rome was, in truth, a city and an empire "sitting on many waters."[107]

Neuhaus follows the same line of thought, affirming that,

> For the writers of the early Christian centuries, such as Augustine and Jerome, Babylon represented the power, arrogance, idolatry, and general wickedness of the Roman Empire. Also for Jews of the period, Rome was the new Babylon, for, like the first Babylon centuries earlier, the Roman Empire destroyed the temple in Jerusalem in A.D. 70. For both Jews and Christians of the first centuries after

---

[106] Juan Stam. "La ramera." Viewed on 2 Nov 2019,
<http://www.juanstam.com/dnn/Blogs/tabid/110/EntryId/330/ Default.aspx. 2011>.
[107] *Ibid.*

Christ, Rome was the persecutor of God's chosen people and was destined to fall.[108]

Without prophets, there is no word from God for the city. In the words of Dutch biblical scholar, Hans de Wit, in exile the text is homeland.[109] Milton Schwantes, a Brazilian biblical scholar, affirms that,

> In the Bible, exile is not just deportation or escape to a foreign land. It is also oppression and unworthy life in one's own land, in the country where one is born. If the prophets had not been strongholds against the oppressors who wanted to occupy the land of God's people, the exiles probably would not have had the strength to dream the dream of life.[110]

Though Babylon says, "I rule as a queen" (Rev 18:7), God declares through God's prophets that the throne is already taken. "And he who was seated on the throne said, 'Behold, I am making all things new'" (Rev 21:5). And finally, "no longer will there be anything accursed, but the throne of God and of the Lamb will be in it, and his servants will worship him" (Rev 22:3).

That is the end of the Babylonian conspiratorial evil system. The news on that day will be, "Fallen, fallen is Babylon the great" (Isa 21:9; Rev 14:8; 18:2). No more this evil and oppressive system, because:

> Great is the Lord and greatly to be praised in the city of our God! His holy mountain, beautiful in elevation, is the joy of all the earth, Mount Zion, in the far north, the city of the great king (Ps 48:1-2).

Conclusion

Ultimately Babylon is not about judgment but redemption of and through God's People. As Christians today, we are called to live, even in our exile, in the tension between the already and the not-yet realities of God's kingdom; between the transcendence and the immanence of the kingdom;

---

[108] Neuhaus, *op cit.*, 9-10.

[109] Hans de Wit states that in diaspora and exile the text is homeland. *En la dispersión el texto es patria: Introducción a la hermenéutica clásica, moderna y posmoderna.* San José, Costa Rica: Editorial Sibila, 2017.

[110] Milton Schwantes. *Sofrimento e esperança no exílio: história e teologia do povo de Deus no século VI AC.* São Paulo: Paulinas, 2007.

between "Your kingdom come" and "Your will be done, on earth as it is in heaven" (Matt 6:10). The New Jerusalem is the paradigm for our prophetic, ethical living. We are not called to live in our not-yet dimension as passive Christians, accepting all the injustices and consequences of an oppressive system that conspires against life and God's *imago Dei*. Our priority is to "seek first the kingdom of God and God's justice" (Matt 6:33). Here is the challenge. "We really can turn Babylon into the New Jerusalem by means of radical reform."[111] This is the radical reformation proposed by God in which the Church is called to participate:

> For behold, I create new heavens and a new earth,
> and the former things shall not be remembered or come into mind.
> But be glad and rejoice forever in that which I create; for behold,
> I create Jerusalem to be a joy, and her people to be a gladness.
> I will rejoice in Jerusalem and be glad in my people.
> No more shall be heard in it the sound of weeping and the cry of distress.
> No more shall there be in it an infant who lives but a few days, or an old man who does not fill out his days, for the young man shall die a hundred years old,
> and the sinner a hundred years old shall be accursed.
> They shall build houses and inhabit them; they shall plant vineyards and eat their fruit.
> They shall not build and another inhabit; they shall not plant and another eat;
> for like the days of a tree shall the days of my people be,
> and my chosen shall long enjoy the work of their hands.
> They shall not labor in vain or bear children for calamity,
> for they shall be the offspring of the blessed of the Lord, and their descendants with them.
> Before they call I will answer; while they are yet speaking I will hear.
> The wolf and the lamb shall graze together; the lion shall eat straw like the ox,
> and dust shall be the serpent's food.
> They shall not hurt or destroy in all my holy mountain, says the Lord (Isa 65:17-25).

There is still hope! God is our hope now and forever! Let us work while it is day!

---

[111] Neuhaus, *op cit.*, 13.

OLD TESTAMENT 244 times	
Books	**Occurrences**
Historical Books – 45 times	
II Kings (28)	17:24, 30 20:12, 14, 17, 18 24:1, 7, 10, 11, 12, 15, 16, 17, 20 25:1, 6, 7, 8, 11, 13, 20, 21, 22, 23, 24, 27, 28
I Chronicles (1)	9:1
II Chronicles (7)	32:31 33:11 36:6, 7, 10, 18, 20
Ezra (6)	2:1 5:12, 13, 14 5:17 6:5
Nehemiah (2)	7:6 13:6
Esther (1)	2:6
Poetic Books – 3 times	
Psalm (3)	87:4 137:1, 8
Prophetic Books – 196 times	
Major Prophets – 193 times	
Isaiah (13)	13:1, 19 14:4, 22 21:9 39:1, 3, 6, 7 43:14 47:1

	48:20
Jeremiah (150)	20:4, 5, 6
	21:2, 4, 7, 10
	22: 25
	24:1
	25:1, 9, 11, 12, 26
	27:6, 8, 9, 11, 12, 13, 14, 16, 17, 18, 20, 22
	28:2, 3, 4, 6, 11, 14
	29:1, 3, 4, 10, 15, 20, 21, 22, 28
	32:3, 4, 5, 28, 36
	34:1, 2, 3, 7, 21
	35: 11
	36:29
	37:1, 17, 19
	38: 3, 17, 18, 22, 23
	39:1, 3, 5, 6, 7, 9, 11, 13
	40:1, 4, 5, 7, 9, 11
	41:2, 18
	42:11
	43:3, 10, 30
	46:2, 13, 26
	49:30
	50:1, 2, 8, 9, 13, 14, 15, 16, 17, 18, 23, 24, 28, 29, 34, 35, 39, 42, 43, 45, 46
	51:1, 2, 6, 7, 8, 9, 11, 12, 24, 29, 30, 31, 33, 34, 35, 37, 41, 42, 44, 47, 48, 49, 53, 54, 55, 56, 58, 59, 60, 61, 64
	52:4, 9, 10, 11, 12, 15, 17, 26, 31, 32
Ezekiel (15)	12:13
	17:12, 16, 20
	19:9
	21:19, 21
	24:2
	26:7
	29:18, 19

	30:10, 24, 25
	32:11
Daniel (15)	1:1
	2:12, 14, 18, 24, 48, 49
	3:1, 12, 30
	4:6, 29, 30
	5:7
	7:1
Minor Prophets – 3 times	
Micah (1)	4:10
Zechariah (2)	2:7
	6:10

NEW TESTAMENT 11 times	
Books	**Occurrences**
Matthew (3)	1:11, 12, 17
Acts (1)	7:43
I Peter (1)	5:13
Revelation (6)	14:8
	16:19
	17:5
	18:2, 10, 21

Chapter 4: Capernaum

by Sarita D. Gallagher Edwards[112]

God's Mission on the Borders

The city of Capernaum encapsulated the reality of many modern border towns; it was multicultural, multiethnic, and multi-religious, and its population encompassed a broad socioeconomic spectrum. Jesus' commitment to live and minister in such a community demonstrates God's heart for all the nations of the world. There are many lessons that we can learn from Jesus' ministry in Capernaum including Jesus' adoption of ministry to and from the margins of society, Jesus' embrace of strategic "roads" of evangelism, and Jesus' contextualization of his message and ministry using the cultural customs, industries, and geography of his community. This chapter summarizes the historical development of ancient Capernaum and the biblical events that took place in the township during the lifetime of Jesus and his disciples. In addition, the significance of Jesus' decision to base his ministry in Capernaum is addressed, as well as missiological lessons that we can learn from this urban context as we seek to contextualize the gospel in the 21st century.

---

[112] Sarita D. Gallagher Edwards holds a Ph.D. in Missiology from the School of Intercultural Studies of Fuller Theological Seminary. Dr. Edwards is professor of religion at George Fox University in Newberg, Oregon. She served as a missionary with CRC Churches International in Papua New Guinea and Australia and teaches in the areas of biblical theology, intercultural studies, world religions, and world Christianity. Sarita's most recent book is *Breaking through the Boundaries: God's Mission from the Outside In* (Orbis Books, 2019). She is also the author of *Abrahamic Blessing: A Missiological Narrative of Revival in Papua New Guinea* (Pickwick, 2014), as well as numerous chapters and articles.

Introduction

After a short drive from the kibbutz, our tour bus pulled up to the ancient seaside town of Capernaum. We had spent the morning visiting biblical sites along the northern coastline of the Sea of Galilee – the Mount of Beatitudes and Tabgha, where Jesus had multiplied the loaves and fishes – and were finishing our excursion in the fishing village of Capernaum, which had served as Jesus' home base during his years of public ministry. Walking along the orderly streets of the ancient settlement with palm trees swaying overhead, it was easy to imagine the ruins filled with the everyday sounds of 1st century fishermen, farmers, Roman soldiers, and merchants going about their daily tasks. Compared with the excitement and chaos of Jerusalem, the pastoral surroundings of Capernaum elicited a natural sense of calm and tranquility.

In considering the centrality of Capernaum in Jesus' ministry, it is intriguing to ask why Jesus chose to live and minister in this remote northern Galilean fishing town. Surrounded by multiple cities of prominence, wealth, and power – Jerusalem, Caesarea, Sepphoris, and Tiberias, among many others – Jesus' choice of a blue-collar frontier town at first seems counter-intuitive. However, in examining the socio-economic history of ancient Capernaum, the theological and missional importance of Jesus' decision becomes apparent.

Description of Capernaum

After traveling through the rocky topography surrounding the city of Jerusalem, the Galilee region of Israel is a relief from the Judean desert's stark and barren landscape, a fertile valley in the midst of the wilderness. The description of the area recorded by the First Century Jewish historian Flavius Josephus still accurately describes the countryside surrounding the Lake of Gennesaret (also known as the Sea of Galilee and Sea of Tiberias). In his account of the Galilean region, Josephus notes:

> Skirting the lake of Gennesar[et], and also bearing that name,
> lies a region whose natural properties and beauty are very

remarkable. There is not a plant which its fertile soil refuses to produce, and its cultivators, in fact, grow every species; the air is so well-tempered that it suits the most opposite varieties. The walnut, a tree which delights in the most wintry climate, here grows luxuriantly, beside palm trees, which thrive on heat, and figs and olives, which require a milder atmosphere. One might say that nature had taken pride in thus assembling, by a tour de force, the most discordant species in a single spot, and that, by a happy rivalry, each of the seasons wished to claim this region for her own. For not only has the country this surprising merit of producing such diverse fruits, but it also preserves them: for ten months without intermission it supplies those kings of fruits, the grape and the fig; the rest mature on the trees the whole year round. Besides being favo[red] by its genial air, the country is watered by a highly fertilizing spring, called by the inhabitants Capharnaum [Capernaum].[113]

Today, the agricultural region near Capernaum continues to be renowned for its olive groves, date farms, vineyards, citrus orchards, and freshwater fishing industry. The original township of Capernaum, however, has long since lain abandoned; it's last full-time residents having left in the 10th century BCE.[114] In order to develop an understanding of 1st century Capernaum, therefore, we must turn to biblical accounts and the archeological research of the 19th-21st centuries. In the following section, these records are examined in order to comprehend the historical development, socio-economic identities, and political significance of Capernaum during the time of Christ.

The Socio-Cultural History of Capernaum

While the ancient city of Capernaum was located on land originally allotted to the tribe of Naphtali in the 13th century BCE (Josh 19:32-39), it was not until the Third Century BCE that the township of Capernaum was established. By the First Century, Capernaum was already a prosperous agrarian town whose economy was supported by the local fishing industry and

---

[113] *The Jewish War,* 3:516-521, translation by H. St. J. Thackeray in Vol. II of *Josephus* in the *Loeb Classical Library* series London: William Heinemann, 1927, 721-723.
[114] John C.H. Laughlin. "Capernaum," *The New Interpreter's Dictionary of the Bible,* Nashville, TN: Abingdon Press, 2006, 564.

agriculture.[115] Surrounded by abundant natural resources, the northern Galilee region benefited from fertile soil, consistent rainfall, and a moderate climate, which in turn supported the cultivation of dates, olives, and citrus fruits.[116] The city's economy was also buoyed by the local fishing industry, which included fresh-water fishing in the Gennesaret, the manufacture and mending of nets, and the restoration and construction of fishing boats.[117] Throughout the region, the construction of both private and public buildings used local building materials.[118] In Capernaum, for example, the original synagogue from the 1st century CE was built with local black basalt stone from the hills north of Capernaum.[119]

In addition to its local commerce, the city of Capernaum advanced due to its strategic position on the *Via Maris* trade route. Extending from Egypt in the south to Damascus in the northeast and Syria in the northwest, the *Via Maris* was the primary trade route between the Mediterranean Sea and Mesopotamia.[120] In addition to international trade, Capernaum was involved in the local trade of fish and produce with the villages and cities along the coastline of the Sea of Galilee.[121] While Capernaum's location was relatively remote – on the northern border of Israel and the easternmost border of the Roman Empire – the city's economy continued to be bolstered over the centuries by local and transnational trade.

In the 1st century, Capernaum was located only three miles from the border between the territories of Herod Antipas and Herod Philip. As such, the city provided a port of entry into both the Galilee (Herod Antipas' territory to the east of the Jordan river) and Golan (Herod Philip's territory to the west of the Jordan) regions.[122] Despite its location on multiple regional and

---

[115] Laughlin, *op.cit.*, 565.
[116] LaMoine F. DeVries. *Cities of the Biblical World,* Peabody, MA: Hendrickson Publishers, 1997, 269.
[117] *Ibid.*
[118] *Ibid.*
[119] *Ibid.*
[120] Laughlin, *op.cit.*, 565.
[121] J. E. Sanderson. *Major Cities of the Biblical World*, Roland Kenneth Harrison, ed., Nashville, TN: Thomas Nelson Publishers, 1985, 74.
[122] DeVries, *op.cit.*, 269.

national borders, Capernaum was not a multicultural city like its neighbor, Tiberias, to the south.[123] Instead, archeological evidence suggests that besides a small Christian population that developed in the 2nd-3rd centuries CE, Capernaum had a primarily homogenous Jewish population up until the 5th century.[124] Nevertheless, as a trading post on the *Via Maris,* Capernaum would have welcomed traveling merchants from around the world in addition to foreign neighbors from the nearby villages interested in the new merchandise.

The Israelite tribes that originally conquered and settled the area, Naphtali and Zebulun, were unable to fully expel the Canaanite inhabitants and as a result the population thereafter became ethnically mixed (Judg. 1:30-33; 2:1-4). After a series of invasions by foreign powers, Galilee was conquered in 732 BCE by the Assyrian king Tiglath-pileser III (II Kings 15:29), who deported many of the Jewish inhabitants and settled Gentiles in their place. Gentile migration to Galilee continued throughout the expansion of the Assyrian, Babylonian, and Greco-Roman empires. As a result, from the 8th century BCE to the end of the 2nd century BCE, the population of Galilee was predominantly Gentile. By the 1st century CE, Galilee had been reincorporated into Israel by king Herod and the Jewish community had repopulated the area. During the Roman occupation, Galilee continued to receive an influx of Gentile migrants largely due to the *Via Maris* trade route and Galilee's strategic position along international borders.

As Capernaum was situated on the northern political frontier of Israel, the town was of strategic importance to both the Roman Empire and the local tetrarchs. On the part of the Roman Empire, the primary objective was that of security, reflected in the stationing of a Roman Centurion and garrison of 100 soldiers in the town (Matt 8:5-9).[125] For the national leaders,

---

[123] Sanderson, *op.cit.,* 75-76.
[124] Vasiluos Tzaferis. "New Archaeological Evidence on Ancient Capernaum," *Biblical Archaeologist,* New Haven, 46:4: 198-204.
[125] Walter A. Elwell and Philip W. Comfort, eds., "Capernaum," *Tyndale Bible Dictionary,* Wheaton, IL: Tyndale House Publishers, 2001, 256.

the issue was the prospect of financial gain. As such, a customs station was established in Capernaum to collect taxes on local and foreign trade. The Roman imperial taxes and fees during the 1st century included custom taxes on products moving from one tax district to another, toll-fees on roads, and the requirement for all commercial fishermen to purchase fishing contracts.[126] In the gospel accounts the healing of the Roman Centurion's servant (Matt 8:5-9) and the royal official's son (John 4:46-54), in addition to Matthew/Levi's role as a local tax collector (Matt 9:9-13), all reflect the military and fiscal importance of 1st century Capernaum within the Galilee region.[127]

The socio-economic growth of Capernaum continued throughout the late Roman period with the city reaching its peak during the 3rd – 5th centuries CE. The prosperity of this period is evident in the size and craftsmanship found in the town's synagogue built in the 4th century CE.[128] At its height, the town's population climbed to around 1,500 people.[129] The expansion of the Islamic Empire in the 7th century, however, impacted the entire region and by the 10th century, Capernaum was reduced to a small and uninfluential village. The town soon after became deserted except for traveling Bedouins and fishermen and remained so until it's rediscovery by archeologists in the 19th century.[130]

The Rediscovery of Capernaum

In the mid-19th century, the site of Capernaum was discovered by the American biblical scholar Edward Robinson. While Robinson uncovered the town's 4th century CE Jewish synagogue, he failed to identify the structure with the city of Capernaum. It wasn't until the British archeologist Charles Wilson's excavations in 1865-1866 that the site called Tell Hum was identified

---

[126] K.C. Hanson. "The Galilean Fishing Economy and the Jesus Tradition," *Biblical Theology Bulletin,* Vol. 27:3, 1997, 104.
[127] Sanderson, *op.cit.,* 75-76.
[128] Tzaferis, *op.cit.,* 198-204.
[129] Laughlin, *op.cit.,* 564.
[130] *Ibid.*

as being Capernaum.[131] Until this discovery, the site was known in Arabic as Tell Hum (the "Hill of Hum") and in Hebrew as Kefar Nahum (the "Village of Nahum").[132] It is possible that the name Tell Hum was an adaptation of Kefar Nahum, the city's designation as recorded in the Midrash.[133] Jack Finegan surmises that Kefar, which means "village," could have been changed to Tell in reference to the dirt mound where the old city laid, and Nahum could have been an abbreviated form of Hum. If that analysis is accurate, the original Hebrew name of Capernaum is still conserved in its Arabic counterpart, Tell Hum.[134]

In 1894 the site of Capernaum was acquired from the As-Samakiyeh Arabs by the Franciscan Custody of the Holy Land.[135] A Franciscan monastery was soon built near the site; however, due to ongoing tensions in the region, a decision was made to bury the synagogue ruins for its protection. In 1905 excavations began again in Capernaum, this time led by the German archeologists Heinrich Kohl and Carl Watzinger with the sponsorship of the Deutsche Orient-Gesellschaft.[136] Since the late 19th century, the Capernaum site has been divided into two parts governed by distinct religious communities. In accordance with the original agreement, the Franciscan Fathers have facilitated the excavation of the western side of the site and the Greek Orthodox patriarch of Jerusalem, the eastern side.[137]

In a series of endeavors led by the Franciscan archeologists Virgilio C. Corbo and Stanislao Loffreda from 1968-1985, a synagogue and the house of Simon Peter were discovered.[138] The 1st century synagogue is believed to be

[131] Jack Finegan. *The Archeology of the New Testament: The Life of Jesus and the Beginning of the Early Church* Princeton, NJ: Princeton University Press, 1969, 51-52.
[132] Laughlin, *op.cit.*, 564.
[133] R.A.S. Macalister. "Capernaum," in Hastings, James, ed., *Hasting's Dictionary of the Bible.* 5th ed. New York, NY: Hendrickson Publishers, 2001, 117.
[134] Finegan. *op.cit.*, 51.
[135] Virgilio C. Corbo. "Capernaum," in David Noel Freedman ed., *The Anchor Bible Dictionary,* vol. 1. New York: Doubleday, 1992, 866.
[136] Finegan. *op. cit.*, 51-52.
[137] Sharon Lea Mattila. "Capernaum, Village of Nahum, From Hellenistic to Byzantine Times," in David A. Fiensy and James Riley Strange, eds., *Galilee: In the Late Second Temple and Mishnaic Periods*, Minneapolis, MN: Fortress Press, 2015, 217.
[138] Corbo, *op.cit.*, 866.

the same synagogue sponsored by the Roman Centurion as referenced in Luke 7:2-5.[139] Built during the Hellenistic period (332-37 BCE), the house was most likely acquired at a later date by the family of Simon Peter.[140] The discovery included several layers of buildings all built upon the original residence. The first building to be discovered was the octagonal Byzantine church, which was uncovered by Gaudence Orfali in 1921 and then eventually excavated by Corbo in 1968.[141] In the 4th century, a new synagogue was built directly on the older synagogue, which was constructed using the distinct black basalt stone from the region. The 4th-5th century church was discovered to have been built upon a small Christian house church, which itself was an extension of the original domestic dwelling. The original house was identified as the remnants of a 1st-century fisherman's lodgings which was later adapted and used as a corporate place of Christian worship as early as the 2nd century.[142]

The identification of Simon Peter's residence and house church is supported by several historical accounts and discoveries on the site. Foremost is the pilgrim Aetheria's account of her 385 CE visit to Capernaum, in which she reported that "In Capernaum out of the house of the first of the apostles a church was made, the walls of which stand until today as they once were. Here the Lord cured the paralytic."[143] This report is supported by the Anonymous Pilgrim of Piacenza who in reference to his visit in 570 CE wrote, "We came to Capernaum into the house of St. Peter, which is a basilica."[144] In addition to these accounts, the decorations and graffiti found on the walls of the house church support the theory that the original residence belonged to Simon Peter. Archeologists additionally discovered Judeo-Christian symbols painted onto the walls of the house church, along with devotional graffiti in Greek,

---

[139] *Ibid.*
[140] *Ibid.*, 867.
[141] Finegan. *op.cit.*, 56.
[142] *Ibid.*
[143] Corbo, *op.cit.*, 867.
[144] Finegan. *op.cit.*, 56.

Latin, Aramaic, and Syriac that had been etched into the plaster by early Christian pilgrims who had visited the site over the next few centuries.[145]

Capernaum in Scripture

According to Matthew, Jesus moved to Capernaum from his rural home-town of Nazareth after his baptism and temptation in the wilderness (Matt 3:13-4:13). The gospel records that Jesus returned to Galilee and relocated to Capernaum upon hearing of the imprisonment of John the Baptist by Herod Antipas (Matt 4:12; cf. Luke 3:19-20). During the next few years, Capernaum became Jesus' home-base and ministry headquarters (Matt 4:13, 9:1; Mark 2:1). Capernaum is later referred to as "[Jesus'] own town" (9:1). It was in Capernaum that Jesus began his public ministry, preaching "Repent, for the kingdom of heaven has come near" (Matt 4:17). Soon after moving to Capernaum, while walking along the Sea of Galilee, Jesus called two sets of brothers to become his disciples: Simon (called Peter) and Andrew (Matt 4:18-19; cf. Mark 1:16-18); and James and John, the sons of Zebedee (Matt 4:21-22; cf. Mark 1:19-20). Jesus also called the future church leader and biographer, Matthew (also called Levi), who worked as a tax collector at the time (Matt 9:9).

While originally from Bethsaida (John 1:44), Simon Peter and his brother Andrew appear to have moved to Capernaum by the time they encountered Jesus. Working as commercial fishermen on the Sea of Galilee, the brothers were business partners with James and John (Luke 5:7-10). The healing of Simon Peter's mother-in-law in Capernaum (Mark 1:29-31) reveals that Peter was married and appears to have lived there with his extended family (vv. 29-30). In Paul's letter to the Corinthians, the apostle refers to Peter's wife, stating that Peter, along with several other disciples of Jesus, took their believing wives with them when they traveled for ministry (1 Cor. 9:5).

---

[145] Corbo, *op.cit.*, 867.

While in Capernaum, Jesus taught in the city's sacred space of worship and public dialogue, the Jewish synagogue (Luke 4:31-37; cf. Mark 1:21-22, John 6:22-59). Luke notes that Capernaum's synagogue was funded and built by the Roman Centurion that sought Jesus's assistance on behalf of his dying servant (Luke 7:1-5). When listening to Jesus teach, the Jewish congregation in Capernaum observed the difference between Jesus' teaching and that of their own rabbis. "The people [of Capernaum] were amazed at [Jesus'] teaching because he taught them as one who had authority, not as the teachers of the law" (Mark 1:21; cf. Luke 4:32). A portion of Jesus' teachings in Capernaum is documented in the gospels. In Matthew 17:24-27, for example, Jesus engages with Peter about the two-drachma temple tax. In Mark 9:33-37, Jesus speaks to his disciples about the need for humility. In John 6:22-59, Jesus speaks to the crowd who followed him across the Sea of Galilee after Jesus miraculously fed five thousand people (John 6:1-14). In this dialogue, Jesus responds to the crowd "I am the bread of life.... I am the living bread that came down from heaven. Whoever eats this bread will live forever. This bread is my flesh, which I will give for the life of the world" (John 6:48-51).

Jesus also taught in private spaces such as residents' homes. After calling Matthew son of Alphaeus as a disciple, for instance, Jesus went and had dinner in the tax collector's home (Mark 2:13-17). During the meal, Matthew's house became filled with many of his tax collector colleagues and other individuals who were considered sinners by the religious Jewish community. The teachers of the law who saw that Jesus was eating with known tax collectors and individuals who were spiritually unclean responded with a thinly veiled rebuke to Jesus' disciples (v. 16). In response to the Pharisees' criticism, Jesus explained that "It is not the healthy who need a doctor, but the sick. I have not come to call the righteous, but sinners" (Mark 2:17). As the news about Jesus spread, the multitudes who came to Capernaum increased and in turn brought with them their sick and those who were demon-possessed. In another private residence in Capernaum, the crowd that came to hear Jesus became so large that a paralyzed man had to be lowered through the roof in order to be brought before Jesus (Mark 2:1-12).

While in Capernaum, Jesus healed the sick, cast out evil spirits, and performed many signs and wonders (Mark 1:23-2:12; Luke 4:33-41). The miracles of healing in Capernaum that are recorded in the gospels include Jesus' healing of a paralytic man (Mark 2:1-12), the saving of the life of a Roman Centurion's servant (Matt 8:5-13; Luke 7:2-10), and the healing of Peter's mother-in-law from a fever (Mark 1:31). It is noteworthy that in the case of the paralytic man, Jesus first forgave the man's sins and then healed his physical ailment as evidence that "the Son of Man has authority on earth to forgive sins" (Mark 2:10). During this time, Jesus also healed several individuals from a distance demonstrating the extent of his power and authority. While traveling through Cana, for example, Jesus encountered a royal official who begged him to come back to Capernaum to heal his son who was dying (John 4:46-53). Granting his request, Jesus replied to the man "your son will live" (v. 50). The official returned to Capernaum to find that his son was healed at the exact time that Jesus had spoken (vv. 50-53). As a result, the royal official "and his whole household believed" (v. 53). In Capernaum, Jesus also cast out many demonic spirits (Mark 1:32-34; Luke 4:31-41). On one occasion, Jesus expelled an unclean spirit from a Jewish man in the midst of the Shabbat synagogue service (Mark 1:21-26; Luke 4:31-37).

As a result of Jesus' teachings and miracles in Capernaum, the news about Jesus reached all of Galilee (Mark 1:28; Luke 4:40-41). From his ministry base in Capernaum, Matthew records that Jesus traveled through all of Galilee "teaching in their synagogues, proclaiming the good news of the kingdom, and healing every disease and sickness among the people" (Matt 4:23). As a consequence, "news about [Jesus] spread all over Syria, and people brought to him all who were ill with various diseases, those suffering severe pain, the demon-possessed, those having seizures, and the paralyzed; and he healed them. Large crowds from Galilee, the Decapolis, Jerusalem, Judea, and the region across the Jordan followed him" (Matt 4:23-25). As Galilee's population was multiethnic and many of its towns were situated on the *Via Maris* trade route, it is most likely that the crowds listening to Jesus included Jews and Canaanites, as well as Phoenicians, Syrians, Romans, and Samaritans traveling through the region.

Even though the residents of Capernaum saw the miracles of Jesus, there were still those who remained in their unbelief. Accordingly, Capernaum is also remembered, along with the nearby towns of Chorazin and Bethsaida, as having been rebuked by Jesus for its stubborn rejection of Christ despite all the miracles they witnessed (Matt 11:20-24; Luke 10:13-15). Jesus reproached Capernaum declaring "And you, Capernaum, will you be lifted to the heavens? No, you will go down to Hades. For if the miracles that were performed in you had been performed in Sodom, it would have remained to this day. But I tell you that it will be more bearable for Sodom on the day of judgment than for you" (Matt 11:23-24).

The Missional Significance of Capernaum as Jesus' Mission Base

In fulfillment of a prophecy given hundreds of years before Christ's birth, Jesus' residence in Galilee facilitated the outworking of God's salvific mission to all the nations of the world. In particular, Capernaum's multicultural population, the city's location on the *Via Maris* trade route, and the vast networking capacity of the fishing industry were all key factors that ensured that the good news about Christ would be heard by both Jews and Gentiles alike.

The Fulfillment of Prophecy

When analyzing the socio-cultural history of Capernaum, the question arises: "Why did Jesus reside in Capernaum during his ministry?" All four gospels note that Jesus lived and worked out of Capernaum, however the gospel of Matthew provides additional insight. As indicated in Matthew, Jesus' move to Capernaum was not arbitrary, but instead, it was a fulfillment of a prophetic word given to Isaiah. In Matthew 4:12-16, the author explains:

Leaving Nazareth, [Jesus] went and lived in Capernaum, which was by the lake in the area of Zebulun and Naphtali – to fulfill what was said through the prophet Isaiah: Land of Zebulun and land of Naphtali, the Way of the Sea, beyond the Jordan, Galilee of the Gentiles – the people living in darkness have seen a great light; on those living in the land of the shadow of death a light has dawned. (Isa 9:1-2)

The author continues that "from that time on Jesus began to preach, 'Repent, for the kingdom of heaven has come near'" (Matt 4:17). Matthew highlights in this passage that Jesus' residence in Galilee was not happenstance, but instead, it was a direct fulfillment of Isaiah's prophecy.

As the missiologist Paul Hertig so aptly inquires, however, "Is [Matthew] simply trying to emphasize through geographical data that Jesus' ministry is the fulfillment of Isaiah 9:1-7, or is he doing something more with the theme of Galilee?"[146] Hertig argues that Jesus' ministry in Galilee extends beyond the fulfillment of a prophecy to reflect the nature and purpose of God's mission to the nations.[147] Hertig explains that "the Galilee theme widens the scope of the mission to include both Jew and Gentile, center and margins, paving the way for a contextualized mission for all nations."[148] Jesus' decision to reside and minister in the Galilean city of Capernaum reflects and facilitates God's salvific mission to both the Jewish and Gentile communities.

In Isaiah 9:1-2, God's mission to the nations is foreshadowed in the metaphor of the Messiah as a "great light" in a land of darkness. A continuation of the Old Testament motif of God and the Word of God as light,[149] the theme of Christ as the light is repeated throughout the New Testament (see John 1:5, 8:12, 12:35-37; I John 1:5-9; Eph 5:14; I Pet 2:9; Rev 21:23). In the case of Isaiah 9:1-2, it is significant that God proclaims that He will dispel the darkness in the multicultural region of Galilee; appropriately

---

[146] Paul Hertig. "The Galilee Theme in Matthew: Transforming Mission through Marginality," *Missiology: An International Review*, Vol. XXV, No. 2 (April 1997), 155.

[147] *Ibid.*

[148] *Ibid.*, 161.

[149] The motif of God as light is a prevalent theme in the Hebrew Scriptures. (See Exodus 13:21; Psalm 18:28, 27:1, 36:9, 119:105, 130; Proverbs 6:23; Isaiah 42:16, 58:8, 60:1-3, 19-20; Micah 7:8-10).

named "Galilee of the Gentiles" (Isa 9:1, Matt 4:15; I Macc 5:15). While the mission of Jesus Christ does bring God's light to the Jews, Isaiah's prophecy foreshadows that God's light will extend even to the Gentiles. This theme is reiterated throughout the New Testament and is expressed again in Jesus Christ's missional declaration in John: "I am the light of the world. Whoever follows me will never walk in darkness, but will have the light of life" (John 8:12).

Proclamation of the Gospel in "Galilee of the Gentiles"

By residing in Capernaum, Jesus' proclamation of God's kingdom was announced to a multi-religious and ethnically diverse community. The phrase, "Galilee of the Gentiles," used by the prophet Isaiah (9:1) and repeated by Matthew (4:15), alluded to the longstanding ethnic diversity of the region. Jesus' residence in Capernaum, one of the most prominent towns in 1st century Galilee, placed him on the international and intercultural borderlands, in the midst of Galilee's socio-cultural and religious diversity.

Foretold and foreordained by God, Jesus' residence in "Galilee of the Gentiles" is a tangible reflection of God's grace extended to the Gentiles. While in Galilee, Jesus engaged with Gentiles throughout his three years of ministry. In Matthew 5:23-25, the gospel writer records that as Jesus taught, preached, and healed people in Galilee, "large crowds from Galilee, the Decapolis, Jerusalem, Judea, and the region across the Jordan followed him" (v. 25). During this period, numerous Gentiles responded in faith to the works and message of Jesus. Jesus was not passive in these encounters, instead he engaged with the Gentiles who came to him with compassion and mercy, granting their petitions for healing. On one occasion in Capernaum Jesus was approached by the Jewish friends of a Roman Centurion, who requested on behalf of the Gentile man that Jesus come and heal the man's servant who was ill, about to die (Luke 7:1-5). When Jesus agreed to go to the Centurion's house, the Roman officer sent another set of friends to tell Jesus that he did not "deserve to have [Jesus] come under [his] roof" for he was unworthy to be in Jesus' presence" (v. 7). Instead, the Centurion acknowledged that just as he had the power to tell the soldiers under him what to do and when to do it, so Jesus had the authority to heal his servant in a similar way (vv. 7-8). "When Jesus heard this, he was amazed at him, and turning to the crowd following him he said, "I tell you, I have not found such great faith even in Israel." Then the men who had been sent returned to the house and found the servant well (7:9-10). The Gentile centurion was one of two individuals, both Gentiles, that Jesus declared had "great faith" (cf. the Canaanite woman in Matt 15:28).

Proclamation of the Gospel through Trade Routes

By ministering in and from Capernaum, a major hub along the international trade route, Jesus enabled the proclamation of his message to the Gentile community. The *Via Maris* trade route that passed through Galilee, on the border, provided a natural, built-in bridge over which the good news about Jesus could travel to the neighboring nations: Syria to the northeast, Phoenicia to the west, and Samaria to the south.[150] Hertig explains that this movement of travelers went both ways:

> Not only did Jesus journey out to the world, but the world journeyed out to him. News about Jesus spread to Syria and large crowds followed Jesus from Galilee, the Decapolis, Jerusalem, Judea, and from across the Jordan (Matt 4:24-25).... Jesus transformed Galilee into God's new center of mission. Jerusalem, the traditional center of God's redeeming work, discovered its need for mobility; Jerusalem crowds journeyed to the margins at Galilee to find salvation.[151]

Without knowledge of the major trading routes through the Galilee region, it is easy to misidentify Jesus' move from Nazareth to Capernaum as inconsequential. This move, however, strategically placed Jesus in the center of a major thoroughfare of transnational trade and commerce. The city of "Capernaum represented a crossroads between local peasantry and international trade," and as such by moving into this cosmopolitan

---

[150] Paul Hertig. "The Multi-ethnic Journeys of Jesus in Matthew: Margin-Center Dynamics," *Missiology: An International Review*, Vol. XXVI, No. 1 (Jan. 1998), 25.
[151] *Ibid.*, 27.

community Jesus made "himself accessible not only to the wider world of Jews but to Gentiles as well."[152] In Capernaum, Jesus' teaching and signs were witnessed by a constant stream of Gentile merchants, soldiers, foreign officials, and travelers, many of whom would have taken the tales of the Jewish rabbi's miraculous feats to their home towns and countries (cf. Acts 8:26-40).

The fishing industry based in Capernaum also provided a vehicle for the spread of the gospel among communities along the Sea of Galilee and in nearby regions. K.C. Hanson notes that "scholars of the Jesus tradition have seriously underplayed the role and significance of the physical and social geography of Galilean fishing on Jesus' development of his network."[153] Hanson explains that the fishing industry in Capernaum influenced where Jesus operated, who Jesus interacted with, and how Jesus communicated his message.[154] A large number of the towns that Jesus visited and ministered in were fishing villages – Bethsaida, Capernaum, Gennesaret, Magdala, Gerasa, and Tyre and Sidon.[155] Additionally, Jesus' social network was made up of individuals connected to the fishing industry: the fishermen Simon Peter, Andrew, James, and John; individuals living in fishing communities; the mother-in-law of Peter; the mother of James and John; Levi; and the townspeople from Capernaum, Tyre, and Sidon.[156] Hanson adds:

> It does not seem to be an overstatement to say that Jesus' proclamation of God's Reign had its primary audience in Galilean fishing villages and towns. This at least partially accounts for his avoidance of Galilean cities (notably Tiberias and Sepphoris) and the snide view of Jesus' activity expressed by Jerusalemite elites. It may also account for the tradition of Jesus drawing crowds from the fishing regions of Tyre and Sidon.[157]

---

[152] *Ibid.*, 25.
[153] Hanson, *op.cit.*, 100.
[154] *Ibid.*, 109.
[155] *Ibid.*, 107.
[156] *Ibid.*
[157] *Ibid.*, 109.

From Jesus' base in Capernaum, the message of Christ was circulated throughout the area by fishermen, on fishing boats, and to fishing communities. The embedded economy of Capernaum's fishing industry strategically provided Jesus with a natural network through which to broadcast his message across the sea in addition to the trade routes that carried his message on land.

Using these trade routes on land and sea, Jesus journeyed from Capernaum to the majority Jewish and Gentile regions. After traveling to the eastern side of the Sea of Galilee by boat, for example, Jesus healed two demon-possessed men from a Gentile community within the Gerasenes region (Matt 8:28-34). Later, while traveling to the fishing towns of Tyre and Sidon, Jesus was approached by a Canaanite woman whose daughter was demon-possessed (Matt 15:21-28). After engaging with her in conversation, Jesus remarked, "Woman, you have great faith! Your request is granted" (v. 28). As in the case of the Roman Centurion in Capernaum, the woman's daughter was healed at the exact moment that Jesus spoke (v. 28). At another time, while traveling along the border of Galilee and Samaria, Jesus healed several lepers, one of whom was a Samaritan, an ethnic group despised by the Jewish community. The narrator makes a point to record that only the Samaritan returned to thank Jesus (Luke 17:11-19).

Contextualized Mission to Contemporary Capernaum

As we consider urban ministry in our contemporary world, there are several insights that we can glean from Jesus' time in Capernaum. First, where Jesus located his mission base and the individuals to whom Jesus ministered should catch the eye of any 21st century church leader. Jesus ministered from a place and among a people group on the margins of society. Jesus purposefully established his ministry in a community that had little political, religious, social, or economic power or prestige (cf. John 7:41, 7:52). Furthermore, in the eyes of the Jewish religious elite, the entire region, including Capernaum, was despised and ridiculed due to its ethnic and religious diversity. Galilee of the Gentiles was considered socially backward, religiously unclean, and ethnically polluted. Yet, it was in Capernaum of Galilee that the long-awaited Jewish Messiah decided to live and minister. In Capernaum, Jesus ate with the despised supporters of the Roman occupation, interacted with individuals who had violated the Jewish law, and spoke to and assisted the religious other. Jesus lived and ministered on and from the margins. In our Christian communities today, what would it look like to follow Jesus' ministry model in our missional contexts? How would embracing Jesus attitude and mindset impact how and with whom we spend our time? How would enacting Jesus' ministry from the margins impact our leadership selection and training, choice of church venue, ministry programs, and networking practices?

Second, Jesus established his ministry in a city strategically positioned to spread the gospel. Capernaum's location on the *Via Maris* trade route along with its fishing network allowed the message of Christ to spread rapidly throughout Israel and the surrounding nations. During the 1st century, the merchants and traders traveling through the fertile crescent were bearers of both resources and news. As such, the teachings, miracles, and parables of Christ reached remote villages and cities long before the early church sent its missionaries in the following centuries. In choosing Capernaum, Jesus chose a city that was able to facilitate his travel to the surrounding towns, but also that would allow people to easily come to him. In the 21st century, the seed of the gospel continues to spread through an ever-increasing set of "roads" including social media, podcasts, television, films, radio, books, magazines, sermons, and relationships, among many other avenues. Each of these vehicles of evangelism requires the Christian believer to step onto the "road" of communication. In your ministry context today, what roads is the Holy Spirit inviting you to step onto? What new avenues of evangelism are within your reach to explore?

Third, Jesus contextualized his message using the cultural customs, industries, and geography of the residents. While living in the community of

Capernaum, Jesus taught with illustrations from the local fishing industry, using parables such as the Parable of the Net (Matt 13:47-50) and metaphors such as the Good Gifts (Matt 7:9-11; Luke 11:11-13) and the Millstone and the Sea (Mark 9:42; Matt 18:6; Luke 17:2). Jesus also invited community members into the center of his ministry, calling several local fishermen to be his disciples (Mark 1:16-20; Matt 4:18-22; Luke 5:1-11). Due to his proximity to the Sea of Galilee, a large portion of Jesus' signs and wonders were also connected to, or adjacent to, the sea: miracles such as the calming of the storm (Mark 4:35-41; Matt 8:23-27; Luke 8:22-25), the feeding of the 5,000 (Mark 6:35-44; Luke 9:10-17), Jesus walking on the water (Mark 6:45-52; Matt 14:22-33; John 6:16-21), the feeding of the 4,000 (Matt 15:32-39), and the two extraordinary catches of fish (Luke 5:1-11; John 21:1-14). Jesus' investment in the Galilean fishing community of Capernaum is noteworthy. Having been raised in the land-locked village of Nazareth, Jesus contextualizes his message and develops a ministry team to reflect his missional context in Capernaum. In our contemporary settings, how can Jesus' cultural contextualization breathe new life into our ministry contexts today? Do our ministry teams, like Jesus' disciples, reflect our city and neighborhood's demographics? And, what are fresh ways in which we can contextualize the gospel to better speak into and reflect our community's socio-cultural, economic, religious, and occupational realities?

Conclusion

By locating his ministry base in Galilee, Jesus established a different kind of kingdom than that of the empires of the world. Instead of working from the centers of political power and wealth, such as Jerusalem, Caesarea, and Tiberias, Jesus' ministry base was in a small fishing village on the northern edge of the nation of Israel and along the eastern borderlands of the Roman Empire. Although the population of 1st century Capernaum was largely Jewish, the witnesses of Jesus' miracles also included local Canaanites, Gentile soldiers, international merchants and traders, and political officials passing through the township. The stories about the Jewish rabbi who cast out evil spirits, healed paralyzed men and confounded the local religious leaders would have been riveting tales told along the *Via Maris* highway from the Mediterranean coastal towns to the Syrian interior.

The fact that Jesus chose to live and minister in this small Jewish town along the transnational trade route to Syria highlights once again the reality that Jesus' ministry was directed to the entire world, not only the Jewish community. As demonstrated repeatedly by Jesus' teachings and actions, the kingdom of God was not restricted to the rich, the well-educated, the powerful, or the ultra-religious person of the day. The kingdom of God was open to all: to the common person, the blue-collar worker, the day laborer, the mother, the fisherman, the soldier, the trader, the Jew, and the Gentile. The kingdom of God welcomed those who lived in country towns as well as those who lived in the mega-cities. Jesus' ministry amongst the rural and urban populations of Capernaum was not less important than what he accomplished in Jerusalem, the capital of Israel. Likewise, the people of Capernaum and the surrounding agricultural towns were just as significant in God's eyes as the leaders and rulers of this world.

The city of Capernaum encapsulated the reality of many modern border towns; it was multicultural, multiethnic, and multi-religious, and its population encompassed a broad socioeconomic spectrum. Jesus' commitment to live and minister in such a community demonstrates God's heart for all the nations of the world. There are many lessons that we can learn from Jesus' ministry in Capernaum including Jesus' adoption of ministry to and from the margins of society, Jesus' embrace of strategic pathways of evangelism, and Jesus' contextualization of his message and ministry using the cultural customs, industries, and geography of his community.

Chapter 5: Corinth

by Jayakumar Christian[158]

God's Mission of Rediscovered Wisdom

The church lives out its theology with sincerity and integrity preaching an alternative ideology. It seeks to demolish the city's domination system and its spiritual obsession with knowledge and wisdom as sources of power by being a counter-narrative community to the city. Christ's church seeks to challenge the mushrooming heresies that set themselves up against the knowledge of God. The church refuses to be co-opted into a system that abuses power and wounds the soul of those on the margins. Called to be a prophetic community in the city, the church lives out the foolishness of the Gospel in God's space in the city.

Introduction

Corinth was politically important, geographically well-placed, and economically strategic. Corinth was a city with two strategically located

---

158 Dr. Jayakumar Christian (Ph.D. in Missiology from the School of Intercultural Studies of Fuller Theological Seminary) provides leadership for World Vision International's Faith & Development efforts from his base in Chennai, India. His publications include *God of the Empty-Handed: Poverty, Power, and the Kingdom of God;* "Toward Redefining Urban Poverty" in Charles Van Engen and Jude Tiersma, eds., *God So Loves the City: Seeking a Theology for Urban Mission,* pp 195-220; and "Innovation at the Margins" in Charles Van Engen, ed., *The State of Missiology Today: Global Innovations in Christian Witness,* 165-177.

harbours,[159] "the master of two harbours"[160] that attracted tourists, traders, and soldiers. The city "rose from the ashes"[161] demonstrating its resilience. Corinth was populated by former slaves, army veterans, and foreigners who were known for their wealth and ostentation. When Paul visited in 50 CE, Corinth was the most beautiful, modern, and industrious city of its size in Greece.

The Mind of Corinth

Corinth was the most influential city in the province of Achaea. It was a city designed for "those who were pre-occupied with the marks of social status."[162] Corinth was an important city, a busy center for trade with both rich and slaves co-existing.[163] There was a growing migrant population triggered by an emerging economy. It was a city obsessed with fame and power. The mix of many economic advantages and diversity of social classes lent itself to the abuse of power[164] and a tendency to discriminate (I Cor 11:17-34).[165] It was a society that was probably obsessed with rights (I Cor 6:12; 10:23), freedom (I Cor 9:19), and authority (II Cor 13:10, II Cor 10:8). It does appear that "secular wisdom – which reflected the code of conduct of the social elite, who jostled one another for power, prestige, and popularity – had its hold on the members of the [Corinthian] church."[166]

---

[159] Corinth was located between two harbors on a narrow strip of land with sea on either side, forming a link between two larger areas of land (an isthmus). One of the harbors provided access to Asia (Cenchrea on the Sarconic Gulf), and the other to Italy (Lechaeum on the Corinthian Gulf). It was a common route for merchants from Italy and from Asia.

[160] Quoted in David E. Garland, *1 Corinthians: Baker Exegetical Commentary on the New Testament.* Grand Rapids, Michigan: Baker Publishing Group, 2003, 1.

[161] Corinth was razed to the ground by Roman wrath in 146 BCE. It remained uninhabited for 102 years after the defeat, only attracting tourists to view its ruins. In 44 BCE Julius Caesar established Corinth as a Roman Colony. *Ibid.,* 1

[162] Garland, *op.cit.,* 4; also read Guthrie, George E. *2 Corinthians: Baker Exegetical Commentary on the New Testament,* Grand Rapids, Michigan: Baker Publishing Group, 2015, 15.

[163] Hilda Bright. *An Easy English Bible Version and Commentary on Paul's First Letter to the Corinthians,* accessed from www.easyenglish.bible

[164] Guthrie, *op.cit.,* 16.

[165] All references from the Bible in this chapter are from the New International Version.

[166] Garland, *op.cit.,* 6.

Corinth was a cosmopolitan mosaic of many cultures. Corinth was a "Greek city by location, the capital of Achaea (which made up most of ancient Greece),...a Roman colony for nearly a century, officially resettled by Romans long after its destruction, with Greek and Latin cultures co-existing. Its citizens, however, viewed themselves as Roman and were proud of their Roman identity."[167] In Corinth, it was common for Jews to take on Roman names (examples: Aquila [I Cor 16:9] and Crispus [I Cor 1:14], Gaius [I Cor 1:14] and Fortunatus [I Cor 16:17]). As a commercial hub, Corinth was also inhabited by Phoenicians and Phrygians from the east.

Corinth was a religious hub with many temples and religious practices. A temple for the goddess of love, Aphrodite, was a main attraction both for tourists and devotees. Many prostitutes in the city were associated with this temple. Corinth became notorious for exploitative sexual behaviour (I Cor 5:1-13; 6:12-20). To live "like a Corinthian"[168] meant to get drunk often and/or to visit prostitutes as a way of life. The mix of religion and sexual promiscuity was common in the city of Corinth.

Corinth was famous for the Isthmian Games. These games were second in importance only to the Olympic Games. Corinthians were known for their cleverness, inventiveness, and artistic sense; and they prided themselves on surpassing the other Greeks in the embellishment of their city and the adornment of their temples. There were many celebrated painters in Corinth, and the city became famous for the Corinthian order of architecture. The city became a popular social hub for all these reasons. The proximity to Athens had a significant influence on Corinth's obsession with theatre, lectures, and professional orators. It was obsessed with knowledge and

---

[167] Craig S. Keener, ed. *The IVP Bible Background Commentary,* Downers Grove, Illinois: InterVarsity Press, 2014, 459.

[168] Corinth was known as a licentious city so that one of the Greek verbs for fornicate was *korinthiazomai,* a word derived from the city's name. It is assumed there were 1,000 sacred prostitutes in the temple of Aphrodite on the Acrocorinth with significant levels of sexual promiscuity sanctioned by religion. See *The Biblical City of Corinth* by David Padfield accessed from www.padfield.com, 2005.

oratory skills. The Corinthian obsession with knowledge was a source of power to earn an edge in their competitive culture.

Corinth's obsession with knowledge, religiously sanctioned sexual promiscuity, proliferation of heresies, and the tendency to use power to discriminate, provides an interesting construct to understand the mind of Corinth. Paul refers to these as the "standards of this world," (II Cor 10:2), worldliness (I Cor 3:1), "standards of this age," "wisdom of this world" (I Cor 3:18,19), and worldly point of view (II Cor 5:16).[169] Paul also suggests that the mind of the city is in direct conflict with the mind of the church and the wisdom of God (I Cor 6:1,4).

Jacques Ellul in the *Meaning of the City* describes a city as a collective whole and points out that a city is much more than the total number of persons.[170] Bishop Leslie Newbigin identifies this as the "spiritual power within, behind or above its visible embodiment.... Long-enduring institutions have something, an inwardness, which can be recognized in those who form the institution at any one time but outlasts and transcends them."[171]

Ellul's description of the collective whole resonates with Wink's description of the city's spirituality as a system of domination that justifies its existence, independence, and dominance. In *Engaging the Powers* Walter Wink suggests that the principalities and powers of every domination system undergird the "spirituality at the center of the political, economic and cultural institutions of their day"[172] and are at the core of persuasive ideologies as well.[173] Wink suggests that an institutionalized system of ideologies is not simply a personification of institutional qualities but an actual spiritual ethos.[174] The mind of the city is the dominating system that we are up against.

---

[169] Also read II Cor 11:3 (serpent's cunningness), II Cor 11:14 (Satan masquerading as an angel of light).

[170] Jacques Ellul. *The Meaning of the City*, Eugene, Oregon: Wipf and Stock Publishers, 1970, 45.

[171] Leslie Newbigin. *The Open Secret*. Grand Rapids, Michigan: GR: Eerdmans, 1989, 202

[172] Walter Wink. *Engaging the Powers: Discernment and Resistance in a World of Domination,* Minneapolis, MN: Augsburg Fortress, 1992, 6.

[173] *Ibid.,* 300.

[174] *Ibid.,* 6.

We confront such a system that is strongly rooted in the spirituality of the city. As for Corinth, its system of domination was entrenched in its obsession with knowledge, power, heresies, and sexual immorality.

The power of Corinth also included the tendency to co-opt all institutions, be it arts, theatre, or religious institutions such as the church.[175] The church ran the risk of being co-opted and instrumentalized by the city for the purposes of the city. Paul in his letters to the Corinthians seeks to address this threat of co-option and articulates the mind of the church as a counter-narrative[176] to the mind of the city. Robert Linthicum points out "Paul's primary concern was to enable these urban churches to act rather than to react to their city....If they could not be assertive in undertaking their ministry in their city and as part of the Roman Empire, they would eventually die." [177]

Corinth demonstrates for us that a city is more than a mere geographical or a demographic entity or merely the sum of its political, social, religious, or economic institutions. The city is a force magnifier. It is the highest aspiration of a nation. It often has the potential to shape the mind of the nation. Its diversity is more than a mosaic of peoples or even an Indian *thali*.[178]

---

[175] George Guthrie referring to the influence of the city on the church in Corinth, suggests that many of the issues in the church "can be traced to their uncritical acceptance of the attitudes, values, and behaviors of the society in which they lived" (Guthrie, *op.cit.*, 15).

[176] Walter Brueggemann in "The City in Biblical Perspective: Failed and Possible" identifies the need for an alternate reading of the city and states that the city is "an ideological construal, grounded in scarcity and brutality, that in principle admits of no alternative tellings of the city. It is the task of church and synagogue to tell an alternative account of the city that concedes nothing to the claims of an ideological telling that, in light of the gospel, is false." (in *Word and World,* Volume XIX, Number 3 Summer 1999; Luther Seminary, St. Paul, MN, 249.)

[177] Robert Linthicum. *City of God City of Satan: A Biblical Theology of the Urban Church,* Grand Rapids, Michigan: Zondervan Publishing House, 1991, 66.

[178] The Indian idea is the opposite of what Freudians call "the narcissism of minor differences"; in India we celebrate the commonality of major differences. If America is a melting-pot, then to me India is a *thali*, a selection of sumptuous dishes in different bowls. Each taste is different, and does not necessarily mix with the next, but they belong together on the same plate, and they complement each other in making the meal a satisfying repast. (Shashi Tharoor: "Indian identity is forged in diversity. Every one of us is in a minority." Accessed from https://www.theguardian.com/commentisfree/2007/aug/15/comment.india).

How then should the Church respond? What are the missiological factors that need to be considered as we respond to the sociology of the city? How do we respond to the spirituality of the city in a manner that reflects the integrity of our faith and theology? How can the church be a disruptive prophetic community in the city "seek the welfare of the city...and pray to the Lord on its behalf" with integrity, recognizing that in the welfare of the city is the welfare of the church, the people of God (Jer 29:7).[179] The church is that prophetic community involved in a dangerous vocation. This bias for being appears to be Paul's bias in his letters to the Corinthian church. Paul is focused on equipping the church to be a prophetic community, a credible counter-narrative to the domination system of the city, Corinth.

Paul's Missional Response to Corinth's Domination System

Paul offers three missiological themes that could mold our response to Corinth's domination system, based on his relationship with the Corinthian church. They are:

- Redefine knowledge as subversive foolishness – God's wisdom is subversive foolishness, a mystery, and we are stewards, not owners of God's wisdom.
- Demonstrate influence from an intentional position of powerlessness – refusing to be co-opted, redefining 'person of influence,' while setting ethical benchmarks.
- Nurture an alternate community – healing broken relationships – the church as an alternate community, with an alternate mantra and alternate frame to understand authority, rights, and freedom.

Redefine Knowledge as Subversive Foolishness

Corinth was visibly obsessed with knowledge as a natural corollary to power. Knowledge was the basis of authority. Within the church, this resulted

---

[179] Ellul, *op.cit.*, 72-78.

in a battle of preference for Apollos over Paul. This obsession with knowledge and power also led to discrimination and humiliation of those on the lower rungs of society. In today's cities, social media speeds the pursuit of knowledge and information. This obsession with knowledge and information not only parades itself as the new wisdom but also parades itself as the alternate truth. Facts and lies are produced at the beck and call of the powerful. Truth gets relativized. As wisdom and truth are tailor-made for people to make a name for themselves, God is eclipsed.

In his engagement with the church, Paul does not undermine knowledge and wisdom. Instead, he places it in its proper perspective. Referring to the city's and the church's desire for knowledge and wisdom (described in I Cor 2:6 as 'wisdom of this age,' "wisdom of the rulers[180] of this age," and "wisdom of the world" [I Cor 1:21]), Paul states that these are "futile and foolish" in the eyes of God (I Cor 3:19,20) and will come to nothing (I Cor 2:6). He goes further to identify the wisdom of the world as being governed by the god of this age which blinds the mind of believers (II Cor 4:4), characterized by the cunning of the serpent (II Cor 11:3) and often parading itself as the "angel of light" (II Cor 11:14).

There are three key themes Paul offers the Corinthian church to construct its theology of knowledge and wisdom and in the process to counter the world's obsession with knowledge.

God's Wisdom is Subversive Foolishness[181]

Paul acknowledges the message of the cross (I Cor 1:24) is foolishness to the world (I Cor 1:18; 23) and a stumbling block to those who seek signs (I Cor 1:23). But he then goes on to describe how God's wisdom is not merely superior to the world's understanding of knowledge and wisdom but will demolish it every argument and pretension against the knowledge of God (II

---

[180] Many scholars believe Paul is referring to the demonic powers that "hold the world in their thraldom" (Garland, *op cit.*, 93).

[181] Note from the editors. This term has been used in conservative, Evangelical parlance. See, for example, Michael Mears Bruner. *A Subversive Gospel: Flannery O'Connor and the Reimagining of Beauty, Goodness, and Truth.* Downers Grove: IVP, 2017.

Cor 10:5) and make foolish the wisdom of the world (I Cor 1:20). It dismantles the knowledge base of the wise, teachers, and philosophers – our information gurus and knowledge high priests of the city (I Cor 1:20). God will frustrate the intelligence of the intelligent (I Cor 1:19); and the foolishness of God is wiser than human wisdom and stronger than human strength (I Cor 1:25). It will shame the wise and the strong and "nullify things that are" (I Cor 1:28). The last word will always belong to God. The knowledge-wisdom parade of the world is temporal; the band will stop its music soon; the parade will end. With this confidence, we seek to demolish the false confidence of the city with knowledge and wisdom that mocks God.

God's Wisdom is a Mystery

Paul provides an interesting and more radical perspective on the purpose of knowledge and wisdom. He suggests that the purpose of wisdom is to know the mind of Christ (I Cor 2:16), knowing God's glory (II Cor 4:6), and being known by God (I Cor 8:3). The world's wisdom falls far short of these expectations of knowledge and wisdom. For the world knowledge as an alternative truth is a source of power in their pursuit of one-upmanship, making humans gods. For the church, our pursuit of knowledge, wisdom, and truth will include knowing the mind of Christ, seeking the fullness of God's glory, and being known by God.

Paul brings another dimension into his reflections of knowledge and wisdom as a mystery (I Cor. 2:7). He suggests that wisdom is a product of the ministry of the Holy Spirit. The Spirit of God knows the mind of God. Paul "asserts that God's wisdom comes through revelation, revelation comes through the Spirit and only spiritual persons receive this revelation."[182] He refers to the wisdom of God as that mystery (I Cor 2:7). We engage with the world "believing and expecting that the Holy Spirit can and will use this dialogue to do God's sovereign work, to glorify Jesus by converting to him

---

[182] Garland, *op.cit.*, 90.

both the partners in dialogue."[183] We seek to engage with the city as ones who have access to this "mystery" not by our righteousness, but by God's mercies.

We are Stewards, Not Owners

In a context where knowledge, information, and wisdom become the private property of the powerful, Paul offers a completely different perspective about Christian understanding. He begins his first letter to the Corinthians by reminding them that they were "not wise, not influential, not noble" (I Cor 1:26) but God "chose the foolish things of the world to shame the wise; God chose the weak things of the world to shame the strong. God chose the lowly things of this world and the despised things – and the things that are not – to nullify the things that are" (I Cor 1:27-29). In his second letter Paul reminds the church that the competence we have "is not our own, but our competence comes from God" (II Cor 3:4-6). Paul states that he "did not come [chose not to come] with eloquence or human wisdom [but rather]... resolved to know nothing while I was with you" (I Cor 2:1, 2). The intentional refusal to use the world's instruments of power is a radical choice. Paul instead chose to preach only Jesus Christ and him crucified. Paul believes the knowledge and wisdom are a gift from God. We are only stewards of this gift. As stewards, we do not use knowledge and wisdom for our self-glorification. Rather we are to stay faithful to the message of the cross – a radical alternative to a world hungering for knowledge, wisdom, and the power that goes with it. When we pretend to be 'owners' truth becomes a bitter experience for everyone around us; when we are stewards we bless many.

To a world obsessed with knowledge, wisdom, and power, Christ, the cross, and the church are disruptive alternatives. The church prophetically demonstrates that Christ and the cross are radically subversive wisdom, a mystery of which we are only unworthy stewards, never owners.

---

[183] Newbigin, *op.cit.*, 210.

Demonstrate Influence from a Position of Powerlessness

Corinth and the Corinthian church promoted a flawed understanding of power, influence, leadership, and greatness. The city has a tendency to create patrons of power in many of our institutions. In the Corinthian church, Corinth's obsession with knowledge and wisdom created many awkward moments for Paul concerning the church which he had nurtured for many years. Paul refers to this pain by constantly reminding the church of his unique relationship with the church. "Surely I am [an apostle] to you" (I Cor 9:2); "I am the least of the apostles" (I Cor 15:9); and "Even though you have ten thousand guardians in Christ,...in Christ Jesus I became your father through the gospel. Therefore, I urge you to imitate me" (I Cor 4:15,16). It almost seems as though the city was successful in creating divisions within the church. Paul challenges this flawed perception of power within the church and the city, based on two key themes to define leadership: influence and greatness.

Refusing to Be Co-opted, Redefining "Person of Influence"

In the Corinthian church, the patronage of the powerful meant at least three key requirements. First, a leader never suffers. "Suffering-leader" was an alien concept for the Corinthian church. Paul through his letter over and over again draws the attention of the church to the many sufferings he had to experience for the gospel (II Cor 1:8-11; 6:3-13; 11:16-33; I Cor 4:9-13; 15:30,31). Paul does not glorify his suffering but in his descriptions, he makes it known that suffering for the gospel was natural and he would not trade it for the patronage of the powerful. Garland in his commentary refers to Paul's listing of suffering as an "ironic critique" of the Corinthian's worldly mindset.[184] Second, the "leader of prestige" would be dependent on the patronage of the powerful, but for Paul, this gracious offer of patronage (II Cor 11:7-9) was not worth selling his soul for. Paul was, after all, a tradesman in the eyes of the elite. Paul served without charge, not creating dependencies.

---

[184] Garland, *op.cit.*, 139.

Paul refers to this refusal as the "sin of humbling". And finally, Paul was not the orator the city and the church would glorify (I Cor 11:5, 6). He did not qualify for this reason as a person of repute. In I Cor 1:11, Paul declares that he did not come to Corinth with a display of wisdom and eloquence. Paul was not going to fall for any of the offers of patronage from the powerful[185]. The city and the powerful in the church used their patronage to instrumentalize others and even the church itself. Paul's refusal to be co-opted was key to being prophetic in the city, a mind-set that would not have gone well with the social elite.

Setting Ethical Benchmarks

During his engagement with the Corinthian church, Paul dealt with critical issues urging the church not to merely follow the best standards in the marketplace but to be the benchmark. Let me cite two instances where Paul demonstrated bench-marking standards. First, his refusal to be dependent on the church for his living – a radical departure from what the church believed was the norm. He would rather work with his own hands (I Cor 4:12). Secondly, his relationship with the church was characterized by "integrity and godly sincerity" (II Cor 1:12).

Demonstrating Integrity and Accountability in Sharing Wealth

The diligence that Paul exercised in handling the generous collection from the Corinthian church for the church in Jerusalem demonstrated integrity and accountability. Paul explains in detail in II Corinthians chapter 8 his modus-operandi in handling their collection. He mentions that Titus, known for his volunteer enthusiasm (II Cor 8:8), and two others who were appointed (II Cor 8:22) by the church (II Cor 8:19), would take charge of these collections. He then mentions that these are required so that no one can criticize us over this large sum of money we are administering. Paul exemplified high standards of integrity, transparency, and accountability –

---

[185] Also read II Cor 3:1; 5:12; 6:4; 12:11; 1:12,14 (you are our boast); II Cor 10:13 (will not boast); II Cor 11:10,12 (others boast) II Cor 11:16ff (boast about suffering); II Cor 11:30 (boast about weakness); I Cor 15:9,10 (least of the apostles).

setting a benchmark for the church and society. We cannot engage the city if our collective and personal lives are not marked with the highest standards of integrity, accountability, and transparency. We need to earn the right to be heard.

Nurture an Alternate Community That Heals Broken Relationships

The Corinthian society and the church were prone to use their passion for power[186] to define their parameters for various relationships. Their religious ceremonies gave way to revelry (I Cor 10:7), sexual immorality, and humiliation of those who had nothing (I Cor 11:22). The church was also struggling with its understanding of rights, freedom, and authority. Paul's teaching on the Lord's Supper counters how the powerful manipulate even religion to fit their purposes. The Eucharist was never meant to be privatized to humiliate those who do not have anything (I Cor 11:20). Paul counters this blatant violation of the Lord's Supper by reminding the Corinthians of Christ's sacrifice, the basis for the Lord's Supper. There are no platforms at the cross of Jesus. Paul's indictment was a sad commentary on how the church internalizes the world's ways and institutionalizes them.[187] Paul provides three key alternatives to the broken relationships, humiliation, and marginalization nurtured by church and society.

The Church as an Alternate Community

Paul presents the church as an alternate community to counter broken relationships in the church and the society. He uses three key aspects of Christian teaching to frame the church's understanding of the alternate community. First, we are a body "one body with many parts" (I Cor 12). He goes on to describe this body as one which God has put together, giving greater honor for those who lacked honor, with no space for division, and

---

[186] Walter Wink provides a helpful frame to understand the world's understanding of power in *Engaging the Powers* (1992). He provides 4 key attributes of power (as the world understands it). 1. requires we value power as an end in itself (p 54), 2. requires society become like the powerful (p 40), 3. acquires a sense of independence, beyond human control (p 41), and 4. wounds the soul of the powerless (p 101).

[187] "Society continually reinforces and justifies the mistreatment of the oppressed group, so that the oppressed tend to 'misbelieve' the same misinformation about itself that the social system as a whole teaches" (Wink *op.cit.*, 97).

expressing equal concern for each other – four key traits of the alternate community. Paul uses the Lord's Supper to describe the new community. This is a supper that signifies the "broken body and shed blood" of our Lord Jesus Christ – as a reminder of his death until he comes (I Cor 23ff). Sacrifice is the foundation of this new community. Secondly, he calls on the church to examine themselves before participating in the supper – not merely an examination of personal/ private sins (although that is important), but he calls on the church to examine their relationships (given the context in which the teaching was situated). There is no place for private parties, idolatry, revelry in the name of religion, and humiliation of those on the lower rungs of society when the church gathers. Thirdly, Paul points to the way the body of Christ demonstrates care for each other through their generosity – the Macedonian church and now the Corinthian church reaching out to the church in Jerusalem in need (II Cor 9:6ff). Generosity is an antidote to hunger for power; not merely a fundraiser. Paul very interestingly mentions equality as a goal of generosity (II Cor 8:14). The church is that continually-being-healed community, in the city.

Love as an Alternative to the World

Paul then introduces an alternate mantra for the church as a radical alternative to the world: love. In his masterpiece on love in I Corinthians 13, Paul was not merely giving a directive to the church. He was summarizing his relationship with the Corinthian church. Paul had lived out Chapter 13 in his relationship with the church. His patient handling of issues, the refusal to gloss over sin in the church (incest, super-apostles), his painful descriptions of suffering and refusal to boast about his ways, his defense of his love for the church as father and apostle, and his constant delighting in the truth, refusing to delight in evil, are examples of his living out the chapter on love. The church is a prophetic community, in the city which 'revels in love,' but is strangely hungry for love.

An Alternate Frame to Understand Authority, Rights, and Freedom

Paul offers an alternate frame to understand authority, rights, and freedom. Paul's painful treatment of these themes in his letter seems to suggest this was an area the church and society were struggling with. For a society obsessed with power and social status, this struggle is understandable. In his investment of life in the Corinthian church, Paul redefines authority, rights, and freedom using five parameters. He recognizes that the use of these may be permissible, but they should

- be beneficial and constructive (I Cor 10:23);
- never be mastered by these (I Cor 6:12);
- never become a stumbling block to the weaker among them (I Cor 8:9);
- always result in building up the others, not breaking them (I Cor 13:10); and
- never hinder the gospel, thus saving some for Christ (I Cor 9:22).

Using the alternate community as his foundational mantra of love and redefinition of the familiar instruments of power like freedom, authority, and rights, Paul provides a strong critique of the city's and the church's tendencies to break relationships, revel in sin, and marginalize many.

The Church Rediscovers the God Space
in Public Discourse in the City

In his letters to the church at Corinth, Paul provides a helpful frame to understand the church in the city. He suggests that the church be fully involved, not leave the city (I Cor 5:10; Cf. Jn 17:15,16), and not even judge the city (I Cor 5:12; 47). Paul does call the church's attention to the sinfulness of the city (I Cor 6:9-11) and that should continue to be scorned by the church (I Cor 6:4). He affirms that the city with all these sins will not inherit the kingdom of God (I Cor 6:9). Paul then positions the church to "become all things to all people so that by all possible means [we] might save some...for the sake of the gospel" (I Cor 9:22, 23). Paul's response to the city and his missiology in the city is focused on getting the church right. His letter to the Corinthian church was embedded in his relationship[188] with a community that is called to be saints (I Cor 1:2; II Cor 1:1).

How then should the Church respond? What are the missiological factors that need to be considered as we respond to the sociology of the city? How do we respond to the spirituality of the city in a manner that reflects the integrity of our faith and theology? How can the church be a disruptive prophetic community in the city that seeks the welfare of the city...and prays to the Lord on its behalf with integrity, recognizing that in the welfare of the city is the welfare of the church, the people of God (Jer 29:7)?[189]

Reflecting on Jeremiah 29:4-7, 10, Jacques Ellul reminds us that we pray for the city as captives. God's directive to God's people appears so illogical: captives pray for the welfare of those who are holding them captive. In this, Ellul suggests, "is our accomplishment...which shows we are not captives like others. This is exactly the line of separation between ourselves and the city."[190] Our job, Ellul suggests, is that "we are clearly told to

---

[188] Paul stayed in Corinth for 18 months (Acts 18:11) around 50 CE, the longest ever, possibly after Ephesus. He must have found the city conducive for his engagement for a few good reasons. The economics of Corinth allowed him to practice his trade of tent making with ease. The high traffic of traders, travelers and tourists who frequented Corinth and the presence of a large migrant population (slaves and free) provided him an opportunity to engage a significant group of people for the gospel. Paul began his ministry with the Jews, reasoning with them in the synagogue (Acts 18:4). When the Jews turned against him, he moved to minister to the Gentiles (Acts 18:6). The Jews then conspired against Paul and accused him of teaching contrary to the law and brought him before Gallio, the proconsul of Achaia (51 CE). But Gallio refused to be a judge over them. The church Paul founded in Corinth was diverse and socially stratified – Jews, Gentile converts, others who feared God as well as some Roman citizens. He then made a second visit in 54 CE. Bible scholars believe there must have been at least four letters that Paul wrote to the Corinthian church. First a private letter (referred to in I Cor. 5:9). The second was first Corinthians. The third letter referred to as a "sorrowful letter" in II Cor. 2:3, 4 and then the fourth was the second Corinthians. Of all the epistles of Paul, the second letter to the Corinthians is considered to be the most personal.
[189] Read Ellul, *op.cit.*, 72-78.
[190] Ellul, *op.cit.*, 75.

participate materially in the life of the city and to foster its welfare. The welfare, not the destruction."[191]

In both Corinthian letters, Paul discusses a third determining factor to govern his conclusions on issues brought to his attention. This determining factor breaks the mold used for many of our public discourses. Most of our public discourses tend to be closed-ended conversations with the individual at the center. With the introduction of this third determining perspective, Paul breaks the common reactive mold. This determining factor is the sum-total of four themes. In his letter to the Corinthian church, Paul offers four aspects that radically change conversation. They are,

- Perfecting holiness out of reverence for God (II Cor 7:1),
- Seeking God's glory displayed in the face of Christ (II Cor 4:8),
- Judging as the Lord who judges (I Cor 4:4), and
- Fixing our eyes on what is unseen or eternal: resurrection (II Cor 4:18).

As Paul develops these four aspects of our public discourse, it becomes obvious that we carry out these public discourses in God's space rather than paternalistically offering some space for God in our debates. The alternative that Paul offers, turns the ground rules for public discourse on its head. These critical theological motifs change the public discourse from navel-gazing reactive conversations to a radically transforming discourse. This God-honoring discourse has four aspects.

First, on issues of sexual promiscuity, abuse of the Lord's Supper, marriage, and idolatry Paul draws attention to the call to holiness – a result of reverence to God.

A second aspect has to do with the glory of God. Recognizing that the god of this age seeks to blind the minds of unbelievers from seeing the glory

---

[191] *Ibid.*, 74.

of Christ,[192] Paul affirms that the power of God's glory in the face of Jesus Christ is much more overwhelming than the schemes of the evil one. Through his letters, Paul reminds us that life is about living for the glory of God (I Cor 10:31) and that marriage is for the glory of God (I Cor 11:7). With this theological motif of the "glory of God," we shift the public discourse from what is permissible and good to what abounds to God's glory – a significant shift.

Third, Paul's reference to the day of the Lord and judgment of the Lord alters the conversation on issues that face the city and the church. He refers to this day in many different ways – the day will bring it to light (I Cor 3:13); in the day of the Lord Jesus (II Cor 1:14; 1:8); until the Lord comes (I Cor 4:5). The reality of "the day" and "judgment" looms large over Paul's counsel to the church in Corinth.

Finally, in II Cor 4:16-18 Paul frames the theme of Christ's resurrection using four opposites: outwardly wasting away, yet inwardly being renewed; light momentary troubles as against earning eternal glory; that which is seen and temporary as compared to the reality of the eternal and unseen; and the eternal hope in the resurrection from the dead. Paul then concludes "therefore we do not lose heart" (II Cor 4:16). In the resurrection, we see not only a new perspective on life's questions but also the death of death. Death and death threats have lost their sting, because of the resurrection (I Cor 15:55,56, 57), a stance that the church is blessed with in its engagement with the city.

The introduction of these four theological motifs (holiness, glory of God, judgment, and resurrection) changes the tone of Paul's conversation with the church and through the church with the city. It is liberating. It transforms the power-driven, right/wrong human-centered conversation to one which would keep us blameless on the day of our Lord Jesus Christ (I Cor 1:8).

---

[192] Read II Cor 4:4. The god of this age has blinded the minds of unbelievers, so that they cannot see the light of the gospel that displays the glory of Christ, who is the image of God.

Conclusion

How then should we pray for the welfare of the city? How should the church engage the city? How do we seek the welfare of the city as a prophetic community that is faith-rooted in our Lord and Savior Jesus Christ? In his incarnational relationship with the church in Corinth, Paul offered four key constructs of a missiology of the local church present in the city as a prophetic community. Paul affirmed that the church should

- Demonstrate the power of subversive foolishness and be credible stewards of the mystery of the wisdom and knowledge of the cross;
- Live and demonstrate its radically different understanding of leadership, influence, greatness, and power in the city;
- Continually nurture itself to be a caring community – a community that is continually healed and become a healing community in the city; and
- Continually repeat our public discourses, our political and faith debates in God's space, not God invited into our space.

The church is not merely an activist organization that preaches an alternative ideology but one which lives out its theology with sincerity and integrity. It seeks to demolish the city's domination system and its spirituality by being a counter-narrative community to the city. We seek to demolish the city's obsession with knowledge and wisdom as an end-in-itself. We seek to call the bluff on the mushrooming heresies that set themselves up against the knowledge of God. We seek to dismantle every argument created to justify moral erosion and sexual promiscuity – the new violence in our cities. We refuse to be co-opted into a system that abuses power and wounds the soul of

112

those on the margins. We are called to be a prophetic community, in the city. We live out the foolishness of the Gospel in God's space in the city.[193]

Chapter 6: Egypt

by Daniel A. Rodriguez[194]

God's Mission Among Displaced Peoples

This chapter offers "an approach to biblical hermeneutics that sees the mission of God as a framework within which we can read the whole Bible."[195] First, I will provide readers with an overview of Egypt and its relationship to the people and land of Israel. Then I will turn my attention to the Exodus, the seminal event involving Egypt that informs our knowledge of God and the mission of God's people. Finally, I will draw practical implications for God's missionary people today. One theme is redemption that reflects the nature of God's mission among and by diaspora communities.

Introduction

Biblical Egypt played an all-important and unique role in the story of redemption including the formation of a missionary people, meant to be a light to all the nations (Isa 60:3). In particular, Egypt was the scene of the

---

[194] Daniel A. Rodriguez, a native of California, is Divisional Dean of the Religion and Philosophy Division and Professor of Religion and Hispanic Studies at Pepperdine University. Since 1979, he has served the Churches of Christ as a minister in Central and Southern California, and as a missionary in Puebla, Mexico. Daniel holds a Ph.D. in Intercultural Studies from Fuller Theological Seminary. He has published numerous journal articles and contributed chapters to edited volumes on the subject of Hispanic evangelicalism. Daniel's book, *A Future for the Latino Church*, challenges the assumption that Hispanic ministry is synonymous with Spanish-language ministry and challenges the evangelical church in the United States to become all things to all Latinos.

[195] Christopher J.H. Wright, *The Mission of God: Unlocking the Bible's Grand Narrative.* Downers Grove: IVP, 2010, 17.

Exodus narrative (Ex 1-15), where Yahweh (YHWH), the God who appeared to Moses, revealed the extent and purpose of divine redemption as well as God's compassion, faithfulness, and greatness. After the Incarnation, the Exodus narrative is the single most important event described in the Bible. Not surprisingly, the Exodus narrative serves as a divine model for interpreting and informing the identity and life of ancient Israel from the wilderness until the return from exile in Babylon. Allusions to the Exodus narrative as well as direct references to it also clearly informed the ministry of Jesus and the mission of the early church. Therefore, I believe it is incumbent upon God's people today to consider the Exodus narrative as a prime lens for understanding the mission of God and its eschatological vision "to bring unity to all things in heaven and on earth under Christ" (Eph 1:10).

Egypt and Israel: A Complicated Relationship

Throughout the Old Testament Egypt is described as an important neighbor of Israel. Mentioned almost 700 times in the Old Testament and 25 times in the New Testament, Egypt is the most frequently mentioned place outside of the land of Israel in the Bible. The relationship between Israel and Egypt was complicated. For example, in the patriarchal period, the Bible describes Egypt as a place of refuge during famine for Abram and Sarai (Gen 12:10-20) and Jacob and his household (Gen 41-46). It was also a place blessed by God's people (e.g., Joseph and Moses. Cf. Gen 41:15-40; Ex 8:8-15). Egypt was also a place where God's people prospered materially and numerically (Ex 1:1-7). However, sometime after the death of Joseph (Gen 50:22-26), Egypt becomes a place of oppression and slavery (Ex 1-15).[196]

More importantly, Egypt was a place where God became known to Israel and the nations[197] by rescuing God's people from socioeconomic, cultural, and religious oppression. "I am the Lord your God, who brought you

---

[196] See James Karl Hoffmeier. *Israel in Egypt: The Evidence for the Authenticity of the Exodus Tradition*, New York: Oxford University Press, 1999.

[197] Ross W. Blackburn. *The God Who Makes Himself Known: The Missionary Heart of the Book of Exodus*. New Studies in Biblical Theology, Downers Grove, IL: InterVarsity Press, 2012, 28.

out of Egypt" (Ex 20:2) becomes the familiar phrase uttered by God in the wilderness.[198] Echoing Yahweh, Moses repeatedly reminds Israel "the Lord brought you out of Egypt with a mighty hand" (Ex 3:9).[199] From the time of Joshua through the reign of Solomon, Israel is continuously reminded that "It was the Lord our God himself who brought us and our parents up out of Egypt, from that land of slavery, and performed those great signs before our eyes" (Josh 24:17).[200]

After the Exodus and throughout Israel's wandering in the desert, Egypt becomes a place that prompts distorted memories among God's rebellious people. For example, in Exodus 16:3, the Israelites grumbled against Moses and Aaron, "If only we had died by the Lord's hand in Egypt! There we sat around pots of meat and ate all the food we wanted, but you have brought us out into this desert to starve this entire assembly to death."[201]

Divine deliverance from Egypt also served as the foundation for the Ten Commandments (Ex 20:1; Deut 5:6) as well as the frequent injunctions "to be holy" in all aspects of life in the Promised Land (Lev 11:44-45). From the days of king Solomon until the end of the divided kingdom, Egypt was both an adversary and unreliable ally in times of trouble (e.g., II Kings 17, 18, 24-25). From Solomon to Jehoiakim, many of the kings of Israel and Judah unwisely relied on Egypt as a refuge from danger (I Kings 11:17-19; 11:40) to defend themselves from Assyria or later from Babylon (II Kings 18:21, 24; 25:26). Egypt became a place of refuge for refugees from Judah after the Babylonians captured Jerusalem. Sadly, they preferred to place their trust in Egypt, a dying nation, rather than in the living God. Jeremiah delivered God's verdict, "I will punish those who live in Egypt with the sword, famine, and plague, as I punished Jerusalem" (Jer 44:13).

---

[198] Cf. Lev 11:44-45; 19:36; 22:33; 25:38; 25:55; 26:13; 26:45; Num 15:41; Deut 5:6; 13:5; Ps 81:10.

[199] Cf. Ex 13:3, 14, 16, 16:6; 18:1; 20:2; 29:46; Lev 11:45; 19:36; 22:33; 23:43.

[200] Cf. Judg 2:1, 12; 6:13; 19:30; 1 Sam 2:27; 5:15; 15:15; 16:12; 24:18; 24:22; 2 Sam 7:6, 33; 1 Kings 8:16, 21, 51; 9:9; 2 Kings 17:7, 36; 1 Chron 17:5, 21; 2 Chron 6:5; 7:22.

[201] Cf. Ex 14:12; Num 11:18-20; 14:3-4; 20:5; 21:5; Deut 4:20; 5:15; 6:21.

The words of Jeremiah 2:36 echo throughout the divided kingdom, "You will be disappointed by Egypt as you were by Assyria." The foolishness and danger of relying on Egypt as a refuge or ally are clearly stated in Isaiah 30:1-3.

> Woe to the obstinate children, declares the LORD, to those who carry out plans that are not mine, forming an alliance, but not by my Spirit, heaping sin upon sin;
> Who go down to Egypt without consulting me;
> Who look for help to Pharaoh's protection, to Egypt's shade for refuge.
> But Pharaoh's protection will be to your shame;
> Egypt's shade will bring you disgrace.

New Testament writers present Egypt in both positive and negative terms. For Joseph, Mary, and the baby Jesus, Egypt was a place of refuge from mortal danger (Matt 2:13-15). However, in Revelation 11:8, Egypt is used symbolically to describe Jerusalem, a place of rebellion, where the "Lord was crucified." However, the final word about Egypt is not Revelation 11:8. It is found in Isaiah 19:18-25, where the prophet assures Egypt that it is as an object of God's mission and will ultimately share in Israel's divine inheritance. "The Lord Almighty will bless them, saying, 'Blessed be Egypt my people, Assyria my handiwork, and Israel my inheritance'" (Isa 19:25). The prophet was given a glimpse into a yet distant future when Israel's enemies in the Exodus and Exile narratives would become heirs with Israel of the blessing of Abraham. But that reconciliation would require the destruction of "the barrier, the dividing wall of hostility," accomplished finally at the cross by Jesus Christ (Eph 2:11-19).

Egypt: Where the Missionary God Became Known

Christopher Wright argues convincingly that the mission of God's people must reflect a commitment to the mission of God revealed: "as Yahweh in the Old Testament, and walking among us in the incarnate life of Jesus of

Nazareth in the New."[202] To embrace that mission, Wright insists that contemporary Christians, like ancient Israel, must know and bear witness to the one living God and Savior. "The church's mission flows from the identity of God and Christ. When you know who God is, when you know who Jesus is, witnessing mission is the unavoidable outcome."[203]

Knowing the one, true God is a persistent theme in Israel's encounter with Egypt. For example, during their sojourn in Egypt, God became known to Abram, Sarai, and the Egyptians, demonstrating God's ability to protect God's people and to judge and punish the nations who threaten them or their mission to bless all the families of the earth (Gen 12:10-20). Three generations later, the Lord is revealed in Egypt through Joseph who interprets Pharaoh's dreams thereby avoiding a national disaster during a prolonged famine (Gen 41:15-32). These earlier manifestations of God's divine nature and sovereignty pale in comparison with the ways Yahweh became known in Egypt during the catastrophic events described in Exodus 1-15,

> Therefore, say to the Israelites: I am the LORD, and I will bring you out from under the yoke of the Egyptians. I will free you from being slaves to them, and I will redeem you with an outstretched arm and with mighty acts of judgment. I will take you as my own people, and I will be your God. Then you will know that I am the LORD your God, who brought you out from under the yoke of the Egyptians (Ex 6:6-8).

"YHWH wills to be known to Israel and the ends of the earth."[204] In Egypt, the God of Abraham, Isaac, Jacob, and Moses makes himself known as "the Lord [who] brought you out of Egypt with his mighty hand" (Ex 13:3). However, before Yahweh rescued Israel from Egypt to begin their long journey to the Promised Land, God's people needed to be educated about the nature and ways of Yahweh (Ex 6:7; 14:29-31). Similarly, Pharaoh needed to be educated about Yahweh's nature and purposes. He asked, "Who is the Lord

---

[202] Christopher J. H. Wright. *The Mission of God's People: A Biblical Theology of the Church's Mission,* Grand Rapids, MI: Zondervan, 2010, 31.
[203] Wright, *The Mission of God,* 66-67.
[204] *Ibid.,* 71, 74.

that I should obey his voice to let Israel go? I do not know the Lord, and besides, I will not let Israel go" (Ex 5:2). God answered Pharaoh's rhetorical question gradually, plague after plague until the decisive night of the Passover.

> At midnight the LORD struck down all the firstborn in Egypt, from the firstborn of Pharaoh, who sat on the throne, to the firstborn of the prisoner, who was in the dungeon, and the firstborn of all the livestock as well. Pharaoh and all his officials and all the Egyptians got up during the night, and there was loud wailing in Egypt, for there was not a house without someone dead. During the night Pharaoh summoned Moses and Aaron and said, "Up! Leave my people, you and the Israelites! Go, worship the LORD as you have requested. Take your flocks and herds, as you have said, and go. And also bless me. "The Egyptians urged the people to hurry and leave the country. "For otherwise," they said, "we will all die!" (Ex 12:29-33)

Yahweh desired to be known to the Israelites as well as to Pharaoh and the Egyptians. What was revealed about Yahweh during the Exodus? First, Yahweh's incomparable nature was made clear. On multiple occasions, Moses spells out the purpose of the plagues: "that you may know there is no one like the Lord our God" (Ex 8:10; 9:14). Second, the Exodus event revealed that Yahweh is sovereign over all the earth. This is evident when Yahweh instructs Moses and Aaron to speak to Pharaoh, "This is what the Lord says: By this, you will know that I am the Lord" (Ex 7:17).[205] Yahweh is the God of Israel and Lord of all nations. As sovereign, Yahweh brings judgment on all the earth (Ex 12:12). The Lord's judgment and punishment of Egypt in the Exodus event illustrates this reality. Third, Yahweh desired that Pharaoh and the children of Israel would know that God is unique. After crossing the sea on dry land, Moses and Israel sang, "Who among the gods is like you, Lord? Who is like you – majestic in holiness, awesome in glory, working wonders?"

---

[205] Cf. Ex 7:5; 8:22; 12:12; 14:4, 18.

(Ex 15:11).[206] Finally, these attributes of God revealed in Egypt were also meant to be proclaimed.

After Yahweh redeems the descendants of Jacob/Israel from Egyptian bondage and oppression, God anticipates becoming known among the nations through those who have been redeemed (Deut 4:5-7). "Having been chosen, redeemed and called into covenant relationship, the people of God have a life to live – a distinctive, holy, ethical life that is to be lived before God and in the sight of the nations."[207] These same ethical implications of redemption find parallels in the New Testament (cf. Matt 5:14-16; I Pet 2:9).

The scope of God's mission was global and timeless. For millennia, every year during the Passover celebration, observant Jews have retold the story of Israel's miraculous redemption from Egypt. Walter Brueggemann argues that the Exodus narrative "has become the defining, paradigmatic account of faith whereby Israel is understood as the beloved, chosen community of YHWH and the object of YHWH's peculiar and decisive intervention in public events." By "paradigmatic" Brueggemann means that "the narrative is seen to make a claim to intense particularity, but a particularity that invites and permits rereading in a variety of circumstances and contexts."[208] One such circumstance concerns a model of redemption that reflects the nature of the mission of God and responds in contextually appropriate ways to mission among and by diaspora communities.

Egypt: Where God Reveals a Model of Redemption

In Egypt, Yahweh revealed a timeless model of redemption. Biblical scholars agree that the original Exodus event became paradigmatic for Israel's later self-identity. For example, Isaiah, among other Old Testament writers, made extensive use of Exodus language reread and reframed for his context

---

[206] Wright, *The Mission of God*, 77-82.
[207] *Ibid.*, 190.
[208] Walter Brueggemann. *An Introduction to the Old Testament: The Canon and Christian Imagination*. First Edition, Louisville, KY.: Westminster John Knox Press, 2003, 54.

(e.g., Isa 43:1-3). A return from exile that resembles the Exodus from Egypt is envisioned in Isaiah 10:21-26; 11:15-16; and 52:4-12.[209]

In the New Testament, Jesus is the second Moses (See Acts 3:22; 7:37 and John 1:47) promised by God in Deuteronomy 18:18-19.

> I will raise up for them a prophet like you from among their fellow Israelites, and I will put my words in his mouth. He will tell them everything I command him. I myself will call to account anyone who does not listen to my words that the prophet speaks in my name.

Jesus of Nazareth understood himself as the second Moses sent "to proclaim freedom for the prisoners and recovery of sight for the blind, to set the oppressed free, to proclaim the year of the Lord's favor" (Luke 4:16-19, cf. Luke 7:18-22). This perspective is most clearly seen during Jesus' final celebration of the Passover meal with his disciples. N.T. Wright observes that the Last Supper "brought Jesus' kingdom movement to its climax. It indicated a new Exodus was happening in and through Jesus himself.... Jesus intended this meal to symbolize the new Exodus, the arrival of the kingdom through his own fate."[210] The Apostle Paul also makes it quite clear that in the death, burial, and resurrection, Jesus Christ has initiated nothing less than a new Exodus (Rom 3-8; I Cor 10:1-13).[211]

Like Moses, Jesus understood he was sent by God to initiate a new Exodus where freedom would be proclaimed for the prisoners and release proclaimed for the oppressed. If Christopher Wright is correct when he asserts that the Exodus event reveals the "grand narrative" of the Bible, then it is not surprising that the gospels are filled with allusions to the Exodus. It also becomes clear why Peter, Stephen, and Philip refer to Jesus as the "second Moses." These observations suggest that Cleophus LaRue is correct when he insists, "We must begin to think through and preach through the

---

[209] Hans M. Barstad, "A Way in the Wilderness. The 'Second Exodus' in the Message of Second Isaiah," *Journal of Semitic studies/Monograph* (1989): 107.
[210] N.T. Wright. *Jesus and the Victory of God,* Minneapolis, MN: Fortress Press, 1996, 557-559.
[211] Daniel Lynwood Smith. "The Uses of 'New Exodus' in New Testament Scholarship: Preparing a Way through the Wilderness," *Currents in Biblical Research* 14, no. 2 (2016), 216-220.

implications of the Exodus."[212] Understanding the nature and purpose of the mission of God revealed in the "paradigmatic Exodus event" is therefore essential to understanding the mission of Jesus and his church today particularly in the context of social injustice and oppression. Christopher Wright concurs, insisting that the Exodus narrative is a "paradigmatic and highly repeatable model" for understanding the nature of Christian mission.[213]

The Exodus and the Relationship
between Social Responsibility and Evangelism

As I am writing this chapter, the COVID-19 pandemic has been eclipsed by nationwide protests and rioting following the death of George Floyd, an unarmed black man in police custody in Minneapolis. Responses to the murder of George Floyd are further dividing our fragile society. On May 31, 2020, the *Los Angeles Times* reported that "The outrage over Floyd's death has done what no other event has done in months: turned the nation's attention from its all-consuming focus on the COVID-19 pandemic."

As a professor at a prestigious Christian university, I have observed a growing social consciousness among many of my Christian students, white as well as those of color. They are becoming keenly aware of the injustice and inequities experienced by those who live at the margin of American society in at-risk and underserved neighborhoods. They are also becoming painfully aware of those around the world who suffer as victims of social injustice, poverty, slavery, human trafficking, preventable diseases, and the HIV/AIDS epidemic. Their passion for engaging in social action and social justice is evident in their growing interest in organizations such as the Peace Corps and the International Justice Mission.

---

[212] Cleopus J. LaRue. "The Exodus as Paradigmatic Text in the African American Community," in Dave Bland and David Fleer, eds. *Reclaiming the Imagination: The Exodus as Paradigmatic Narrative for Preaching,* Ashland, OH: Chalice Press, 2009, 127.
[213] Wright, *The Mission of God,* 275.

When I question my socially conscious students about the "spiritual dimensions" of their commitment to social justice, I frequently receive the following response, "God hasn't called me to evangelize, he has called me to help the poor and fight against social injustice." This truncated view of Christian mission and service is characteristic of the historic tendency to embrace what Ron Sider calls "Lopsided Christianity." In the following paragraphs, I will examine the proper balance between evangelism and social responsibility based on the paradigmatic Exodus narrative.

Many Christians, inspired by the Great Commission texts in the New Testaments (e.g., Matt 28:18-20, Luke 24:46-47 and Acts 1:8) have concluded that the most important tasks entrusted to Christians include preaching the gospel, making and nurturing disciples, and planting indigenous reproducing churches. Sider has observed, "They are strong on personal evangelism but with little or no passion for justice for the poor and liberation for the oppressed."[214] The focus of this "vertical approach" is on life after death, on preparing people to stand confidently "in Christ" before God on Judgment Day. The assumption is that the world is like a slowly sinking ship, and the objective is to convince the passengers of that fact and get them into the lifeboats (i.e., the church) as soon as possible.

Others, inspired by Jesus' so-called "Nazareth Manifesto" (Luke 4:16-21), as well as his public ministry (Luke 7: 18-23), and his call for social responsibility (Matt 25: 31-46; Luke 10:25-37), have concluded that the most important tasks entrusted to Christians include engaging in social action and social justice. They are quick to point out that "God's idea of redemption was comprehensive" addressing political, economic, social, and spiritual injustice and oppression.[215] Inspired by the Exodus narrative, the focus of this "horizontal approach" is on life before death, on "acting justly and loving

---

[214] Ronald J. Sider. *Good News and Good Works: A Theology for the Whole Gospel.* Grand Rapids, MI: Baker Books, 1999, 16.
[215] Wright, *The Mission of God*, 268-272.

mercy" (Mic 6:8). The unspoken assumption is that people need bread for life before they will ever be concerned about the Bread of Life.

In *Good News and Good Works*, Sider has sadly observed, "each group uses the other's one-sidedness to justify its continuing lack of balance."[216] In response to lopsided Christianity, we need a biblical perspective that inseparably interrelates and intertwines evangelism and social responsibility without equating or confusing the one with the other. We need to articulate a biblical perspective that challenges the false dichotomy between evangelism and social responsibility. Christopher Wright insists that the Exodus narrative provided the "biblical foundation for a holistic understanding of Christian mission" needed to respond to lopsided Christianity.[217]

The rationale for the Exodus is stated clearly throughout the narrative. In Exodus 3:9-10, the Lord tells Moses, "And now the cry of the Israelites has reached me, and I have seen the way the Egyptians are oppressing them. So now, go. I am sending you to Pharaoh to bring my people the Israelites out of Egypt." Observe that the Lord is liberating Israel from misery, suffering, and oppression. However, two verses later the Lord explains that Israel is being liberated for something: worship. "And God said, 'I will be with you. And this will be the sign to you that it is I who have sent you: When you have brought the people out of Egypt, you will worship God on this mountain'" (3:12). In Exodus 6:6-7, the Lord reiterates the "holistic" rationale for the Exodus.

> Therefore, say to the Israelites: I am the LORD, and I will bring you out from under the yoke of the Egyptians. I will free you from being slaves to them, and I will redeem you with an outstretched arm and with mighty acts of judgment. I will take you as my own people, and I will be your God. Then you will know that I am the LORD your God, who brought you out from under the yoke of the Egyptians.

---

[216] Sider, *op cit.*, 17.
[217] Wright, *The Mission of God*, 303.

The Lord reminds Moses that Israel was redeemed to know him and become his people, his servants. After Israel is delivered from the hands of the Egyptians we are told in Exodus 14:31, "And when the Israelites saw the great power the LORD displayed against the Egyptians, the people feared the LORD and put their trust in him and Moses his servant." In the Exodus narrative, the Lord liberates Israel from misery, suffering, and oppression. However, the Exodus narrative also reveals his desire to liberate them for obedience, worship, and service to him as their one true God. When God enters into a relationship with Israel after the Exodus, it takes place in the context of a reciprocal covenant typified by the theme "I will be your God, and you will be my people" (Cf. Ex 6:7; 19:5-6; Lev 26:12; I Pet 2:9-10).

The Old Testament reveals the devastating consequences when the people of Israel forgot they had been liberated. The scriptures remind us that if people are only liberated from oppression and not also for devotion and service to God, they inevitably become oppressors. In the book of Amos, the Lord's judgment is against those who were "brought up out of Egypt" (2:10). They had become like Egyptians, denying "justice to the oppressed" (2:6-7). The oppressed had become oppressors. This is the inevitable result of only liberating people from oppression and not for devotion and service to the God of Moses and Jesus.

We must also recall that most of those comprehensively liberated from Egyptian oppression and injustice were destined to perish in the wilderness rather than enter the Promised Land because they failed to honor and serve the God who liberated them from slavery and oppression. Likewise Jesus, the second Moses, indicated that the oppressed as well as those who oppress them, must "stop sinning" and put their trust in God as Lord and Savior, or they too would "die in their sins" (John 5:14; 8:24). This will not happen simply by Christians showing mercy and doing justice. Neither will it happen by only preaching the gospel. We must embrace "the kind of comprehensive redemptive response to human need that God demanded."[218]

---

[218] Wright, *The Mission of God's People*, 112.

Egypt: The Context of God's Mission Today

In the New Testament, Egypt is the place from which God led his people Israel (Heb 3:16; 8:9; 11:26-27). The Exodus narrative, particularly the years in the wilderness, provide warnings for the early church (I Cor 10:1-11). Like many Old Testament prophets, New Testament writers utilize Egypt as a potent theological symbol for the early church. Egypt continued to fulfill a dual role as a place of refuge and a place of oppression. In Matthew 2:15, Egypt was a place of refuge for Mary, Joseph, and the baby Jesus. Cared for by another Joseph, Jesus must flee to Egypt to avoid certain death. When the threat is over, Jesus returns to the Promised Land, fulfilling the prophecy in Hosea 11:1, "When Israel was a child, I loved him, and out of Egypt I called my son." The final reference to Egypt in the Bible is symbolic. In Revelation 11:8, Egypt symbolizes Jerusalem, the rebellious capital of the antichrist, "where also their Lord was crucified."

Egypt: A Symbol of Injustice and Oppression Today

Egypt has continued to be a powerful symbol of "slavery and oppression" for those who profess faith in the God of Abraham, Joseph, Moses, and Jesus Christ. Richard Hughes reminds us that in the days of Tyndale, English Protestants drew a parallel between England and ancient Israel. Later in their migration to New England, Puritans found the parallel even more compelling. Centuries earlier, God had led the Jews out of Egypt, through the Red Sea, and into the Promised Land. God led the Puritans out of England, across the Atlantic Ocean, and into another promised land. The Puritans made the most of this comparison. In the Puritan imagination, England became Egypt, the Atlantic Ocean became the Red Sea, the American wilderness became their land of Canaan, and the Puritans themselves became the new Israel.[219] By the early nineteenth century, the myth was becoming deeply rooted in the American psyche and found one of its greatest proponents in Thomas Jefferson. For example, in his second inaugural

---

[219] Richard T. Hughes. *Myths America Lives By*, 1st edition, Urbana, IL: University of Illinois Press, 2004, 32.

address in 1805, Jefferson once again appealed to the image of ancient Israel as a model for the United States. "I shall need the favor of that Being in whose hands we are, who led our fathers, as Israel of old, from their native land and planted them in a country flowing with all the necessities and comforts of life."[220] The belief that Americans, more precisely White Anglo-Saxon Protestants, constituted a chosen people gradually turned into the belief of America as a chosen nation. According to Hughes, it was not difficult for the myth of the chosen nation to become the country's Manifest Destiny, a badge of privilege and power that justified the oppression and exploitation of those not included among the chosen, for example, Native Americans, Black Slaves and later the Spanish speaking Catholic inhabitants of the southwest.[221]

Conversely, slaves brought to the new world from Africa starting in the early 17th Century, saw themselves as Joseph, forcibly brought to Egypt, that is North America, where white slave masters, masquerading as Christians enslaved and oppressed them for centuries.[222]

> No single story captures more clearly the distinctiveness of African American Christianity than that of the Exodus. From the earliest days of colonization, white Christians had represented their journey across the Atlantic as the Exodus of a New Israel; slaves identified themselves as the Old Israel suffering bondage under a new Pharaoh. [223]

The Exodus narrative serves a similar purpose for today's immigrants, especially those from Latin America. Daniel Carroll reminds us that the Old Testament stories about migrations, Exodus, and exile have "the potential to be a divine mirror, where they see themselves and identify with its descriptions and characters. Immigrants can actually 'live' the text's scenes

---

[220] *Ibid.*, 35.
[221] *Ibid.*, 37, 41.
[222] David Kling surveys the biblical Exodus and then turns to various African-American understandings and expressions of Exodus themes in the context of slavery, emancipation, migration, the civil rights movement, and black liberation theology. See David Kling. *The Bible in History: How the Texts Have Shaped the Times,* New York: Oxford University Press, 2004, 193-230.
[223] Albert J. Raboteau, "African Americans, Exodus, and the American Israel," in Larry G. Murphy, ed., *Down by the Riverside: Readings in African American Religion 8,* N.Y.: NYU Press, 2000, 20.

because they have gone through similar experiences and have dealt with comparable emotions, tensions, and challenges." Sadly, instead of arriving at the Promised Land, many immigrants from Latin America find themselves working long hours with low pay and few benefits. In many respects, they discover that "they have left one Egypt for another." Like the Hebrews in Egypt, the majority culture fears their numbers and their being different, although they want their labor.[224] Sadly, blind patriotism, hyper-nationalism, xenophobia, and anti-immigrant rhetoric are disqualifying many 21st century believers from participating with moral authority and integrity in the mission of God, especially among diaspora communities. Sharing a similar concern for what he calls the "scandal of ideological captivity" within the church, Wright challenges Christians in the United States to ask if they have simply "absorbed the dominating cultural and national worldview" and then baptized it with a Christian veneer.[225]

Living in Egypt Among the Latin American Diaspora

One unwelcome consequence of appropriating Exodus themes in missions among and by the Latin American diaspora has been the reluctance on the part of Hispanic[226] churches dominated by foreign-born[227] Latinos to accommodate the needs of the growing number of native-born[228] English dominant Latinos. In his study of Hispanic Protestant churches, Edwin Hernández noted that sociologically, traditional Spanish speaking churches

---

[224] M. Daniel Carroll R. *Christians at the Border: Immigration, the Church, and the Bible*, 1st edition, Grand Rapids, MI: Baker Academic, 2008, 87.
[225] Wright, *The Mission of God's People*, 283.
[226] Hispanic, Latino/a, Latinx. These terms are used interchangeably to refer to all individuals of Latin American ancestry or with ties to the Spanish-speaking and Portuguese-speaking world who reside either legally or illegally within the borders of the United States of America. Any prolonged debate over which term should be used is self-defeating because any one of the terms ultimately fails to deal with the complexity of the Hispanic existence in the United States.
[227] Foreign-born, first-generation and immigrant-generation. These terms will be used interchangeably to refer to all individuals of Latin American ancestry who have legally or illegally immigrated to the United States.
[228] Following the precedent established by the U.S. Census Bureau and the Pew Research Center, Native-born Latino and U.S.-born Latina will be used synonymously to refer to those Latinos born in the U.S., Puerto Rico or other U.S. territories and those born abroad to at least one parent who was a U.S. citizen.

help foreign-born Latinos adapt to life in the United States while at the same time serving as "an important mechanism for sustaining cultural values, language, and practices."[229] Consequently, for some churches dominated by foreign-born Latinos, incorporating English language programs and ministries to accommodate the preferences of native-born Latino teens and young adults undermines their efforts to sustain and reinforce the values, language, and practices of the Latin American diaspora. Similarly, Daniel Sánchez has observed that many immigrant parents pressure their pastors to help them "preserve the Hispanic language and culture."[230] In response, visionary and missional pastors try to help reluctant foreign-born parents and members to recognize that they are often more concerned with conserving their ancestral culture and language than with the spiritual welfare of their children and grandchildren.

In addition to the commitment to preserve the culture and traditions of the Latin American diaspora communities, there are also significant theological presuppositions that strengthen the resolve to resist the call to accommodate the linguistic and cultural preferences of native-born, English dominant Latinos. For instance, Christians are called to be holy in all their conduct (I Pet 1:14-16) which above all else is characterized by "nonconformity" to the pattern of this world (Rom 12:2). Too many first-generation Hispanics, their cherished traditions, and prohibitions are not viewed as "cultural preferences," but rather as reflecting the value of personal and communal holiness (la santidad), "without which no one will see the Lord" (Heb. 12:14). Therefore, for many first-generation Latino Christians, it is untenable to consider accommodating the younger generation's needs and preferences, many of which have been influenced by secular society. Samuel Solivan-Román sheds additional light on this theological source of resistance.

---

229 Edwin I. Hernández. "Moving from the Cathedral to Storefront Churches: Understanding Religious Growth and Decline among Latino Protestants," in David Maldonado Jr., ed., *Protestantes/Protestants: Hispanic Christianity within Mainline Traditions*, Nashville: Abingdon, 1999, 223.
230 Daniel R. Sánchez. *Hispanic Realities Impacting America: Implications for Evangelism & Missions*. Fort Worth, TX: Church Starting Network, 2006, 85.

He argues that many Hispanic evangelicals "understand themselves to be the bulwark against death and the forces of evil that are overwhelming the world. They are a fortress against the cultural forces that seek to destroy them and their value system, a system that they understand as reflecting the values of the kingdom of God and their Lord Jesus Christ."[231]

In all fairness to the immigrant generation, frustrated native-born Hispanic Christians are often unable or unwilling to see their subculture and the broader American society through the eyes of foreign-born Hispanic Christians. Many Spanish dominant Latinos do not equate the United States with the Promised Land or the "Chosen Nation" as do many American Christians, including many U.S. born Latinos. Instead, many foreign-born Latinos draw analogies between their experience in the United States and that of the Hebrews in Egypt. Like the sons of Jacob (Gen 46-50), many Hispanic immigrants leave their beloved homelands and come to the United States (i.e., Egypt) for one primary reason: to survive. They come to the United States because here they can carry on until they are in a position to return to their *patria* (homeland) to live out their dreams. In the meantime, like the descendants of Jacob, they resolve to maintain a necessary distance from the Egyptians (i.e., Anglo Americans) and their materialistic and decadent culture, pejoratively referred to as *"el mundo"* (the world).

Consequently, Latino evangelicals, especially the foreign-born, feel compelled to create spiritual as well as cultural ghettos like the land of Goshen (Gen 46:28) where they can sustain and reinforce the culture, values, language, and practices of their *patria* while they "live in exile" surrounded by a foreign, hostile and worldly society. Seen sympathetically from this standpoint, incorporating English and accommodating the cultural preferences of highly assimilated Latinos is tantamount to opening the doors of the church to "the forces of evil that are overwhelming the world."[232] Many

---

231 Samuel Solivan-Román. "Hispanic Pentecostal Worship," in Justo L. González, ed.,
 ¡Alabadle! Hispanic Christian Worship, Nashville, TN: Abingdon Press, 1996, 45.
232 *Ibid.*

well-meaning and pious first-generation Hispanic Christians sincerely believe they must resist assimilation and acculturation, including encouraging the use of English in the church. From the standpoint of many English dominant, native-born Latinos, the ethnocentrism and anti-American bias of the immigrant generation inadvertently reinforces the paradox of living in two hostile worlds. As a result, young U.S. born Latinos are unintentionally excluded from the church in favor of the foreign-born and second-generation Latinos who embrace "the value system of their native country – rural, monolingual – embodying conservative Hispanic values."[233] Of course, when it comes to ethnocentrism and nativism, first-generation Latinos do not have a corner on the market. As we have seen above, members of the dominant group in the United States have very similar self-understandings. Today a growing number of evangelicals are speaking out against the worst consequences of cultural superiority and ethnocentrism endemic in most societies, including those that appropriate the identity of Israel in the Exodus narrative as analogous to their own.

Every Society Today is Egypt

Many missiologists correctly assume that humans create all cultures; therefore, all cultures have inherent strengths and weaknesses. Gailyn Van Rheenen reminds us that "All cultures simultaneously demonstrate the original goodness of the creation and the satanic brokenness resulting from the Fall. Cultures exhibit both a proclivity to sin, which alienates them from God, and attributes of goodness, reflecting divine presence."[234] All cultures including Anglo-American, African-American and Hispanic cultures (plural) are what Sherwood Lingenfelter calls "palaces" and "prisons of disobedience." They are "palaces" because they provide human beings with "comfort, security, meaning, and relationships." However, they are also "prisons of disobedience" because they restrict our freedom to live the abundant life we

---

[233] Manuel Ortiz. *The Hispanic Challenge,* Downers Grove, IL: InterVarsity Press, 1993, 63.
[234] Gailyn Van Rheenen. *Missions: Biblical Foundations and Contemporary Strategies,* Grand Rapids, MI: Zondervan, 2014, 240.

were created for, the life provided for by Jesus Christ (John 10:10). Instead, every culture sets barriers between people, God, and others. As such, God judges every culture.[235] This rejection and rebellion against God is often manifest in what we call "religion" (cf. Rom 1:18-23). Consequently, in word and deed, Jesus challenged the traditional ideas, behavior, products, and institutions of his society and culture. This is obvious not only in the Sermon on the Mount (Matt 5-7) but also in his critique of the teaching, behavior, and institutions of the religious leaders of his day (Matt 15:1-20; 21:33-46; 23:1-36). Ultimately, it cost him his life. The same is true of many believers who took the gospel from Jerusalem to the ends of the earth (Acts 1:8). Implied in the message that Jesus is the only mediator between God and humanity (John 14:1-7; Acts 4:8-12; I Tim 2:3-7) is a critique of every culture, including Anglo-American, African-American and Hispanic cultures, as "prisons of disobedience."

Conclusion: The Church as a Colony
of Resident Aliens Living in Egypt

In their ground-breaking counter-cultural ecclesiology, Hauerwas and Willimon offer a biblical corrective to the cultural superiority and ethnocentrism prevalent among many first-generation Hispanic evangelicals and dominant group Christians in the United States. Concerned with the nature and purpose of the church in a post-Christendom context, the authors ask, "What does it mean for us to live in a culture of unbelief?"[236] They insist that to be a Christian, is to accept "the invitation to be part of an alien people who make a difference because they see something that cannot otherwise be seen without Christ." To be a disciple of Jesus Christ implies joining "a countercultural phenomenon, a new *polis* called church."[237]

---

[235] Sherwood Lingenfelter. *Transforming Culture: A Challenge for Christian Mission*, 2nd edition, Grand Rapids, MI: Baker Academic, 2004, 20.
[236] Stanley Hauerwas and William H. Willimon. *Resident Aliens: Life in the Christian Colony*, Nashville: Abingdon Press, 1989, 115.
[237] *Ibid.*, 24, 30.

Hauerwas and Willimon insist that the political and ethical response of the church as a colony of "resident aliens" (Phil 3:20-21; Heb 11:13; I Pet 1:17; 2:11-12) is informed by the *telos*, the end. "It makes all the difference in the world how one regards the end of the world. "End" not so much in the sense of its final breath, but "end" in the sense of the purpose, the goal, the result."[238] The end, the goal towards which the Christian colony moves is nothing less than the "unity to all things in heaven and on earth under Christ" (Eph 1:9-10). The mechanism by which this reconciliation of all things and all peoples takes place is the death, burial, and resurrection of Jesus Christ resulting in a new household, which ends all particularisms, including the hostility between white and black, rich and poor, native-born and immigrants as well as Jew and Gentile. The result is a new *polis*, a new society, the church.

> Consequently, you are no longer foreigners and strangers, but fellow citizens with God's people and also members of his household, built on the foundation of the apostles and prophets, with Christ Jesus himself as the chief cornerstone. In him the whole building is joined together and rises to become a holy temple in the Lord. And in him you too are being built together to become a dwelling in which God lives by his Spirit (Eph 2:19-22).

The Exodus narrative must shape the church's mission. As we embrace Egypt as the context of every mission effort today, we commit ourselves to make God known among the nations. We proclaim in word and through our transformed lives that he is incomparable, sovereign over all the earth, and unique among the man-made gods that compete for our devotion (Deut 4:5-7). Through the power of the Spirit of Christ, we reject lopsided Christianity and incarnate a holistic model of redemption that liberates all humans from every form of oppression so that together we live "for the praise of his glorious grace" (Eph 1:6, 12, 14). Embracing our identity as a colony of resident aliens living in Egypt will also help us recognize how much we have

---

[238] *Ibid.*, 61.

in common with people of color and with undocumented immigrants living in a racialized and anti-immigrant society.

Finally, the church as a colony of resident aliens embraces the opportunity to teach kingdom values that transcend culture and society to our children, teens, and young adults, especially to those coping with life at the margins of U.S. society (i.e., Egypt) in at-risk underserved neighborhoods.[239] We do so by embracing an "exodus shaped mission" and message that proclaims the superiority of the kingdom of God to any human culture or society, including American.[240] Furthermore, as we challenge the socially constructed barriers that keep us apart we rehearse before a divided world the multinational, multiethnic, and multilingual celebration envisioned in Revelation 7:9-10.

> After this, I looked, and there was a great multitude that no one could count, from every nation, from all tribes and peoples and languages, standing before the throne and before the Lamb, robed in white, with palm branches in their hands. They cried out in a loud voice, saying, "Salvation belongs to our God who is seated on the throne, and to the Lamb!"

[239] Juan Francisco Martínez. *Walk with the People: Latino Ministry in the United States,* Nashville: Abingdon Press, 2008, 14.
[240] Wright, *The Mission of God,* 275.

Chapter 7: Ephesus

by Mary Motte[241]

God's Mission of Peace and Reconciliation
Amidst Beauty, Myth, and Poetry

The ancient city of Ephesus offers us rich images of beauty, myth, and poetry. From the images of antiquity, the Acts of the Apostles, and Paul's letter to the Ephesians, we continue to discover dynamic missionary themes. Christians today, across divisions and cultures, are seeking spaces of peace and reconciliation through a genuine appreciation of the imagery found in Ephesus. The people who inherited the richness of ancient Ephesus have much to teach Christians who are today called to missionary participation in the peace of God and the reconciliation wrought by Christ. In the multifaceted aspects of the imagery of Ephesus, we can gain a deeper connection to the heart of God.

---

[241] Sister Mary Motte (PhD in Education from Boston College) is a Franciscan Missionary of Mary (FMM) and Director of the Mission Resource Center for the FMM in North Providence, Rhode Island. She collaborates in various intercultural/ecumenical study/writing/research projects. Her numerous publications include "Issues in Protestant-Roman Catholic Discussions of Theology of Mission," in Charles Van Engen, Dean S. Gilliland, and Paul Pierson, eds., *The Good News of the Kingdom;* "Historical Perspectives on Catholic Mission Theology," in Robert L. Gallagher and Paul Hertig, eds., *Contemporary Mission Theology: Engaging the Nations;* "Emergence of New Paths: The Future of Mission in Roman Catholicism," in Charles E. Van Engen, ed., *The State of Missiology Today: Global Innovations in Christian Witness;* and "Signs of a Future Transformation in Mission," in *IBMR*, Vol. 43, Issue 1, January 1, 2019.

Introduction

Entering into the vibrancy of an ancient city through the insights from a different time provokes a deeper search for the logic that would underwrite the human endeavor. Stephen Fry argued for the validity of such an effort:

> We haven't arrived at our own moral and ethical imperatives by each of us working them out from first principles; we have inherited them, and they were born out of blood and suffering, as all human things and human beings are.[242]

Ancient Ephesus, the ministry of Paul, and the development of Gentile followers of Christ offer insights that continue to prod for a deeper understanding of mission. Lamin Sanneh observed that "through the Gentile church Paul encountered an unsettling reality about the seriousness of God's irrevocable design to draw all people to the divine."[243] The unsettling reality of God's irrevocable design applied to the experience of Ephesus. Its ancient reality and its encounter with apostolic sources lead to evidence of missiological themes with relevance for mission in the present time.

Important Factors that Shaped Ancient Ephesus

In 4 BCE Duris of Elea described Ephesus as "the most besung of all Ionian cities."[244] This image of beauty and poetry explains why this city, the western boundary when traveling from India, is mentioned over 500 times in Greek literature. The Temple of Artemis, dedicated to the Goddess of the Hunt (Diana), and one of the seven wonders of the world, was among its treasures. Ephesus was also the capital of possibly the richest province of the Roman Empire.[245] As documented by recent excavations, Ephesus was founded as an Attic-Ionian colony in the 10th century BCE on a hill now known as the Ayasuluk Hill. Greek mythology names Androcles, a Prince from Athens, as

---

[242] https://www.theguardian.com/theobserver/2006/jul/09/featuresreview.review.
[243] Lamin Sanneh. *Translating the Message: The Missionary Impact on Culture.* Maryknoll, NY: Orbis Books, 1989, 24.
[244] Jerome Murphy-O'Connor, op. *St. Paul's Ephesus: Texts and Archaeology.* Collegeville, MN, Liturgical Press. 2008, xiii.
[245] *Ibid.*

the founder of Ephesus at the place indicated through the oracle of Delphi in the tale "A Fish and a Boar will Show you the Way":

> The story goes that around the 10th Century BCE, Androcles, son of Athens' king, Kodros, was leading one of the migration convoys. An oracle of Apollo predicted that a fish and a boar would show the location of a new settlement. Soon after while Androcles was frying, a fish fell out of the pan and a startled boar hiding in the bushes ran. Androcles followed the boar and killed it. The location where the boar was killed, was where the city of Ephesus was established.[246]

As king, Androcles united the twelve cities of Ionia, forming the Ionian League.[247] The city became more prosperous during his reign. He died in a battle against the Carians. Androcles and his dog are depicted on The Hadrian temple frieze, dating from the 2nd century CE. Greek historians Pausanias, Strabo and Herodotus, and the poet Kallinos attributed the mythological foundation of the city to Ephos, queen of the Amazons.[248]

Murphy-O'Connor introduces a deeper understanding of the Ephesus that Paul would have known and, in doing so, he makes an interesting comparison that enables a re-ordering of priorities in the work done on ancient texts. The rich history of Ephesus found among the ancient writers of Greece and Rome and their consequent syntheses bring together the invaluable and numerous sources of information about Ephesus. However, as Murphy-O'Connor notes:

> These summaries leave the city's personality in shadows. For grasping the ethos of Ephesus there is no alternative to the first-hand accounts of visitors. These reflect the moods the city inspired in the writers and small things that caught their fancy.[249]

Encountering this reflection of the moods of the city requires delving back in time to be able to touch contemplatively into the feelings, the beauty,

---

[246] https://roadrunnersguidetotheancientworld.com/ephesus/.
[247] Carl Roebuck, "The Early Ionian League," *Classical Philology*, Vol. 50, No. 1 (Jan. 1955), pp. 26-40. Published by: The University of Chicago Press, Stable URL.
[248] https://en.wikipedia.org/wiki/Ephesus.
[249] Murphy-O'Connor, *op.cit.*, xiii.

the joys, the sadness, and the fears of the people living at a particular time. Through such human efforts, we discover more about these people, who, though very different from us, can reveal something, perhaps unknown to themselves, or expressed in a very different way, about divine care and concern for them as well as the complexity of divine actions. Springing from an innate sense of the sacred, these intimations of the divine can lead us to learn to see in a new way, in a contemplative way, starting from our gospel conviction of God's love for every person.

> In contemplative prayer, we move beyond language to experience God as Mystery. We let go of our need to judge, defend, or evaluate, plugging into the mind of Christ which welcomes paradox and knows its true identity in God.... Contemplative prayer, remaining silently and openly in God's presence, "rewires" our brains to think non-dually with compassion, kindness, and a lack of attachment to the ego's preferences[250].

Through contemplation, we come to know that there is no separation between sacred and secular. All is one with Divine Reality. We can ponder the goodness we see and trust that God leaves no people without evidence of God in some way. Such a new way of seeing allows us to perceive the insights of different ancient historians who wrote about Ephesus, as possible ways of understanding what over time had shaped, at least in part, the context in which the Gospel would be proclaimed and received.

The first historian of ancient Ephesus, Strabo, was born in Pontus in 64 or 63 BCE. He was wealthy, which afforded him the opportunity of an all-embracing Greek education and the possibility of travel throughout life. *Geography*, his masterpiece that survives, opens with a description of the Iberian Peninsula: "whose Sacred Cape is the most westerly point, not only of Europe but of the whole inhabited world." [251] He then continues moving east "to the most remote peaks of the mountain chain that form the northern boundary of India." Strabo's first reference to Ephesus occurs in the context

---

[250] https://cac.org/about-cac/contemplation/.
[251] *Ibid.*, 5.

of his treatment of Transalpine Gaul.[252] Ephesus is credited with having a strong religious influence in the area, with its famous temple in honor of Artemis. The statues of Artemis, made in Ephesus, were sent to Marseilles as well as other areas. The statue of Artemis on the Aventine Hill in Rome came from Ephesus.[253] Strabo also writes about two of the famous buildings of historic Ephesus, namely, the Library of Celsus and a theatre capable of holding 25,000 spectators.[254]

The early history of Ephesus combines both fact and myth. The story of the Amazons and their role in the development of Ephesus is a case in point. The Amazons were fierce warrior women who inhabited the edges of the known world. According to Greek mythology, they were archenemies of the Greeks. The Amazon Queens dueled with Heracles and Achilles. The Athenians were believed to have defeated the dominant Amazon army. History records that Cyrus of Persia, Alexander the Great, and Pompey, general of Rome fought Amazons. Adrienne Meyer has recently published an extensive study, *The Amazons,*[255] in which she researches both mythology and history to discover as far as possible the identities of these women who were "barbarian archers on horseback," who led warring raids, who hunted and who prized their feminine freedom and independence.[256] Meyer, in her extensive investigative work, offers a wide-ranging account of warrior women who are found in myth and history. These women were part of the ancient world stretching from the Mediterranean to the Great Wall of China. Recently, the remains of battle-scarred female skeletons buried with their weapons have been found in archeological digs. This evidence proves that women warriors did exist.[257] By working to discern relations between classical myth and art, and between nomadic traditions and scientific archaeology, Meyer discovered

---

252 *Ibid.*
253 *Ibid.*, 7.
254 *Ibid.*, 197.
255 Adrienne Meyer. *The Amazons: Lives and Legends of Warrior Women Across The Ancient World*. Princeton, NJ: Princeton University Press.
256 *Ibid.*
257 *Ibid.* 63 ff; see also https://www.smithsonianmag.com/history/amazon-women-there-any-truth-behind-myth-180950188/#RJLjczbYaLEWreUd.99.

surprising details and new insights about the lives and legends of the women known as Amazons. Meyer reminds us that there were as many Amazon love stories as there were war stories. Warrior women such as the Amazons among the Greeks were also found in nomadic cultures and have been the material of tales in ancient Egypt, China, Central Asia, Persia, and India. Strabo indicates that the Amazons were the founders of Ephesus. Except for Pliny, other ancient scholars state only that the shrine of Artemis was begun by the Amazons.

The reason for including this information about the Amazons is that these ideas probably offer at least some hints about the way of thinking in Ephesus. These ideas probably contributed to later personality developments among the Ephesians, influencing some thinking in Ephesus. The fact that the story of the Amazons was both myth and fact, given the recent discoveries mentioned above, questions the influence of women in the history of Ephesus. The fact that both myth and fact constitute proven traditions about the Amazons, can add insights about the tensions existing between women as secondary participants in history, albeit essential contributors to a society, and women as leaders and equals among male counterparts. The high place accorded Artemis among the ancient Ephesians represented in cult and art suggests the esteem accorded women. It is possible that the tensions around the role of women and the stories of the Amazons have been energetic memories influencing history going forward. Both the dynamic of myth and the force of actual historical reality are major stimuli that shape who a people become and eventually how they interact with new sources that arise among them. The shrine of Artemis in Ephesus, a female goddess, was widely known and had regular visits from people in surrounding areas. In large measure, the shrine's popularity was due to mythology. Murphy—O'Connor affirms that for the Ephesians, the cult of Artemis was a "rock-bottom element in their collative and individual identities":

> Artemis permeated the consciousness of the Ephesians to the point that it was a rock-bottom element in their collective and individual identities...but the fact that...particularly Ephesus

was the domain of Artemis is perfectly articulated by Himerios. When the leader of the Muses divided all the earth beneath the sun with his sister, although he himself dwells among the Greeks, he appointed that the inheritance of Artemis would be Ephesus.[258]

A letter from Apollonius of Tyana to the Ephesians describes the impact of the temple and illustrates how Artemis had permeated the consciousness of the Ephesians[259] when he affirms, "Your temple is thrown open to all who would sacrifice, or offer prayers, or sing hymns, to suppliants, to Hellenes, barbarians, free men, to slaves."[260] This openness, an attitude of welcome to all who came is a significant attribute of the Temple of Artemis in the context of the early times of Ephesus. The value placed on religious freedom through openness toward the other is an indication of a value held by the people.

Because Greek temples were sacred, the people of antiquity accepted that they were places of asylum. The temple was a place where one could find a safe shelter. Eventually, civil power began to give grants of immunity, which meant that the temple authorities had to review the cases presented for asylum.[261] Another important characteristic of Ephesus was its location near a body of water. Over time the silt from the Cayster River moved the coastline further away.[262] The harbor was called Sacred Harbor because of its closeness to the Temple of Artemis. There were difficulties caused by silting, yet the harbor remained in use until the late Roman period. Some records indicate the people living in Ephesus were from a variety of origins.[263] History has also preserved some of the occupations of the people. They were silversmiths, doctors, bakers, wine dealers, wool dealers, garment sellers, towel weavers, hemp dealers, cobblers, temple builders, carpenters, sawyers, knob-turners, surveyors, and workers in the private baths.

---

[258] Murphy-O'Connor, *op.cit.*, 17.
[259] *Ibid.*
[260] *Ibid.*, Letter #67, 21.
[261] *Ibid.*, 16.
[262] *Ibid.*, 26.
[263] *Ibid.*, 27.

Ephesus eventually had its first Roman roads which were marked by seven milestones with Aquillius' name. He made Ephesus the capital of the new province instead of Pergamum.[264] Strabo notes there were two main roads, one of which was called the common highway, and served both military and commercial purposes. We should note here that Paul would have traveled this road in 52 CE when he went from Galatia to Ephesus.[265] Cicero records that Ephesus was the entry to Asia and all places further east. Cicero's experience was typical of that of Roman officials and all who engaged in business in the eastern provinces.[266] Also, Cicero's accounts of his journey are a valuable source since they give an indication of the time needed for the journey by Paul, who traveled the same road through Apamea, Synnada, Philomelus, Iconium, and Cybistra, and then east and south through the Cilician Gates, to the principal opening in the Taurus mountains that brought him to Tarsus. Paul also took this route with Barnabas when he traveled to evangelize Iconium, Lystra, Derbe, and Antioch in Pisidia (Acts 13-14), two more times on his second journey (Acts 16-18) and later when he traveled to Ephesus (Acts 19:1).[267]

As we conclude this section, we can lift some of the specific contributions the history of Ephesus provides as background to the evangelization by Paul and the early Christians. We could mention

- the emphasis on the beauty of Ephesus, the most besung of all Ionian cities;

- the importance to the people of the Temple of Artemis, a female goddess; and,

- the stories related to the Amazon warrior women and what this suggests about the roles of women living in a society in which these barbaric women warriors and their independence were highly valued.

---

[264] *Ibid.,* 35.
[265] *Ibid.,* 37.
[266] *Ibid.,* 56.
[267] *Ibid.,* 57.

The city also enjoyed the position given it by its location on an important harbor, and that many people frequently traveled through Ephesus. Fish was an important element in the diet of the people of that time, along with olive oil that was easily available. Many of the great scholars of ancient times spent time in Ephesus. According to the apostles, big cities like Ephesus, Smyrna and Laodicea would help them spread their message in the Western World. The Ephesians, even in ancient times, had a sense of welcome, of freedom of belief as seen in the views expressed in the temple with regard to both welcome and asylum. There seems to have been a level of wisdom and knowledge among many of the people reflected in the decisions made. The Ephesians were surprisingly modern in their social relations. They allowed strangers to integrate, and education was valued. This overview, however brief and lacking great detail, provides us with some insight into the kind of environment the early Christians would have encountered. This is not to suggest that these characteristics of ancient Ephesus necessarily became actual references to the later proclamation of the gospel. Rather these characteristics penetrated the inherited makeup of the Ephesians into Apostolic times. These features would have been part of the Ephesian identity which prepared in the Ephesians a certain capacity to hear the Word when proclaimed to them.

Ephesus had its history of conflicts, of runaway slaves, of learning, and of originalities that were valued, treasured, feared, or despised by its ancient peoples. Undoubtedly due to its location, Ephesus in the classical Greek era was one of the ten cities in the Ionian League. In 129 BCE it became part of the Roman Republic. Its people also figured significantly in Christian history that eventually took root in Ephesus. We will now look at some of the biblical sources that give us further insight into the religious history of Ephesus.

Apostolic Sources Related to Ephesus

The overall testimony of the ministry of the Apostles is evident throughout the New Testament. In particular, a major source for grasping a deeper intuition about mission as gradually understood and lived by the first companions of Jesus is found in the Acts of the Apostles, which may be considered the first missiological text of the Christian era. Its people also figure significantly in the Christian faith that eventually took root in Ephesus. In the Christian era, Paul's presence in Ephesus and the Letter to the Ephesians confirm the existence of a community. John the Apostle and Ignatius of Antioch would have traveled through Ephesus. In the seven letters of the Apocalypse, John offers further insights into developments among the Ephesian Christians. Some Christian stories indicate that Mary, Mother of Jesus, may have gone to Ephesus to live towards the end of her life.

The Ephesians also figure significantly in shaping the Christian faith that eventually took root in Ephesus. We will now look at two biblical sources: The Acts of the Apostles and the Letter to the Ephesians. While these give further insight into the religious history of Ephesus, they also offer missionary insights through the development of core themes. Beginning with the Acts of the Apostles we enter into the heart of the evangelizing witness in Apostolic times.[268] Bevans and Schroeder tell us that the first disciples were convinced that they were called as well to proclaim, to serve, and to embody the same gospel of forgiveness, graciousness, generosity, inclusiveness, and justice that Jesus had preached, served, and witnessed to in his earthly ministry.[269] John Kilgallen explains further,

> Paul, the Apostle to the Gentiles, leads the way in the information of the first Christian community in Ephesus. His tireless efforts to make the Message known which is recounted in his three missionary journeys recorded in Acts were very successful. After about two years in Ephesus, a

---

[268] Stephen B. Bevans and Roger P. Schroeder. *Constants in Context: A Theology of Mission for Today.* Maryknoll, NY: Orbis Books, 2004, 10-31.
[269] *Ibid.*, 12.

significant community has become followers of the Good News. Yet, Paul was a "complicated Apostle", who was recognized as a genius even in ancient times. He often expressed himself in ways difficult to understand. Readying oneself to read Paul means readying oneself to stand in the presence of utter devotion – first as a Pharisee, then as a follower of Christ. It is hard to imagine a Pharisee to be other than stubborn, ready to make great sacrifices, able to go it alone, if necessary. Such was Paul.[270]

Paul lived in the cultural context of the Greco-Roman world and was imbued with Mediterranean culture. He was surrounded by the overriding reality of the Roman Empire; and he was a Jew. Capturing insight into Paul as a person involves recognition of his general Jewish worldview as well as the four dimensions of Jewish unity in diversity at his time, i.e. submission to Rome; some common boundary markers; an apocalyptic orientation in theological thinking found among many Jews; and various Jewish schools of thought.[271]

Paul was born a Jew, lived a Jew, and died a Jew. It was, therefore, obviously, as a Jew that he experienced the once-crucified Jesus as the resurrected and exalted Lord. Paul did not set out to found a new religion, but to call Jews and especially Gentiles to confess the Jewish Messiah, sent by the one true God, YHWH, as the Lord. In retrospect, we can of course say Paul was a 'Christian' – one who confesses and follows Jesus as Messiah and Lord. But we must do so without forgetting the inherent Jewishness of this very term ("Christian" from *christos*) and of the great Christian apostle, Paul.[272]

Gorman points out that the Acts of the Apostles is an important source to take into consideration in tracing Paul's apostolic ministry because it presents a coherent narrative of Paul's missionary activity following his Damascus Road experience.[273] The church emerges from mission in the Acts

---

[270] John J. Kilgallen, sj. "A Complicated Apostle: Who was St Paul?"
    https://www.americamagazine.org/issue/675/ article/complicated-apostle.
[271] *Ibid.*, 27.
[272] *Ibid.*, 52.
[273] *Ibid.*, 55.

of the Apostles.[274] Following this line of thought, Bevans and Schroeder propose a study of Acts that will confirm that the church only comes to be as it understands and accepts mission anywhere and everywhere in the world.[275] Citing David Bosch, they note that mission might also be called the "Mother of the church," since the Christian church grew out of the apostolic proclamation of the gospel and is alive in the act of proclamation.[276] These are important considerations in looking at Paul the Apostle because it connects experiences of the present time with the missionary ministry of Paul as well as others, in a way that is dynamic and life-giving. In writing Acts, Luke indicates that what makes the church is mission, and the reality at the heart of the church is the impulse of the Spirit for the increase of the Word.[277] The Apostles firmly seized that first aspect of apostolic faith by believing that Jesus was indeed the image of the invisible God (Col 1:15), and the Word made flesh (cf. Jn 1:14). Sources for this affirmation can be found in Acts 2:36; 4:8-12; 8:5, 35; 10:34-42; 28:30.[278] These affirmations are also clearly stated in the Pauline texts: Gal 2:15-20; 1 Cor 1:23-24; Rom 5:15-19; 2 Cor 5:19-21; Eph 1:7-10.[279]

In the Acts of the Apostles Luke writes of Paul's time in Ephesus. Beginning around the year 50 CE Ephesus became an important center for Christians. The Apostle lived there from 52 to 54 CE. At the beginning of his time in Ephesus, Paul went to the Jewish synagogue, where he preached. But the stubbornness of some in the synagogue frustrated him, and after about three months he left when they belittled the Way. He took his disciples with him and went to the lecture hall of Tyrannus (Acts 19:9).

According to Acts, Paul came down to Ephesus where he found some disciples. The first question he asked them as if they received the Holy Spirit

---

[274] Bevans, Schroeder, *op.cit.*, Chapter 1.
[275] *Ibid.*, 10.
[276] *Ibid.*, 11.
[277] *Ibid.*, 11 quoting from Lucien Legrand, op, *Unity and Plurality in Mission: Mission in the Bible*. Maryknoll, NY: Orbis Books, 1990, 91.
[278] Bevans, Schroeder, *op.cit.*, 11.
[279] *Ibid.*, 11.

when they became believers. They answered that they had never even heard that there was a Holy Spirit. Paul then asked how they were baptized, and they answered with the baptism of John.[280] Paul then explained that John baptized with the baptism of repentance, and then invited them to believe in the one who was to come after John, that is Jesus. They were then baptized. Then Paul laid his hands upon them and the Holy Spirit came upon them, and they spoke in tongues and prophesied. They were about twelve men.[281] Paul continued for two years and all those living in the province of Asia heard the word of the Lord, Jews, and Greeks alike.[282] The following comment indicates how striking the action of God was through Paul: "When a cloth that touched his skin was applied to the sick, their diseases left them and the evil spirits came out of them."[283]

Turning to the Letter to the Ephesians,[284] the author expresses a theological vision about the mission of the Church in the world, of which Christ is the head (Eph 4:15). Its purpose is to be the instrument for making God's plan of salvation known throughout the universe (Eph 3:9-10).

> This ecclesiology is anchored in God's saving love, shown in Jesus Christ (Eph 2:4-10), and the whole of redemption is rooted in the plan and accomplishment of the triune God (Eph 1:3-14). The language is often that of doxology (Eph 1:3-14) and prayer (cf. Eph 1:15-23; 3:14-19), indeed of liturgy and hymns (Eph 3:20-21; 5:14).[285]

With regard to the authorship and audience of the Letter to the Ephesians, Gorman notes,

> In my opinion, Paul's mind is the main genius behind the letter, and I will refer to the author as Paul. Nevertheless, it is also likely in my view that the apostle, following the conventions of his day, gave a scribe (perhaps Tychicus: cf.

---

280 Acts of the Apostles, 19:1-3.
281 Acts, 19:4-7.
282 Acts, 19:8-10.
283 Acts, 1:11-12.
284 The letter of Paul to the Ephesians was once thought to have been composed by Paul in prison but more likely may be the work of one of Paul's disciples who possibly wrote the text sometime before 90 CE while consulting Paul's letter to the Colossians.
285 *The New American Bible*, 2010. "Introduction to The Letter to the Ephesians," *in loco*.

6:21-22), some leeway in composing the letter. My interpretation of the text, however, is not greatly affected by this position. With respect to the question of audience, if Ephesians was intended as more of a circular letter...that would simply broaden the intended original audience, which would mean more churches than just those in Ephesus would have heard this version of Paul's gospel of peace.[286]

Ephesians holds up the unity between Jews and Gentiles within God's household (Eph 1:15-2:22, especially Eph 2:11-22). But it notes clearly that the concern is not with the church for its own sake but rather as the means for mission in the world (Eph 3:1-4:24). The members receive gifts from Christ that will lead to growth and renewal (Eph 4:7-24).[287] While Ephesians differs in style from other known Pauline texts, it does carry forward the message of Paul.[288]

Possible Implications for Mission Praxis Today

The brief survey of ancient Ephesus provides evidence of some practices from the pre-Christian era which remain meaningful in the present as we journey with the people to whom we are sent. This is not a question of syncretism but rather an opportunity for genuine appreciation of the gifts from God, e.g., goodness, respect, appreciation of others. This action opens the space for dialogue with the other. In the letter that Apollonius of Tyana wrote to the Ephesians, he grasped the powerful influence the temple of Artemis had on the people, and described how the temple was thrown open to all who would sacrifice, or offer prayers, or sing hymns and includes suppliants, Hellenes, barbarians, free men, slaves.[289] This respect for and welcome to all who would sacrifice or offer prayer or sing hymns would be an expression from the past that challenges creative acts of respect and welcome

---

[286] *Ibid.*
[287] *Ibid.*
[288] Michael Gorman. *Becoming the Gospel: Paul, Participation and Mission.* Grand Rapids: Eerdmans, 2015. 183.
[289] Murphy-O'Connor, *op.cit.*

in today's mission contexts. It is an encounter the deeper meaning of which Pope Francis frequently explores.

> Since encounters help the faith to grow, Christians need to approach those in need, build bridges, serve those who suffer, care for the poor, anoint with patience those nearby, comfort those who are discouraged, and bless those who harm us. In this way, we become living signs of the Love we proclaim.[290]

The ancient Ephesians also understood their place of worship as a place of asylum. The present struggles and tragedies confronting unwanted immigrants question the commitment and vision of many who call themselves Christian, yet do not recognize asylum. Welcoming the stranger, the immigrant, the abandoned affirms mission as a way of going forward today.[291] The place of women illustrated in the appreciation of many Ephesians for Artemis and the Amazon women invites the intuition that women played a significant role in society at that time. Both Protestant and Catholic missionary traditions bear many accounts of the important and heroic contributions made by women in their collaboration in the gospel. At other times they bear the scars of prejudice against women.

Another deep value that filled the Ephesians concerning the shrine of Artemis was that this place was sacred. The mouth of the river was also referred to as Sacred. As Christians, we are continually challenged to respect and discover the underlying realities that make something sacred for people to relate to the sacred in new contexts. This is not to worship false idols, but rather to discern what is the moving force that touches the people so deeply, which opens them to listen to the word that can lead them into new insights of what is sacred in the experience of the Good News.

As Paul prepared to leave Ephesus after about a two-year stay, there was a riot of silversmiths which is reported in Acts 19:23-41. Paul had worked intensively while in Ephesus and his preaching led to a growth in the number

---

[290] https://www.vaticannews.va/en/pope/news/2019-09/pope-francis-evangelization-love.html.
[291] Pope Francis. *The Joy of the Gospel*. Rome, 2013. 11.

of followers. That riot of the silversmiths was economically based because their livelihood was rooted in the production of silver statues of Artemis, which was threatened by the significant increase in Christians. Here is evidence of the effectiveness of Paul's preaching in Ephesus:

> Artemis is the thread that holds together Demetrius' speech to the silversmiths, the riot at the theater, and the town clerk's speech at the end. The incidental details that make up the narrative all point in the same direction: in the city of Ephesus, in Asia, and the whole world, the God of the Christians is challenging the power and supremacy of the goddess of the Ephesians.[292]

The process of building the Church involves both space and time leading to the completion of Christ's body, the Church, whose various manifestations across time are necessary for its completion.[293] The Letter to the Ephesians invites us to journey into the missiological experience of the fullness of God.[294] Raymond Brown stressed the importance of Ephesians: among the Pauline writings, only Romans can match Ephesians as a candidate for exercising the most influence on Christian thought and spirituality.[295] Further, the Letter to the Ephesians is possibly, according to Brown, one of the most influential in Christian understanding of peace and peacemaking. The Letter relates to us what God has done in Christ and completed in his death, and what God desires to do in and through the hearers of the letter which is to affect the reconciliation of people to God and one another. This indicates that,

> God now uses the church to make known, in word and deed, the reconciling death of Christ. As elsewhere in the Pauline corpus, we will see that the *vertical* (people's relationship with God) and the horizontal (peoples' relationship with one another) dimensions of salvation are inseparable. Also, inseparable...are the twin realities of the church's centripetal

---

[292] C.L. Brinks. "'Artemis of the Ephesians:' in Light of Goddess Worship in Ephesus." *The Catholic Biblical Quarterly*, Viol.71, no. 4, 791.

[293] Andrew F. Walls. *The Cross-Cultural Process in Christian History*. Maryknoll, NY: Orbis Books. 2002. 74.

[294] Michael Gorman. *Becoming the Gospel: Paul, Participation and Mission*. Grand Rapids, Mn., 2015. 181-186.

[295] *Ibid.*, 181, as quoted from Raymond E. Brown. *An Introduction to the New Testament*. Anchor Yale Bible Reference Library. New York: Doubleday, 1998, 620.

activity and its centrifugal activity in the world – both of which are aspects of its participation in the *Missio Dei*....Ephesians also testifies to the peacemaking work of the one God as the inseparable activity of three persons: Father, Son, and Spirit.[296]

The church's mission of inclusivity and universality has its roots in the Old Testament, particularly in the vision of the prophets. God's election of Israel was never for its own sake, but always so that, in it, all nations would receive a blessing.[297] Ephesians pleads with the community to maintain that which God has brought into being: the unity of the Spirit in the bond of peace (Eph 4:3). The letter stresses the practices of mutual edification that honor and please God's Spirit (Eph 4:29-32). The image of the church, truly a missiological image in Ephesians, is ultimately a way of seeing the church as a place of realized peace. This church is inclusive by nature of all those who make it up, even if their natural secular habitat would place them at odds with one another.[298] Herein lies the mission of the church, namely to bring this countercultural peaceful gift and calling into a transformative relationship in its concrete cultural existence.[299] Peace is a central concern in Ephesians.

We learn now that the Christ-shaped community of peace, of people reconciled to God and to one another, has a task in the world, the same sort of task given to heralds long ago: to announce the good news of peace: not just any peace, but God's peace, the shalom of God's victorious salvation.[300]

Conclusion

Peacemaking is wearing God, putting God on, dressing in God's attributes, all understood Christologically. This means essentially taking part in the life of God, making peace in and through Christ.

We are transformed into the likeness of God when and as we embody – and thus become – the gospel of peace. Such embodiment will be proactive and involve movement, for

---

[296] Michael Gorman, *op.cit.*, 182.
[297] Bevans and Schroeder, *op.cit.*
[298] *Ibid.*, 186.
[299] *Ibid.*
[300] *Ibid.*, 205.

that is, after all, the purpose of shoes. The gospel must be not taken into the world but walked into the world, incarnationally...it is participation in the missional life of the triune God. Such a missional vocation requires prayer...for it to be faithful and effective (Ephesians 6:18a, 18b, 19-20).[301]

As we conclude, the images of Ephesus return and we can legitimately ask to what end this description of an ancient city? What is the relationship between those people who inherited the richness of ancient Ephesus and Christians who are today called to missionary participation in the peace of God and the reconciliation wrought by Christ? From the images of antiquity, the Acts of the Apostles, and the Letter to the Ephesians, we continue to discover dynamic missionary themes. Christians today, across divisions and cultures, are seeking spaces of peace and reconciliation through genuine encounters.

---

[301] *Ibid.*, 206.

Chapter 8: Nineveh

by Mary Glenn[302]

God's Mission of Love and the Enemy

Nineveh is one of those biblical cities we love to hate. Located in modern-day Iraq, Nineveh is mentioned throughout the Old Testament and is prominently featured in the prophetic books of Nahum and Jonah. Some have used the metaphor of the body to describe the sickness of Nineveh. The city's embrace of wickedness has afflicted its body, its state of well-being and existence. Jonah is often criticized for resisting God's call to bring the Lord's message of love and hope to Nineveh. One may understand and relate to Jonah's resistance to this call because he saw the city as undeserving of God's presence, blessings, and forgiveness. God changed his mind after the Ninevites turned from their evil ways. Jonah refused to see Nineveh in any other way but as an 'evil city', even proclaiming he would rather die than see this city spared. What did God see in Nineveh that others did not? Why was it important for the Lord to call Jonah to be on mission in this ancient city? As we read about the city of Nineveh through the lens of God's heart and mission, we gain insight into how God sees people and places as well as the hope he holds for them.

---

302 Mary Glenn (D.Min. from Bakke Graduate University) is an educator, chaplain and bridge-builder. Mary loves cities, and regularly leads urban immersions in the city she loves, Los Angeles. An affiliate professor with Fuller Seminary, Mary has also served as a law enforcement chaplain since 2000, currently serving with the LA County District Attorney's Office, is a police chaplain trainer and an ordained pastor with over 20 years of pastoral experience. Mary is co-president of Cities Together, a faith based non-profit organization that builds bridges and resources leaders in seeking God's peace in their cities.

Introduction

This chapter provides a historical, cultural, and religious overview of the ancient city of Nineveh. Nineveh was the oldest populated city of ancient Assyria, settled as early as 6000 BCE. It is considered "a principal city and last capital of Assyria. The ruins are marked by the mounds called Kuyunjik and Nabi Yunus on the river Tigris opposite Mosul in Iraq."[303] Nineveh, the capital of the Assyrian empire, was one of the cities founded by Nimrod after leaving Babylon (Genesis 10:11).[304]

Ashur, Nineveh, and Urbilum were considered the key cities of the Assyrian Empire. Those who migrated to this region included Semitic and southern Mesopotamia tribes. "The Assyrians then returned to other regions and succeeded in incorporating all of Mesopotamia into the empire for a short period before the Hittites recaptured a large part of it. During this period, the Assyrians adopted the use of the Babylonian dialect, as it was considered more advanced."[305] The Assyrians possessed a strong military. All socioeconomic classes of society were involved in war activities. The empire's greatest period was from 1200-1000 BCE.[306] As the use of military force increased, domestic rights decreased including the status of women. Marriage contracts favored men and minor offenses could be punished with slavery.

Nineveh: A City of History, Culture, and Religion in the Ancient World

Nineveh's context and history are complex and multi-faceted. It was the religious center of the goddess Ishtar who symbolized fertility and love. The city rose to importance as a result of this worship. The city was built on a fault line, and after experiencing earthquakes, had great damage to its

---

[303] D. Wood, & I. Marshall. (1996). *New Bible Dictionary* (3rd ed. / ed.). Leicester, England: InterVarsity Press, entry: Nineveh, p. 836.

[304] Some scholars dispute Nimrod as the founder of Nineveh and instead state the country Assyria (translated "Ashur") as the founder.

[305] Cynthia Clark Northrup. *Encyclopedia of World Trade: From Ancient Times to the Present.* Vol.1, New York: Routledge, 2014, 70.

[306] *Ibid.,* 71.

infrastructure including the first Ishtar temple. Kings ruled this area, building new palaces and temples. After surviving occupation and battles, the city was rebuilt by king Sennacherib. He made Nineveh[307] his capital around 705 BCE, building a new palace, protective walls around the city, streets, structures, parks, and gardens as well as systems of irrigation, canals, and dams that controlled the flow of the river through the city. More than 120,000 people lived in Nineveh at this time,[308] double the number of inhabitants in the city of Babylon.

Nineveh was a city of prominence, forward-thinking, filled with ambition and pride. It championed infrastructure, innovation, and technology. In spite of this flourishing, rulers, civil wars, and infighting led to mass death and deportation. Assaults launched by the Babylonians, Elamites, Medes, and Scythians weakened the city of Nineveh. The siege of Nineveh came at the hands of the king of Akkad and the king of Media during the summer of 612 BCE. After the king of Assyria died, the city was plundered. All of this eventually resulted in the tragic demise, desolation, and end of Nineveh. God's judgment on their pride is detailed in Isaiah 10 and their destruction prophesied by Zephaniah. "The fall of the great city of Nineveh as predicted by the prophets of Nahum and Zephaniah occurred in August 612 BCE. By 605 BCE, the Assyrian kingdom officially ended and the empire of Babylonia was on the rise. The city was left to fall into the heap of desolate ruin (Nah 2:10-3:7), a pasturing place (Zephaniah 2:13-15), giving the citadel its modern name of Tali Kuyunjik,(mound of many sheep). By the time Xenophon and the retreated army passed in 401 BCE, it was already an unrecognizable mass of debris."[309]

Nineveh, said to take three days to traverse, was a gateway to the fertile plains from the mountains. They had one of the first aqueducts of its kind. The city cultivated wheat, barley, grapes, and was home to large

---

[307] Described in the book of Jonah as taking three days to cross.
[308] Wood, *op.cit.*, 837.
[309] *Ibid.*, 837.

botanical gardens and even a zoo. Nineveh was a hub for world trade and was considered the greatest city in the world for almost two centuries. It was the intersection of the worlds of India and the Mediterranean, frequented by merchants selling goods in the city including pepper and spices from India as well as silk, blue fabric, and embroidery. The Tigris River served as the waterway for trade. Nineveh was known not only for its geography and trade but also for its library and advanced Assyrian language. As a religious center, fertility, growth, and prosperity were worshipped, desired, and invested in. Nineveh was cultured, collaborative, advanced in every way and intent to be a forerunner in what a city could and should be.

The Jonah Story and Beyond

Nineveh is no doubt an important city in God's mission in the world. Beyond the story told in the book of Jonah, the city gives insight into understanding the power of names, labels, and metaphors. Likened to a body, described as an evil city and known for its wickedness, Nineveh provides a glimpse into the role of cities in the story of humanity and their relationship with God. The city first enters into the stage of God's mission in Genesis 10: 8-12:

> Cush became the father of Nimrod; he was the first on earth to become a mighty warrior. He was a mighty hunter before the Lord; therefore it is said, "Like Nimrod a mighty hunter before the Lord." The beginning of his kingdom was Babel, Erech, and Accad, all of them in the land of Shinar. From that land he went into Assyria, and built Nineveh, Rehoboth-ir, Calah, and Resen between Nineveh and Calah; that is the great city.[310]

Even though Nineveh is mentioned elsewhere, the story of Jonah has seared Nineveh is our memories. The story brings to mind a big fish, a pouting prophet, and a forgiving God. The book of Jonah leaves no doubt that Nineveh was thought of as an evil city that deserved destruction. The city's inhabitants

---

[310] *New Revised Standard Version* (NRSV) translation.

did not care to know right from wrong. Sometime between 786-746 BCE, the Lord called Jonah, son of Amittai, to prophesy against Nineveh. He initially resisted God's mission. In response to hearing God's call to repent, the people fasted and turned from their evil ways.[311] Surprising Jonah, God spared the city from destruction. God's change of heart did not sit well with Jonah who protested, pouted, and proclaimed he would rather die than see this city spared. Jonah's response spoke more to who he was rather than who Nineveh was. As Jonah retreated in anger, he found shelter under a vine to await the outcome of Nineveh (Jonah 4:5). God provided the plant to shade him. And then God provided a worm to chew and wither that same plant. God challenged Jonah's anger by reminding Jonah who was the Creator and who had the right to be angry in this situation. In the end, God's reason for sparing Nineveh was not based on its unique and innovative ethos. God cared for Nineveh because of the people and animals, God's handiwork.

Body as a Metaphor for Nineveh

Body as a metaphor for Nineveh is found three times in the book of Jonah: Jonah in the body of the whale, the city of Nineveh as a body, and the plant that provided shade to Jonah as well as the body of the worm that ate the plant. The first and last examples bring attention to the key usage of the metaphor, the city. Nowhere is the metaphor of the city as body illustrated more concretely than in the book of Nahum who also prophesied against Nineveh. Nahum describes the city as a healthy body in its health. The people of Nineveh were the bodies of the city. The speaker shifted the referent from city-as-structure to city-as-people.[312] (Nahum 3:18-19)

In describing the city as a body, Nahum personified the city and was able to connect the (physical) activities of the city to the city's inhabitants and then to the readers. "As with the life story of Jerusalem, the body image of

---

[311] Some scholars say there is no external evidence for the repentance of the people of Nineveh. Wood, *op.cit.*, 837.
[312] Karolien Vermeulen. "The body of Nineveh: the conceptual image of the city in Nahum 2-3." *Journal of Hebrew Scriptures*;Volume 17, Article 1, 2017. 7.

Nineveh is used consistently, creating the story of a strong and healthy body becoming a sick and bereaved corpse.... The frequent use of actual body parts further emphasizes a bodily understanding of the city space."[313] Nahum described the shift from a seemingly healthy city entity to one that was ill, empty, and bereaved.

Nahum in three brief chapters, describes Nineveh's descent into wickedness and illness, even denoting it as the city of blood/bloodshed (Nahum 3:1) and the wicked city (Nahum 2). "The image of the city as a body is more than the mere result of human cognition. As Dobbs-Allsopp stated concerning Jerusalem, the enemy city in the text is a blend of cognition and creativity. It draws the far away near and renders the foreign familiar so that the reader can fully experience the death of the villain Nineveh."[314] The sickness of the body (of the city of Nineveh) was further illustrated with the reference to locusts (used as similes or marked metaphors) in describing the power and strength of Nineveh while foreshadowing the downfall and ultimate destruction of Nineveh.[315] The audience of the time would understand this reference as they were familiar with locusts and their behavior of clearing the land and then flying away, not thinking twice about the destruction they caused. Nahum suggested that Nineveh and locusts shared a life cycle where they could devour, multiply, shed their skin, and fly away (Nahum 3:15-17).[316]

About 150 years separate the book of Jonah and the book of Nahum. Nahum attempted to encourage the southern kingdom of Israel (Judah and Benjamin) that hadn't been captured by the Assyrian empire to not give in to them. Nahum tried to convince them that Nineveh would be destroyed. The hope was that the people of Judah would trust in God rather than an empire (Assyrian) that had no emotional concern for what it had left behind. The use

---

[313] *Ibid.,* 3.
[314] Vermeulen, *op.cit.,* 17.
[315] Willie Wessels. "The metaphorical depiction of Nineveh's demise. The use of locust as a 'marked metaphor' in Nahum 3:15-17." *Scriptura 116* (volume 2), 2017, 246.
[316] *Ibid.,* 250.

of locusts to describe the power of Nineveh and the Assyrians involved looking ahead to their coming doom. Even the strong and powerful would fall. The judgment and justice of God was promised and guaranteed in the book of Nahum. In comparison to the kingdom of Assyria, God provided safety and was a stronghold of justice and righteousness rather than the Assyrian's cruelty, pursuit of power, and self-satisfaction. Instead of destruction and doom, God reigned and brought life. Only God's power, authority, and kingdom prevailed and stood the test of time. God forgave Nineveh the first time and eventually the city was left in ruins. Was this city determined and destined to be the "evil city"?

Was Nineveh to be Perceived Only as an Evil City?

Unquestionably Nineveh played an important role in ancient biblical history. The question is whether or not its contribution was limited to its wickedness. Would Nineveh only and always be known as the 'evil city'? Nineveh was labeled an evil city in its time. In addition to being the religious center of Ishtar worship (the goddess who symbolized fertility and love), it was a city that was known for its wickedness. It played a key role in a war-making empire that stripped protections for its most vulnerable residents, including women. Was it possible for a city like Nineveh to reinvent itself, becoming the city God hoped it would become? Or was Nineveh always doomed to be a haven for evil and darkness? In Jonah's call to Nineveh, we find a God who saw something Jonah and we might fail to see; a city that was never beyond the love and salvation of God.

God loves even the most despised cities. Could it be possible that Nineveh and her people's identities were not found in their behavior (disobedience, not knowing right from wrong, and wickedness) but found in their belovedness as God's image-bearers? God sent Jonah to preach a message of repentance to Nineveh (Jonah 3:1-2). He initially obeyed (Jonah 3:3). Jonah determined that Nineveh was a God-forsaken people and place (Jonah 3:4). One might ask why Jonah was hoping for this outcome? Why would someone find comfort in another's suffering (whether caused by themselves or others) and revel in God's punishment of a city? Upon hearing the message and call for repentance, the king of Nineveh put on sackcloth and proclaimed a fast in the city. The king led by example in calling the people to turn from their evil ways (Jonah 3:6-7). When Jonah questioned the compassion of the Lord, God asked why he should not have concern for this great city with over 120,000 people and animals (Jonah 4:11)? The Lord had compassion for the city, his heart was moved and he even called Nineveh a great city. In Jonah 4: 11 God says, "And why shouldn't I feel sorry for a great city like Nineveh with its 120,000 people in utter spiritual darkness and all its cattle?"[317] God's posture towards Nineveh can guide how we perceive, pray for, and engage with our cities.

Nineveh was called a "great city" due to its size as well as its advancements and accomplishments.[318] Was Nineveh forever to be branded a city of evil? Is it possible that the city held a deeper purpose and meaning despite its choices and actions? When cities are labeled as "the other," it is more difficult to see the interconnectedness of our lives. Jonah did not see the residents of Nineveh as worthy of being spared. He saw no connection between his life and theirs. Imagine if Jonah was able to see how interconnected and interwoven his life was with the Ninevites? Would there have been a different outcome for him and the city? Cities too often carry a variety of labels which can be a result of reality, fear, dislike, and even hatred.

Jonah preferred to die rather than see God turn his heart from anger to love towards Nineveh because they repented and turned from their evil ways. Maybe it was time for Jonah to not only learn about God's grace but also his own perceived labels. Sociologist Brené Brown taught us that when people see each other as "the other", less human and even morally inferior, dehumanizing behavior is made possible. The dehumanization of others creates moral exclusion. Labels, words, and language precede and can even

---

The Living Bible
Jonah 1:2.

precipitate this kind of action. "Dehumanizing and holding people accountable are mutually exclusive. Humiliation and dehumanizing... are emotional self-indulgence at (its) worst. And if our faith asks us to find the face of God in everyone we meet, that should include the politicians, media, and strangers on Twitter with whom we most violently disagree." [319] To prevent this kind of harm, it is important for God to be the lens that one uses to view and engage with the city and her people. Scripture and a missiological approach provides a new way of seeing others.

God called Jonah to be on mission with God in Nineveh and to prophesy to the city. God is the God of second chances. God loves cities and calls people to seek peace in the city (Jeremiah 29). This story reminds us that no one is beyond the love of God. All matters and God intends for all to hear of and respond to the message of love and call to repentance. In Jonah 3:5 the people of Nineveh believed God after fasting and having a change of heart and behavior. In response, God "changed his mind" (Jonah 3:10). God's heart was impacted by how a city turned from its wicked ways towards God.

God Creates and Holds Love and Hope for Place

God loves places and cities. Cities are mentioned over 1,200 times in the Bible. Genesis 1:1, "In the beginning when God created the heavens and the earth" (NRSV) tells us that the first thing God created was location, place (the heavens and the earth). In addition to creating place, God dwells in place and that is where we find God. This is most tangibly exemplified in the life of Jesus. "The Word became flesh and blood and moved into the neighborhood" (John 1:14). [320]

Place (and cities) reveal where God is found.

> In the city there is grit but there is also grace.... In a city...we have God's face all around us, if we look for it—not in the sky, but the faces of others. Whether we are talking about Los Angeles or Louisville or Bakersfield or Bend, cities can show

---

[319] Brown, Brené. *Braving the wilderness: the quest for true belonging and the courage to stand.* New York: Random House. 2017, 76.
[320] The Message translation.

us how varied we are as human beings: varied in ethnicity, race, age, style, health. We might think the cityscape hides God, but in a unique way, a metropolis (and place) reveals God's presence through the diversity of His children, for all are created in God's image."[321]

Cities are sacred spaces for us to be found by God and with each other. In his book, *The Land: Place as Gift, Promise, and Challenge in Biblical Faith*, Walter Brueggermann proposes that land is foundational to our faith[322] and is where our faith is lived out.

In addition, place holds particularity, history, stories, and memories. "Place memory encapsulates the human ability to connect both the built and natural environments that are entwined in the cultural landscape."[323] Place connects us to our history and our place in God's story, as well as provides a sense of purpose and meaning. "The fact that we construct meaning from our geography is both practical and theological."[324]

In place, God's presence and characteristics are made known. God created place and he invites us into God's mission in place. God is a missionary God. God's mission doesn't take place in a vacuum but is set in a context, place. God's intent for Nineveh and all cities is for reconciliation, restoration, and transformation. God's purposes are the reconciling of the cosmos to Godself (II Cor 5:19) through the sending of Jesus Christ and the activity of the Holy Spirit. Christian mission originates in the activity of God. So the impulse for mission is not primarily the converting of souls or the expansion of the church but participation in God's cosmic purposes for a new order of relationships at all levels in the universe governed by justice, love, peace, and grace. Place is part of God's redemptive mission. God is an

---

[321] Marcy Heidish. *Soul and the city: finding God in the noise and frenzy of life.* Colorado Springs, Colorado: WaterBrook Press, 2008, 4.
[322] Walter Brueggermann. *The land: place as gift, promise and challenge in biblical faith.* Minneapolis, Minnesota: Augsburg Fortress Publishers, 2003, 3.
[323] Dolores Hayden. *The power of place: urban landscapes as public history.* Cambridge, MA: The MIT Press, 1997, 46.
[324] David P. Leong. *Race and place: how urban geography shapes the journey to reconciliation.* Downers Grove, Illinois: Intervarsity Press, 2017, 23.

inclusive God who utilizes place to connect us to him and to each other, maybe something God was attempting to teach Jonah. In God, we find belonging as a community in place. "This kind of geographic transgression – this habitual crossing of color, class, and gender lines – is what continually characterizes Jesus' faithful ministry of inviting his followers to consider a new kind of belonging and a new kind of community that would embody this unusual belonging in the world."[325]

Cities enable place identity and our connection to each other. Systems and injustices in place influence and impact its residents. David Leong outlines how the relationship between geography and land impacts our relationships with each other and the places we live in. Cities can hold systemic challenges and injustices as well as hope for change. "A deep reading of both the scriptures and the city is essential to understanding the signs of the times."[326] It is important to remember that no matter what cities and place currently embody, God holds hope, mission, and reconciliation for place. This principle includes the city of Nineveh. "This restored Eden nourishes and heals all the people who dwell there, and the whole story has come full circle."[327] The book of Revelation unfolds the vision of a restored city (the New Jerusalem) and a place that is the new kingdom of God. Jeremiah 29 explores how God's love for place extends to God's people and their role in God's mission of seeking God's peace for creation.

As we develop a theology of place, we become more committed to the community in which we live and to seek its shalom. Shalom is a comprehensive concept that expresses society as God intended it to be, including a sense of wholeness, harmony, joy, and justice. Peacemaking enables the church to maintain the integrity of its witness and commitment to the city while operating in a pluralistic civic setting.[328] How do and can we embody this shalom of God in the places we are called? In response to this

---

[325] *Ibid.,* 56.
[326] *Ibid.,* 29.
[327] *Ibid.,* 73.
[328] Mark Gornik. *To live in peace.* Grand Rapid, MI: Eerdmans, 2002.

concept of God's shalom economy, all have a call and responsibility to participate in God's peace-building and peace-making in place. Actions and behavior have impact beyond an individual.

God's mission in Nineveh was unique. The first thing that marks this mission as unique was that this mission wasn't just about Nineveh; it was also about Jonah as the agent of God's mission. Even though Jonah was the messenger, it was important for him to hear and receive the word of the Lord. As much as God hoped for the transformation of Nineveh, God hoped for Jonah's heart to be transformed in how he viewed others. In fact their transformation was intertwined. Their stories were connected, maybe even mutually interdependent. As much as Jonah would want to deny it, he needed Nineveh as much as Nineveh needed him. They could learn from each other about God's mission and love. Scripture describes how humans in the church make up the different parts of the body. In using this metaphor of the body in this context, Jonah and Nineveh are members. How could this insight have shifted the way they engaged with and saw each other as well as their responsibility to each other?

The second unique aspect of God's mission in Nineveh is the tension of God's judgment and grace. Jonah was eager to hold Nineveh's feet to the fire, to hold them accountable for their evil acts. God is a God of judgment as much as a God of grace. "Through his death and resurrection, Jesus offers redemption and transformation of the old Jerusalem into the new City of God. This is an eschatological reality that John would later refer to in Revelation 21. True to God's form of response throughout the history of Israel, there is always grace in the midst of judgment; in the end, there is a rewriting of the story of Jerusalem."[329] His grace and judgment are not meant to be dissected and divorced. When Jonah preached repentance to Nineveh, they repented, much to the disapproval of Jonah. The city of that time and generation is

[329] Charles Van Engen, "Constructing a theology of mission for the city," in Charles Van Engen and Jude Tiersma-Watson. eds., *God so loves the city: seeking a theology for urban mission.* Eugene, Oregon: Wipf and Stock Publishers, 1994, 242.

spared the wrath of God for that moment. Jonah hoped for only judgment for Nineveh, not for mercy. This choice impacted Jonah, how he related to God, and how he related to others. "In the end, Jonah's strange encounter with God brings about the deconstruction and re-mystification of the superficially simple tale of Nineveh's repentance and salvation."[330] It isn't as simple and clear cut as Jonah or possibly we would like it to be.

Third, God is the one who orchestrates transformation. God alone holds the ultimate authority. As Jonah protested his loss of shade from the tree as well as God's sparing of Nineveh, he declared he would rather die. God's point was that Jonah didn't make either the tree or the city, so if anyone had a 'right' to have emotions, it was God. God reminded Jonah that God was in charge and held all of eternity.

Everyone in the story of Nineveh played a role. God alone is sovereign, all of the time, throughout time. God invites us to join God on a mission. We are made in God's image. We are to imitate God. Let's be clear, none of us are God.

> So, by the end of the story, human folly is once more exposed. Within the narrative, no person has been immune from it: prophet, sailors, foreigners, the Hebrew community that created the story and adopted it into its literary canon, any reader, and any writer of the established genres utilized. Only God, whose superior wisdom dictates benevolence rather than human (sometimes hypocritical) justice, is depicted as unperturbed by personal and seemingly theological considerations.... To be truly human is to partake of divinity not only through orthodox sentiment. To be in God's image, to be sanely judgments, is to forsake legalism and become understanding and merciful. Jonah, prayer, and all, remains the butt of the story."[331]

---

[330] Alan Cooper. "In praise of divine caprice." In P. Davies and D. Clines, eds., *Among the prophets: Language, image, and structure in the prophetic writings.* Sheffield, England: Sheffield Academic Press, 1993, 153.

[331] Athalya Brenner. "Jonah's poem out of and within its context," in P. Davies and D. Clines, eds, *Among the prophets: Language, image, and structure in the prophetic writings.* Sheffield, England: Sheffield Academic Press, 1993, 191-192.

The books of Jonah and Nahum give insight for engaging with God's mission as well as bringing attention to the challenges and choices of engagement. Do we choose to be like Jonah or God? Do we see the worst or hope for the best? Nineveh challenges us to accept that our peace and wholeness are intertwined. It reminds us that God holds justice and mercy in tension in a way that honors both, and God acts as a sovereign agent to bring transformation to the world. The challenge is for human beings to extend grace, speak truth, and leave the judgment to God.

> God wanted Nineveh to know that he doesn't give up on them even if they give up on themselves. No matter how egregious the sin, God still loves people, those he created.... "To this end, one hopes (against all human inclination) to model, not the 'one false move' God but the 'no matter whatness' of God. You strive to live the black spiritual that says, 'God looks beyond our fault and sees our need.'" [332] Nineveh was a great city, an innovative city, a city that embraced evil, and a city that turned from its wickedness.[333] The 'no matter whatness' of God solidified the fact that Nineveh and her people were loved by God. Engagement with God's mission in place (including reflection, applied theology, and relationship with) can lead to renewal and transformation of a city and her people. "The interweaving of reflection and action offers a transformation of all aspects of our missiological engagement with the city. This leads us back to a faith commitment, a loving engagement, and a hopeful envisioning of ways in which we pray we may retell the story So we return to where we began, and boldly proclaim the retelling of the story (Revelation 21:2-3)."[334]

Conclusion

What can be learned from Nineveh about who God is and what God's mission is in the city and is for us today in our cities? As a city of importance, Nineveh is more than just the story of Jonah. It's more than a sick body, an evil city, a forsaken people. Cities like Nineveh and her people are not the sum of the labels they wear nor their acts of evil. God extends love to places,

---

[332] Gregory Boyle. *Tattoos on the heart: the power of boundless compassion*. New York: Free Press, 2011, 52.
[333] Matthew 12:41, Luke 11:32.
[334] Charles Van Engen, *Op cit.*, 263-264.

offering hope, forgiveness, and a new lease on life. The story of exiled Israel in Jeremiah 29 demonstrates how we might partner with God and follow God's mission to seek peace, even among and in the land of those we might consider as our enemies. As God called Jonah to mission in Nineveh, God calls each one of us to mission in our cities. Nineveh reminds us that God's heart is bigger than ours, God's economy has room for everyone, and no one is excluded nor left out from God's mission. God invites and calls the Church to love people, places us and reimagines what place can become. The body of Christ is the living organism bearing God's lifeline and heartbeat in cities, places, and the world. And God's beat goes on.

Chapter 9: Philippi

by Enoch Jinsik Kim[335]

God's Mission of Hope Amid Distress and Suffering

God's mission in the city can be found as we see God's message for the Christians in Philippi. God gave the Philippian church the message of purpose in suffering, value of relationship, and new hope through Christ. Paul wanted to gear the interests of the Philippians to the sufferings of Christ, and he taught them that Christ overcame suffering through humility. The citizenship of heaven that Paul introduced allowed them to expect new things the world could not offer. In Philippians, Paul juxtaposes heavenly citizenship over against Roman citizenship, which many church members could not obtain. Paul reminds the Philippian Christians that all those in authority would one day kneel before Jesus. The gathering of Christians indicated a community that was even greater than that of Roman citizens. The moment we truly become apostolic messengers in our communities and live as salt and light, we become our own minority in this world and society. To the cities where Christians are the minority, the Lord offers purposeful suffering, great unity, and new hope.

---

335 Enoch Jinsik Kim earned his Ph.D. at Fuller Theological Seminary, where he serves as a full-time associate professor in Communication and Mission Studies and a chairperson of the Korean Doctor of Missiology Program. Selected publications include *Mission Strategy in the City* (Pickwick), and *Receptor-Oriented Communication for Hui Muslims in China* (ASM Monograph Series).

Introduction

Like other cities in Macedonia, Philippi was a Roman-dominated Greek territory. In this chapter, I will identify a missional theme associated with Philippi that flows from God's heart for the city. God's mission in the city can be found as we consider the Apostle Paul's interaction with that city and we begin to understand God's message for the Christians in Philippi. This study of Philippi will enable us to identify a missional theme that cities and their churches in similar situations need to hear.

Philippi

The first appearance of ancient Philippi and its residents on record is 490 BCE regarding the Thracian tribe. They owned gold and silver mines in Mount Pangaion and resided near the area.[336] Later, the Athenians and Greek colonists from Thasos competed to occupy the gold mines, and in 360 BCE, the Thracians founded a colony there and called it Crenides (or Datus). The indigenous Thracians then strongly resisted Thasos, who occupied them, and as matters worsened, the Thracians asked the Macedonians for help. As a result, the Macedonian king, Philip II, occupied the Crenides area in 356 BCE. After that, Crenides took the name of Philip II, and the city was called Philippi.[337]

In 42 BCE after the battle between Octavian and Antony, Philippi became a Roman colony with a permanent settlement of discharged veteran soldiers and their families.[338] In 30 BCE, Octavian became Roman emperor, and named the city *Colonia Lulia Philippensis* and then *Colonia Augusta Julia Philippensis*. By the time the Apostle Paul first visited Philippi (49 or 50 CE), there were diverse people groups and long developed and preserved entities in the culture and identity of the people.

---

[336] The record of the Thracian tribes first appears in 490 BCE, when Xerxes, the Persian emperor passed through the region before invading Greece.

[337] Lilian Portefaix. *Sisters Rejoice: Paul's Letter to the Philippians and Luke-Acts as Seen by First-Century Philippian Women.* Stockholm: Almqvist & Wiksell, 1988, 60.

[338] *Ibid.*, 60.

The industry of Philippi was based on agriculture. It had a population of approximately 15,000 inhabitants[339] organized in social structures that included diverse ethnicities and classes that were intermixed due to its long colonial history and strong Roman influence.[340] In what follows, I will identify the geophysical, socio-ethnic, politico-economic, and religious features of Philippi.

Geophysical Features

Philippi was located east of Macedonia, close to the border with Thrace. On the west lay the Strymon River and on the east the Nestos River. The north and south of the city are blocked by mountains, with Mount Pangaoin (location of the gold and silver mines) in the southwest. Further south lay the Mediterranean Sea and on the Mediterranean coast was the port city of Neapolis. The Apostle Paul and his team later entered Philippi through this city. In the center of Philippi was an east-west road called *Via Egnatia* that ran through the city and was the main road connecting Rome with all its eastern colonies.[341] The fact that *Via Egnatia* was built to pass through Philippi indicates how much the Roman Empire was relationally close to Philippi. As a result, Philippi became a city with a strong Roman political influence compared to other colonized Greek cities.

During Philip II's reign, the mines in Mount Pangaion were abandoned, though some small pits remained nearby. As the gold and silver industry died down, Philippi's economy began shifting to agriculture. The land around Philippi was fertile and produced abundant harvests.[342]

Ethnic Population and Social Composition

Philippi was a city with unique characteristics in ethnic population and social composition. Traditionally the residents mainly consisted of indigenous Thracians and descendants of colonial Greeks. Each of these tribes

---

[339] Peter Oakes. *Philippians: From People to Letter*. Society for New Testament Studies
      Monograph Series 110. Cambridge: Cambridge U. Press, 2001, 65.
[340] *Ibid.*, 70.
[341] Barbara Levick. *Roman Colonies in Southern Asia Minor*. Oxford: Clarendon Press, 1967, 5
[342] Portefaix, *op.cit.*, 61.

preserved and practiced their own culture and language in their territories. The local language retained the Greek identity, while religion was the center of the Thracian people.[343] After Rome occupied Philippi in BCE 42, numerous Romans immigrated to the city.[344]

By 50-60 CE, the ethnic population of Philippi was mainly Greek and Roman. There was a sense of divergence between the two due to an economic and political imbalance. Philippi's population at the time could be estimated to have been around 15,000.[345] Peter Oakes estimated the social composition of the city of Philippi in 50 BCE, by utilizing Richard Rohrbaugh's urban system of a pre-industrial city.[346] Oakes estimated the proportion of Romans and Greeks living in Philippi was 40:60. The 40% indicates that Philippi had a much higher proportion of Romans than did other cities on former Greek territories. The people residing in and out of Philippi were made up of 5 tiers. According to Oakes' calculation, the service class is 37%, slaves 20%, colonist farmers 20%, the poor 20%, and elites 3%.[347]

The highest strata and citizen class were Romans. There were several strata within Philippi's Roman community. They were the grandchildren or great-grandchildren of the early colonist soldiers and peasants. The Romans could be divided into at least three levels: *liberti*, Roman citizens, and natives.[348] *Liberti* was the largest group and composed of freed slaves of colonists. The next group was made up of the Roman citizens who moved to Philippi after colonization. These were retired veteran soldiers who owned houses and land in the area. For the Romans, Philippi served as a military outpost for approximately 100 years. However, because Philippi was distant from the military front, it later became a place where soldiers lived with their

---

[343] *Ibid.*, 67.
[344] Oakes, *op.cit.*, 50.
[345] *Ibid.*, 47.
[346] Richard, L Rohrbaugh. "The Pre-Industrial City in Luke-Acts: Urban Social Relations." In Jerome H. Neyrey, ed. *The Social World of Luke-Acts: Models for Interpretation*, Peabody, Mass.: Hendrickson Pub, 1991, 130-132.
[347] Oakes, *op.cit.*, 50. These estimates can vary slightly depending on the society, whether that was a high slave society, high poor society, or high colonist farming society.
[348] *Ibid.*, 71-72.

families, bought property, accumulated wealth, and established their lineages. The soldiers who remained were retired. They owned farms and did not return to the Roman mainland. The last Roman group consisted of the natives, or Greeks, who were citizens of Philippi, though their numbers were not large.

The Greek-speaking population included several groups.[349] The first were the indigenous tribes with their Thracian names and religious habits. As Hellenized groups, they were active in economic affairs. They successfully accumulated wealth through frequent trade with the outside world. The tribes also practiced traditional Greek polytheism and used their wealth to build up idols and shrines throughout the region. The second group was the descendants of Thracian and Macedonian colonists from the 4th century BCE. They came to the area bringing Thracian and other Eastern religious practices with them. In addition to these two groups, there were migrant workers from various parts of the Hellenistic world. This included slaves, brought from the Greek-speaking East.

The Political and Economic Dimensions

From the politico-economic angle, more than other colonial cities, Philippi was strongly influenced by Rome.[350] Rome ruled the city directly, such that Roman influence was evident throughout the city, including Philippi's economy. Most of the farms surrounding the city were Roman owned.[351] Greek economic activities were subject to the Roman system and under heavy surveillance.

In Philippi, there were descendants of indigenous people who had been there for centuries. They were relatively lower-middle-class people, who mainly maintained small shops and factories. Later, Greek migrants began to arrive from Asia Minor. These immigrants were mainly engaged in commerce, importing goods from abroad.[352]

---

[349] *Ibid.*, 73-74.
[350] *Ibid.*, 33.
[351] Portefaix, *op.cit.*, 67.
[352] *Ibid.*, 67.

Religion and Social Cohesion

When the Apostle Paul entered Philippi, there were already several religions and faiths that had existed there for hundreds of years. For example, the slave girl that the Apostle Paul encountered in Philippi made her masters much money by predicting the future revealing how people trusted fortune-telling.[353] Portefaix summarizes the religious diversity embedded in Philippi's history as follows.

> When the Romans arrived, they brought their religion to Philippi. There existed already the cults of the Thracians and the Greek colonists, and in addition, some Oriental cults had been brought into Macedonia in the 3rd cent. B.C., presumably by businessmen from Alexandria and Asia Minor. The Roman religion, however, was leavened with Greek myths and ideas and soon it absorbed the old Greek cults in Philippi. On the other hand, the Thracian religion (found particularly in the countryside) survived. It had maintained its distinctive character during the Greek and Macedonian colonisations and...it influenced the Roman cults in various ways.[354]

The people of Philippi worshipped various Greek gods, a general phenomenon throughout Ancient Greece. Archaeological analysis provides a great deal of information regarding Philippi's spiritual environment and rituals. Good resources concerning their religious life are found in the images appearing as reliefs on the acropolis of Philippi or as statues and busts in the forum. Of these images, 140 portray women, while only 19 portray men. Of the 140 women, 90 of them were of Diana (or Artemis), 42 unknown, 2 of Athena, 3 of Kybele, and 3 of the Lunar Deity.[355] In other words, the Philippians at the time submitted more to goddesses than gods, and among the goddesses, Artemis was given the most attention.

---

[353] Acts 16:16.
[354] Portefaix, *op.cit.*, 70.
[355] Jason T. Lamoreaux. *Ritual, Women, and Philippi: Reimagining the Early Philippian Community.* Matrix: The Bible in Mediterranean Context. Eugene, OR: Cascade Books, 2013, 43.

The stone reliefs in the city of Philippi alone are insufficient to fully understand Artemis' meaning and influence upon the people. By examining Artemis' immense influence upon the entire Mediterranean region during the Classical Roman period, we can more effectively understand its impact on the lives of the Philippians. The religious activities that centered on the goddess were more than simply religious; they significantly impacted people's daily lives. Every time Philippians went through life passages, they needed Artemis' blessings and feared her curses as well. Artemis thus naturally became a significant entity for women who were closely involved in life passages of their families.[356]

All the rituals performed for Artemis were community events. Through dedications, washings, wedding ceremonies, and appeasements, people became recognized members of the community. Every time a child was born, a family member died, or a woman was undergoing physical transformation, women had to deal with the associated pollution and curses. Each time they passed the purification process in front of the community, they could once again qualify as members of the community and restore their status.

In the history of mission, we have learned that when Christianity enters a new culture where the religious practices are integral to the social cohesion, it disrupts the social cohesion provided by those religious practices. The threat of losing the social cohesion often gives rise to religious persecution of the new Christians.

One statue discovered in central Philippi reveals evidence of promoting Roman emperors to godhood and its strong impact on the lives of individuals during the First Century CE. It is mentioned that in a monument

---

[356] Informative and helpful sources are Lamoreaux, *op.cit.*, 125; Matthew Dillon, *Girls and Women in Classical Greek Religion*. London: Routledge, 2008; Helen King. *Hippocrates' Woman: Reading the Female Body in Ancient Greec.* online resource; London: Routledge, 1998; John Howard Oakley and Rebecca H. Sinos. *The Wedding in Ancient Athens*. Wisconsin Studies in Classics; Madison, WI: U of Wisconsin Press, 1993; Valerie A. Abrahamsen. *Women and Worship at Philippi: Diana/Artemis and other Cults in the Early Christian Era*. Portland, ME: Astarte Shell Press, 1995.

in Philippi, there is an inscription of the emperor cults in honor of Augustus (27 BCE-14 CE), Claudius (4-54 CE), and Vespasian (69-79 CE).[357] The inscription refers to Augustus as *Aequitas Augusti*, implying he was at least the equivalent of other goddesses.[358] Philippi was the only city of the region where Augustus was described as *Aequitas Augusti*. This indicates the magnitude of Roman influence in Philippi. The imperial cult elevated the position of the Roman Empire to a cosmic level, and Rome became a god-ruling nation, at least to the Romans. As a result, the edict of the emperor became a command of a god, not of a man, and Rome was recognized as a nation worthy of ruling the world.[359] Philippi's economy and culture were influenced by Greek ideas, politics, and institutions coupled with Roman power, and their religion originated from the various Mediterranean cults.

The Church is Born in Philippi

During his second missionary journey, Paul visited Philippi with Silas, Timothy, and Luke. Paul originally planned to go to Phrygia and Galatia, but in Troas, he had a vision of a Macedonian man, realized the guidance of the Holy Spirit, and decided to go to Philippi. Then Paul and his companions met Lydia, who was a dealer in purple dye and cloth from the city of Thyatira, a slave girl who predicted the future, and a jailer and his family. After the conversion of the jailer and his family, the meetings held in Lydia's house became Macedonia's first church, the Philippian Church.[360]

After observing the social environment of the Philippian Church, a few presuppositions may help to understand the church. Numerous women appear in Acts 16, which introduces much of the Philippian Church's background. Looking at the scope of Lydia and the jailer's activities, Philippi's first church appears to have been located within the town of Philippi. The

---

[357] Lamoreaux, *op.cit.*, 94.
[358] *Ibid.*, 94.
[359] Warren Carter, *The Roman Empire and the New Testament: An Essential Guide*. Nashville: Abingdon, 2006, 7. See also Peter Garnsey. *Social Status and Legal Privilege in the Roman Empire*. Oxford: Clarendon, 1970, 22-23. Garnsey is quoting Suetonius: *Divus Augustus*, p.89.
[360] Acts 16.

demography of Philippi and examples of other churches founded by Paul suggest that the church was socially and ethnically diverse. In light of the emergence of many women and the religious circumstances of those days, the Philippian Church had much to do with the lives of women.

It seems that the role of female leadership, such as Euodia and Syntyche,[361] was strong in the Philippian church.[362] In the Macedonian region, traditionally having women in leadership was relatively common.[363] In addition to leadership, the story of the church's founding and indications in the book of Philippians suggests that the proportion of women in the church was high. In the early church, when the gender ratio was unbalanced, various issues arose. This sometimes occurred when women were the only believers in their family. This at times became a serious problem for a newly converted woman, especially in places like Philippi where Christianity was a new concept, and in a setting greatly rooted in Hellenistic scholarship, culture, and cult. In addition, since ancient society was collective-oriented, considerable courage was required for one to leave an existing group and enter a new one.[364]

Lydia, a businesswoman, was the first woman to come in contact with the gospel in Philippi.[365] Though the book of Acts does not reveal much of her personal life, we can deduce more about her by examining her profession. Purple dyeing at the time was a foul-smelling job as it used animal urine. Therefore, she likely dyed clothes in the suburbs rather than in the crowded city center.[366] Her house was likely outside the city because her house was

---

[361] Phil 4:2.
[362] Carolyn Osiek. *Philippians, Philemon. Abingdon New Testament Commentaries*; Nashville, Tenn.: Abingdon Press, 2000, 26-27.
[363] Ben Witherington, III. *Friendship and Finances in Philippi: The Letter of Paul to the Philippians. The New Testament in Context*; Valley Forge, Pa.: Trinity Press International, 1994, 107-108.
[364] Philip Francis Esler. *The First Christians in Their Social Worlds: Social-Scientific Approaches to New Testament Interpretation*. 1 online resource. London: Routledge, 1994, 29-30. http://public.eblib.com/choice/ publicfullrecord.aspx?p=178577.
[365] Acts 16: 12-15.
[366] Peter Oakes quotes John J. Pilch, *Visions and Healing in the Acts of the Apostles: How the Early Believers Experienced God*. Collegeville, Minn.: Liturgical Press, 2004, 118. http://catdir.loc.gov/catdir/toc/ ecip0414/2004001513.html.

probably near her workplace. According to the book of Acts, Paul and Lydia met near a river, outside the gates. Philippi would have had gates on its east and west sides through which the *Via Egnatia* ran. Outside each gate, lay a river. As Lydia and her family received Jesus through Paul's team, they provided the team lodging at her house. This indicates a likelihood that the members of the early church were part of Lydia's social network.

The Composition of the Philippian Church

Examining the few people who appear in Philippians and Acts offers only a limited understanding of the composition of the Philippian Church and its dynamics. However, an understanding of the social environment of the time, through the sociological data mentioned earlier, can allow us to realistically speculate the Philippian Church's composition and its dynamics. To help us visualize the Philippian Church's membership configuration, Peter Oakes suggests three issues that the Philippians of the time faced.[367]

First, to become a church member, Philippians had to have spatial accessibility. Spatial accessibility refers to the distance from which the Philippian church can be reached. In Philippi, Paul worked mainly within the city or near the city border. Naturally, it would not have been easy for farmers on the outlying farms to access the church. Because peasants, who commuted to their farms while residing in the city, and slaves both were distant from their family members, they are also not considered as those brought to the church by family members. Considering this, the people who contacted Paul, most likely, were those who were living in the city.

Second, to become church members, Philippians had to have social accessibility. In the book of Acts, though Paul had chances to meet with high officials, those were rare occasions even for Paul. Likewise, Paul did not encounter much of the lower class, such as slaves, either. The people who Paul mostly met were from Philippi's common social class. It is also presumed that

---

[367] Oakes, *op.cit.*, 57–59.

these people can be a social chain that led others who are similar in background to the early church.

Peter Oakes introduces the composition of the Philippian Church's population model. He calculated that 40-42% of the church were Romans and 58-64% were Greeks. Members of the church were estimated to be 39-43% service class, 16% slaves, 15-23% colonist farmers, 21-25% poor class, and 1% elite class.[368] It is obvious that service workers, who owned small shops or assisted in others' work, constituted the church's highest percentage. However, Philippi was unique in that it had a high proportion of colonist farmers. This was because Philippi was a much smaller city compared to Corinth, Ephesus, or Antioch. As a result, the city of Philippi was accessible even to farmers on the outskirts.[369] In addition, many who owned houses in the city and commuted to their farms in the suburbs or those who lived on farms and visited their relatives in the city. Because Philippi was the most developed place it worked as the center to the extended areas.

Third, religious accessibility was a formation factor of the early members of the Philippian Church. Philippi was a society deeply rooted in Greek culture and religion. The Greeks had no reason to leave the religion of their own community. The Romans were also well-acquainted with Greek religion and its imperial cult. Therefore, it was difficult for the mainstream population to be attracted to the new faith that Paul brought in. For this reason, we may speculate that the first church members were persons quite interested in religion. The elites who firmly practiced Roman traditional religion, people open to eastern religion, immigrants from Asia Minor, or those absorbed in Judaism are in these categories. Since the church typically grows by existing members' invitation to people with similar social backgrounds, it is likely that Paul's early contacts did so as well.[370] As a result,

---

[368] *Ibid.*, 61.
[369] Wayne A. Meeks. *The First Urban Christians: The Social World of the Apostle Paul.* New Haven: Yale University Press, 1983, 9.
   http://www.gbv.de/dms/bowker/toc/9780300032444.pdf.
[370] Robin Lane Fox. *Pagans and Christians.* New York: Harper Collins, 1986, 319.

we can assert that, later, the readers of Paul's letter to the Philippians, were able to fully empathize with the circumstances of the early contacts.

Suffering, Unity and New Hope

God has a unique heart and a redemptive plan for each city. God loves the people in the city and understands their joys, sorrows, and struggles. Such themes are formed by each of the city's unique histories. When the historical background combines with the social environment and its people and their lives, a unique urban theme is created. God desires to create a unique redemptive plan for each of these unique themes. To do so, God gathers God's people and creates a church within the city where God intends to execute God's plan with them. Therefore, the message God gives to the church is not an independent message for the church alone. Rather, as part of the community, the church should receive it as God's heartfelt message for the whole city.

The message to the Philippian church had to do with joy in the midst of suffering. This is because the Philippians at the time were undergoing various sufferings. This was evident in the Apostle Paul's letter.[371] There are at least four areas that display the Philippians' sufferings. First, Paul states that their sufferings were similar to what he had previously experienced (Philippians 1: 27-30). And he advises them not to live with fear but to live a life worthy of the gospel.

Second, writing either from house arrest or from a prison in Rome, Paul alludes to the Philippians the climax of his suffering, his death. The phrase "poured out" (2:17) is enough to imply his death. By doing so, Paul illustrates the extent of suffering given to a Christian (Philippians 2:17-18).

---

[371] Peter Oakes claims that the theme of suffering appears throughout the entire book of Philippians. He specifically points out the following scriptures: thanksgiving (1:7); the report (1:12-26); the call to steadfastness (1:30); the call to rejoice together (2:17); possibly the report of Epaphroditus (2:27); the argument about trust in the flesh (3:10); the appreciation for the gift (4:12-14). Christ's suffering appears in 2:6-8, 3:10, Epaphroditus's suffering is discussed in 2:26-30, and Philippian's suffering in 1:7, 1:28-30. 2: 17-18. Oakes, *Philippians*, 78.

Third, Paul acknowledges that the Philippian Christian community was subjected to persecution and worldly humiliation (Philippians 2:15-16; 3:20-21). As the whole city operated under the stable and firm cultural, religious, and political systems that Rome and Greece had built over centuries, it is natural for the members of the newly launched small Christian community to feel inferior knowing they were in the minority. Furthermore, the church faced a crisis as its future was questionable under state persecution. In response, Paul advised the Philippian Church not to fall into the minority complex but rather believe that their true citizenship is in heaven. This reminded Christians that the citizenship of heaven offered much more than that of Roman citizenship, which was envied by all Greeks at the time. In other words, the power of the Philippians to overcome their sufferings came from their identity, which belonged not to the state system but heaven.

Fourth, the church was under severe trials and extreme poverty. Paul was aware that the churches of Macedonia were in dire economic hardships (II Corinthians 8:1-5, Philippians 1:7). Paul reveals the hardships of the church at Philippi, to one of the churches in Macedonia, asking them to bless them as "all of you share in God's grace" with Paul. (1:7).

What, then, were the sufferings of the Philippians? The believers in Philippi suffered in many ways from social, religious, relational, and economic difficulties. In other words, the believers experienced the various sufferings of a minority, who are very new and an awkward group in front of the Greco-Roman society. Church members did not simply attend new meetings but even shifted their previous relationships and habits. Of course, this resulted in difficulties with existing groups.

Women could have been misunderstood by their unbelieving husbands and then demanded to explain their new ways of life. Slaves, who may have made up 16% of the church, could have experienced conflict with their masters who had control over their life and death. How would the slaves have explained their newly discovered life to their masters who have never heard about the Christian community? Young people with the new faith also could have been persecuted by their unbelieving parents. It was also inevitable for the Philippian church members, of which 39-43% were of the service class, to suffer heavy economic and social damages. Service sector workers either maintained small stores or were employees of others. The shopkeepers' customers were part of networks that may have been connected through various cult activities and close relationships. Customers who had built this credit were also members of various cult activities that the owners originally partook in. If the converted shopkeeper stopped the cult activity and joined a new group of Christians, the community would feel betrayed and become skeptical of the owner.

The conflict would not have ended with merely an emotional problem. The owner would become increasingly alienated from various social and economic activities. Especially when stores removed their shrines, this sent various messages to society. In addition, refusing to eat meat from their idolatrous sacrifices was interpreted as more than a dietary restriction but as disrespect for the community. Whether this resulted in the whole town disapproving of the Jewish tradition or societal vigilance against the new faith, the shop owning families suffered. Furthermore, the Christian shopkeeper also faced difficulty and hatred when evangelizing. People around them believed that the shopkeepers had deceived their beloved family members into a new cult.

In the midst of such suffering, God gave the Philippians a message of unity. The theme of unity was desperately needed due to the suffering which overshadowed the church. Therefore, the unity produced by cherishing one another was a powerful force that helped overcome the daily sufferings of the Christian community.

The Bible teaches that this unity can be understood only after we realize the suffering that Christ received. To do this, Paul utilizes a three-fold explanation to demonstrate how the Philippians should deal with suffering: Christ's suffering, Paul's suffering, and the Philippians' suffering. Paul, who had already experienced similar suffering, encouraged the Philippians to imitate him.[372] Instead of emphasizing his own defense or recent accounts like he did in his other epistles, Paul introduced himself to the Philippians as a model for them to follow.[373] However, Paul did not introduce himself as merely someone who experienced suffering. Rather, it was to introduce Christ, who suffered as well. Paul wanted to gear the interests of the Philippians to the sufferings of Christ, and he taught them that Christ overcame suffering through humility.[374] This was why Paul regarded whatever he boasted about as garbage and stated that to learn to resemble Christ and join his death was what he wanted most.[375] When such humility is present, unity is achieved and suffering can be overcome.[376]

Paul emphasized the value of being within the Jesus community (Philippians 3:7-9). To the Philippians, who were anxious about their disconnect with external communities, Paul says that past careers and accomplishments of the world were all rubbish. Paul says it is all for attaining the resurrection from the dead through knowing Christ, and the power of his resurrection (Phil 3:10-11).

Paul claims that the authority of Jesus extends over "heaven and earth" (2:9-11) and also Rome. As their social connections were cut off, the Philippians, who faced social and economic difficulties, had to remember that God was greater than all of Rome. This helped the Philippians realize that Christ was the ultimate honor and resurrection that they needed, more than any economic assistance (Philippians 2:6-11).

To have new hope, the Philippians first had to have faith in the resurrection. Though everyone suffered, this was a time when daily suffering was heavier for women, who were affected more directly by people's life and death and all the life passages of the family. A woman's life consisted of high

---

[372] Paul introduces himself in Philippians 1:12-26 and 3:4-16.
[373] Philippians 2:6-8.
[374] Philippians 2:6-8.
[375] Philippians 3:10-11.
[376] Savoring Peterlin. *Paul's Letter to the Philippians in the Light of Disunity in the Church.* Supplements to Novum Testamentum, Leiden: E.J. Brill, 1995, 63.

infant mortality and the constant death of loved ones.[377] Whenever there was birth or death, Philippian women always performed rituals to Artemis. Under this cultural environment, the women who first entered the Christian community were viewed as traitors of Artemis and thus cursed. Consequently, they were blamed for surrounding deaths and stillbirths and fell victim to gossip. To them, Paul gave the message, "to live is Christ, and to die is gain" (Philippians 1:21), and death is no longer a punishment for wrongdoing but rather a benefit as an insider and one of the followers of Jesus.[378] This transformed the notion of death from the traditional retribution and curses into a positive pathway to Christ and resurrection.

The news of the citizenship of heaven was enough for the Philippians to have new hope. The Philippians who refused the civic ritual to Artemis suffered from social isolation and pressure, and economic hardship. As time went on, after they gave up on the blessings of fertility and gifts from Artemis, they likely began to question to what extent their Christian community would protect them. It is also likely that the church members felt the burden of rejecting the imperial cult and Roman system. But the citizenship of heaven that Paul introduced allowed them to expect newer things the world could not offer. This heavenly citizenship was juxtaposed to Roman citizenship, which many church members could not obtain, and reminded the Christians that all authority knelt before Jesus, and therefore, the gathering of Christians indicated a community that was even greater than that of Roman citizens.[379] God gave the Philippian church the message of purpose in suffering, the value of close relationships, and new hope through Christ.

Conclusion

God has a unique heart and a redemptive plan for each city. God loves the people in the city and understands their joys, sorrows, and struggles. Such

---

[377] Sarah Iles Johnston. *Restless Dead: Encounters between the Living and the Dead in Ancient Greece*. Berkeley: U of California Press, 1999, 42.
[378] Lamoreaux, *op.cit.*, 105.
[379] *Ibid.*, 125.

themes are formed by each of the city's unique history. When the historical background combines with the social environment and its people and their lives, a unique urban theme is created. God desires to create a unique redemptive plan for each of these unique themes. To do so, God gathers God's people and creates a church within the city where God intends to execute God's plan with them. Therefore, the message God gives to the church is not an independent message for the church alone. Rather, as part of the community, the church should receive it as God's heartfelt message for the whole city.

Today there are many Christian groups who, like the Philippians, begin the early stages of Christian experience in their cities. Many of these cities have built powerful national, religious, or cultural systems over time. Those early Christians lived as a minority and suffered threats of disconnection from their societies. Because of their faith, they also have experienced suffering, insecurity, and social injustices. I was personally raised under the strict Confucian culture of Korea, and my mother was the first Christian in the family. My father and relatives were embarrassed because my mother and I were Christians, and we were disrespected because of our faith. Consequently, my mother had to pretend not to believe in front of her relatives for 20 years. We had to partake in family sacrifices and could not reveal our faith in front of our relatives. The message my mother and I needed at the time was the suffering for Christ, unity among Christians, and seeking the hope of Heaven. Later, when I served as a missionary in China, the locals I nurtured were mostly people first to believe in all of their families' history. They, like the Philippians, also suffered from fear and loneliness. The message for them and us is, once again, the suffering for Christ, unity among Christians, and the hope of heavenly citizenship.

Chapter 10: Rome

by Robert L. Gallagher[380]

God's Mission That the Wolf and
The Lamb Live and Eat Together

In the messianic age, God's lambs are to live and eat together with the wolves of this world as the kingdom unfolds on earth in proclaiming and demonstrating the Savior's love. The power and magnificence of the Roman wolves is the opposite of the lambs of God serving in humility. Jesus Christ sent his lambs to the harvest field among wolves to bless them with kingdom peace and rest. By loving our enemies, we have an opportunity to dispense God's kindness and mercy. Thus, we should wash the feet of Rome by living and eating together in the wolf's lair, knowing that she could turn and consume us with her strength and splendor. An awareness of the metaphors of God's mission in biblical Rome provides an opportunity to transmit the missional findings to a variety of cultural contexts.

Introduction

The Son of God, the incarnate source of all grace-how had he proclaimed his divinity? By humility, by adoration, and love

---

[380] Robert L. Gallagher (Ph.D., in Intercultural Studies from Fuller Theological Seminary) is a professor emeritus of intercultural studies at Wheaton College Graduate School in Chicago where he has taught since 1998. He served as the president of the American Society of Missiology (2010-11), an executive pastor in Australia (1979-90), and a theological educator in Oceania since 1984. His publications include co-editing *Contemporary Mission Theology: Engaging the Nations* (Orbis Books 2017) and co-authoring *Encountering the History of Missions: From the Early Church to Today* (Baker Academic 2017) and *Breaking through the Boundaries: God's Mission from the Outside In* (Orbis Books 2019).

of God. "Love, love, love," the Capuchin repeated, "humility and love, humility of the nothing before the all, love and adoration of the all by the nothing."[381]

This chapter is a missiological reflection of God's mission in 1st century Rome using a missiological hermeneutic that synthesizes an understanding of the city through metaphor. To explain mission in Rome I will explore the metaphors of the humble servitude of the lamb impacted by the oppressive power of the wolf.[382] My attention is on three perspectives of the city. First, I will describe the historical perspectives of Rome with its distinctive personality and influence. Next, the chapter will explore the biblical perspectives of the city delving into the scriptural texts. Lastly, I will address missiological perspectives together with contemporary implications.

Historical Perspectives of Rome

Ancient Romans explained the earliest history of their city through the story of the twin founders suckled by a wolf.[383] This story of the city's origin shows how Romans thought about themselves since the wolf became the quintessential metaphor of Rome and its empire. The myth involving the

---

[381] Aldous Huxley. "On the Road to Rome." In Samuel Cummings, ed., *Golden Legends: Great Religious Stories from Ancient to Modern Times*, New York: Pellegrini & Cudahy, 1948, 496-508, esp. 499-500. In Huxley's short story, Father Joseph, a Capuchin priest, is fulfilling God's mission by walking bare foot from his convent in Paris to Rome sent by his superiors to deliver letters from King Louis XIII of France (1601-1643; r. 1610-1643) to the Bishop of Rome, Pope Urban VIII (1568-1644; p. 1623-1644) between 1641 and 1642.

[382] For a description of the messianic kingdom where the wolf and the lamb live and feed together, see Isaiah 11:6; 65:25. "The Wolf and the Lamb" is a renowned story in *Aesop's Fables* by the Greek storyteller Aesop (c. 620-564 BCE). The fable is about tyrannical injustice in which a victim is falsely accused and killed despite an appropriate defense.

[383] Antiquity widely adopted the wolf symbol of the city. For instance, in 295 BCE a statue of the wolf suckling the twins was at the foot of the Palatine Hill in Rome. Another power-symbol of the city of Rome is the outstretched eagle, which symbolizes the immense strength and territorial expansion of the Roman Empire. Often seen atop a legionary standard with its outspread wings, this fierce hunting bird represented the dominant span of the empire. After General Gaius Marius (c. 157-86 BCE) renovated the Roman army in 104 BCE, two years later the eagle became the official emblem of the Roman legion, and remained so, even after Christianity became the imperial religion in the fourth-century CE. Furthermore, long after the imperial capital had moved from Rome in the West to Constantinople in the East, the Byzantine Emperor Isaac Kommenos (1007-1061 CE; r. 1057-1059 CE) adopted the double-headed eagle as his symbol in representing the power of the Roman Empire over both the East and West.

wolf drew from an understanding that the wolf-is passive in times of peace yet becomes vicious when aggravated. This symbol represents the identity of Rome. The fable of its founding on rape, infanticide, and murder prophesied the future of the city.[384]

Corralled within its seven hills, the city hugs the east bank of the Tiber River some 18 miles from the port of *Ostia Antica*. Originally, Rome was a meeting-place of the Etruscan states rather than the home of a particular people, which later attracted clan-communities from throughout the Mediterranean. These groups eventually welded into a homogenous political entity. From the 3rd century BCE, immigration came largely from provincial Greeks and Italians. Nevertheless, by the 1st century CE, a river of migrants flowed into the city from Africa, Asia Minor, Egypt, Spain, and Syria.[385]

For over two hundred years, a series of seven kings governed Rome from 753 until 509 BCE when it changed into a republic ruled by a senate (509-27 BCE). Then for the next 500 years, the Roman people conquered much of Italy and the Mediterranean, together with North Africa and Britain, establishing the dominance of its language, Latin. Rome became a naval power in the 3rd to the 2nd centuries BCE by defeating Carthage in North Africa and controlling the Mediterranean Sea. The wolf further extended her domination by the military conquest of Asia, Bithynia, and Cilicia, followed by Egypt, Greece, Macedonia, and Syria, with Corinth ravaged in 146 BCE.

---

[384] The story unfolds with the twins Romulus and Remus from Alba Longa in Central Italy. According to legend, the brothers were the sons of a vestal virgin raped by Mars, the god of war. Their great-uncle Amulius overthrew their grandfather, King Numitor, and ordered the infant twins thrown into the River Tiber. Instead of drowning the brothers, a servant abandoned them on the riverbank where a wolf rescued, raised, and suckled them in her cave. Later, Faustulus, a shepherd, accidentally found the twins, and with his wife nurtured them in their home. When they were old enough, the brothers returned to their hometown, and reinstated their grandfather as king. Together the brothers built a city, but after an argument, Romulus killed Remus. In 753 E, the Etruscan city adopted the name of the victor.

[385] Juvenal (c. 55-c. 138 CE), the Roman satirist writing around 110 CE, supports the notion of large immigration waves to Rome by stating, "My friends, I cannot stand a Rome full of Greeks, yet few of the dregs are Greek! For the Syrian Orontes has long since polluted the Tiber, bringing its language and customs, pipes and harp-strings, and even their native timbrels are dragged along too, and the girls are forced to offer themselves in the Circus" (*Satire III*: "And what about all those Greeks," 60-63; quote, 62).

The republic ended with a series of power struggles with Augustus eventually becoming the first Roman emperor who established the Roman Empire, which lasted for over 400 years (27 BCE-395 CE). The city of Rome was perpetually warring and conquering until the end.

First Century Rome

In New Testament times, Rome was flourishing with economic, social, and political growth.[386] The international aristocracy manifested their wealth through suburban villas and country estates as the Caesars gave the city lavish public buildings together with economic benefits and entertainment for the masses.[387] The city attracted goods, foods, and diplomatic connections, as well as literary and artistic expressions, from every region and state in the empire.[388]

By 64 CE, Rome boasted the most prestigious architectural structures in the Mediterranean world such as the palace of Augustus, the temple of Diana, and the theater of Pompey (capacity of 40,000 people), as well as the Circus Maximus (capacity of 150,000 people) and the Pantheon. The public buildings of Rome were magnificent in their ornamentation, and together with the sumptuous houses of the powerful, flaunted international dominance. The arches, columns, and temples commemorating the deeds of valor of the Roman state stood not so much as memorials to individuals, but

---

[386] In studying the New Testament era for a socio-cultural understanding of Rome, see James S. Jeffers. *The Greco-Roman World of the New Testament Era: Exploring the Background of Early Christianity.* Downers Grove, IL: InterVarsity Press, 1999, 14-18; Vernon K. Robbins. "The Social Location of the Implied Author of Luke-Acts." In Jerome H. Neyrey, ed., *The Social World of Luke-Acts*, Peabody, MA: Hendrickson Publishers, 1991, 329-30; and vănThanh Nguyễn. "Missionary Churches in Acts: A Model of Intercultural Engagement with the Nations." In Robert L. Gallagher and Paul Hertig, eds., *Contemporary Mission Theology: Engaging the Nations*, Essays in honor of Charles E. Van Engen. American Society of Missiology Series, No. 53. Maryknoll, NY: Orbis Books, 2017, 142-43.

[387] The people of Rome were supplied bread and circuses by the government. From 58 BCE, the state gave citizens a free distribution of wheat and water, together with cheap wine, and free admission to chariot racing, gladiatorial contests, and theatrical performances.

[388] D.B. Saddington. "Rome." In R.K. Harrison, ed., *Major Cities of the Biblical World*, Nashville, TN: Thomas Nelson, 1985, 208-22.

as a remembrance to an energetic, constructive, and conquering people. As Philip Schaff explains:

> The Romans from the first believed themselves called to govern the world. They looked upon all foreigners as enemies to be conquered and reduced to servitude. War and triumph were their highest conception of human glory and happiness.... With vast energy, profound policy, unwavering consistency, and wolf-like rapacity, they pursued their ambitious schemes, and became indeed the lords, but also, as their greatest historian, Tacitus says, the insatiable robbers of the world.[389]

The magnificence of the imperial capital founded on rape, infanticide, and murder was in sharp contrast to the staggering urban social problems. For the majority of Romans, living conditions were appalling as they toiled among a densely cloistered arrangement of buildings. Over one million people lived in tenements sometimes three to four stories high that were prone to collapse or burn, framed by streets of bedlam: narrow, filthy, inadequate sanitation, and crowded with unrelenting commerce, traffic, and danger amassed from every corner of the empire.[390]

Jewish Population of Rome

Jewish migrants were present in Rome by 139 BCE. Seventy-seven years later, their numbers increased significantly when General Pompey brought to the city a large number of Jewish slaves.[391] By the 1st century, there were over 40,000 Jews in Rome. The Jewish population lived in seven

---

[389] Philip Schaff. *History of the Christian Church: Apostolic Christianity, A.D. 1-100*. Vol. 1, rev. 3rd ed. Grand Rapids, MI: Eerdmans, [1858] 1994, 80.

[390] For a missiology of transformation as an appropriate mission theology of the city, see Stephen E. Burris. "Mission Theology in the City: Sowing Urban Seeds of Shalom." In Robert L. Gallagher and Paul Hertig, eds., *Contemporary Mission Theology: Engaging the Nations*, Maryknoll, NY: Orbis Books, 2017, 45-53., and Charles Van Engen and Jude Tiersma, eds. *God so Loves the City: Seeking a Theology for Urban Mission*. Monrovia, CA: MARC, 1994.

[391] Because of the large number of foreign-born Jewish slaves in Rome, it is probable that in the churches of Rome there were many slaves and former slaves. Romans 16:10-11 references the servants of the households of Aristobulus and Narcissus. Since most of the slaves were of foreign origin in first-century Rome, it is reasonable to deduce that Nero, in crucifying Christians, still followed the Roman law that prohibited the crucifixion of Romans. This then suggests that many of the Christians were alien residents.

communities each with its synagogue and council of elders. These were some of the poorest sections of the city across from the Tiber River near the Circus Maximus. As foreign residents, they experienced racial discrimination even though the authorities allowed them to meet in synagogues and observe the Sabbath. Nonetheless, imperial decrees expelled the Jewish people from Rome on three occasions.[392]

The Christian faith in Rome may have first gained traction within the Jewish synagogues as a sect of Judaism.[393] The biblical origins of the church are obscure, however, since there is no direct mention of its beginnings. At Pentecost in Acts 2, there is a reference to devout Jews and proselytes visiting Jerusalem from Rome who on returning to their city may have established a believing community within the Jewish enclave (2:10).[394]

Paul's letter to the believers in Rome has a Jewish flavor because the city's synagogues had nurtured the Christian faith.[395] The association with the synagogues suggests that a plurality of house churches developed from the Jewish communities, and not the growth of one church. Paul's greeting (Rom 1:7) acknowledges the singular nature of the church in Rome, all the while mentioning five households in chapter 16.[396] The church's Jewish ethnicity explains Paul's apologetic defense of his theology (6:1-2) and mission strategy (15:14-24). To the Jewish Christians of Rome who were critical of Paul's

---

[392] The Jewish expulsions from Rome—although not permanent—were in 139 BCE (Valerius Maximus), 19 CE (Tiberius), and 49 CE (Claudius). See E.A. Judge. *Social Distinctives of the Christian in the First Century.* Peabody, MA: Hendrickson Publishers, 2008, 28-30.

[393] The break with Jewish tradition came after Nero's persecution of 64 CE blaming the followers of Christ for the fire in the metropolis. Paul's letter to the church in Rome gives evidence of the predominance of Jewish believers in the city such as Andronicus and Junia (16:7), and Herodion (16:11), as well as greetings from Lucius, Jason, and Sosipater, his fellow-Jewish traveling companions (16:21).

[394] For a missional perspective of Pentecost, see Eddie Gibbs. "The Launching of Mission: The Outpouring of the Spirit at Pentecost (Acts 2:1-41)," in Robert L. Gallagher and Paul Hertig, eds. *Mission in Acts: Ancient Narratives in Contemporary Context,* Maryknoll, NY: Orbis Books, 2004, 18-28.

[395] See Romans 1:16; 3:1-30; 9-11. Archaeologists estimate that there were at least 13 synagogues in Rome.

[396] The five households of Romans 16 are Priscilla and Aquila (5); Aristobulus (10); Narcissus (11); "and the brothers with them" (14); "and all the saints with them" (15).

ministry, he needed to explain his apostolic calling and emphasize the spiritual worthiness of his anticipated visit to Jerusalem (15:25-33).

Religion of Rome

The final historical feature of Rome is its religious makeup. The conviction of Rome affected the way Paul approached sharing the gospel in his letter to the churches based on the city's policies towards foreign religions, including Christianity. The belief of the megalopolis was originally animistic involving the worship of the spirits of forests, rivers, and mountains. Later the city's beliefs incorporated Etruscan Hellenism by reducing the gods to human form (Jupiter, Mars, and Juno), and foreign cults such as Cybele (Asia Minor), Isis (Egypt), and Mithra (Persia). Religious exclusivism was unknown in the city's outlook. Even so, Romans viewed all imported religions with suspicion since they believed that foreigners caused social disorder. Hence, the Senate had to approve the religions. These observances did not mean that Rome abandoned the traditional state religion. As immigration brought new cults to Rome, the city simply reinterpreted traditional practices.[397]

When Christianity entered Rome, the wolf's den, a large temple located on Capitoline Hill dedicated to Jupiter and Juno dominated the city landscape. This public worship paralleled private worship in the home with shrines of dead family members, and gods of the family cupboard (spirits who affected a family's home and daily life) acting as constant reminders of the connection between the temporal and spiritual worlds. All the public and private religious rituals needed to lie within the political laws of the city.[398] If a citizen of Rome followed the correct ritualistic observances of the city's

---

[397] Jeffers, *op. cit.*, 73-76.
[398] See Ruth B. Edwards and Mark P. Reasoner. "Rome: Overview," in Craig A. Evans and Stanley E. Porter eds. *Dictionary of New Testament Background*, Downers Grove: IVP, 2000, 1010-18. They argue for an interpretation of Romans based on the notion that the citizens considered religion as a matter of the law. Thus, Paul argues in legal terms beginning with God's general moral law (2:14-16), the Jewish law (3:21; 10:4), and political law (13:1-7). Paul's contextualization of the gospel is based on the law as seen in his awareness that his audience knew the law (7:1), and his focus on questions of the law (2:12-27; 4:13-16; 7:1-3), rather than reflecting on an emphasis of the Torah, especially to a largely non-Jewish audience.

legislature, they could obtain the "peace of the gods."[399] This led to the understanding that the gods were rational beings, a foreign notion to most imported goods.[400] The vocational priesthood of the state religion reinforced this idea by acting as advisors to the city's administrators.[401] The religion of Rome was a concern of the state even though there was no dictated system of theology. There was a tolerance of all national deities, as long as they did not attack polytheism as a whole. Life in Rome was full of religious rituals with membership to a specific religious group based on occupation or ethnic background.[402] Thus, the churches in Rome were unusual since they were composed of people from a variety of socio-cultural and ethnic backgrounds.

Biblical Perspectives of Rome[403]

Even though Paul did not establish the church in Rome (Rom 1:8-15; cf. 15:20), he declared that he intended visiting the city many times[404] before eventually coming to the metropolis around 60 CE, and discovering a flourishing and influential Christian society (Acts 28:14-15; Phil 1:12-17).[405] Paul felt it necessary to obtain the commendation of the Roman community supports the notion of the church's influence around the Mediterranean world (Rom 15:22-24). It was not an idle statement when Paul said, "Your faith is

---

[399] The Roman approach to religion, which was not necessarily establishing a personal relationship, is in direct contrast to Paul stating that believers have peace with God through faith in Jesus Christ (Rom 5:1-2).

[400] In Romans, Paul underscores the rationality of God in dealing with human reason in the following ways: the Lord gives over those who reject him to their own depraved minds (1:28); the human mind can be against God (7:20-24); and giving oneself completely to God in your body is a reasonable action that produces a renewed mind (12:1-2).

[401] The priesthood of Rome advised the political senate regarding the divine will, setting the calendar, establishing the state religious law, making war via religiously appropriate methods, and protecting and interpreting sacred texts. The latter discernment served to allow foreign religions into Rome.

[402] See Acts 6:9 that talks about the Synagogue of the Freedmen in Jerusalem (former slaves who were Cyrenians, Alexandrians, and from Cilicia and Asia).

[403] For scriptural examples that mention the city of Rome (Gk. *Rhōmē*, meaning "strength"), see Acts 2:10; 18:2; 19:21; 23:11; 28:14, 16; Romans 1:7, 15; and pertaining to Rome, see John 11:48; Acts 16:21, 37, 38; 22:25, 26, 27, 29; 23:27; 25:16; 28:17.

[404] See Romans 1:13; 15:22-23; and Acts 19:21; 23:11.

[405] The letter to the church at Philippi is one of seven letters written by Paul during his imprisonment in Rome. In Philippians 1:15, he refers to a rival group preaching Christ to make it difficult for him in prison. This reference suggests that Paul did not start or organize the city church. Cf. Acts 28:14-15.

being reported all over the world" (Rom 1:8). He believed that Roman Christianity came within the jurisdiction of his Gentile calling (Rom 1:11-15); and this motivated the apostle to write to and visit the largely Gentile church.[406]

Rome was a pivotal city for Paul.[407] The apostle could not ignore the strategic significance of the churches in Rome. Located in the capital of the civilized world, they had strong connections to Jerusalem, and through their varied cultural groups had inroads to the wider empire. Although the churches in Rome had a strong Jewish element, they were mostly composed of various Gentile factions derived from the immigration patterns of previous decades. Therefore, Paul refers to God interacting with all humanity, both Jew and non-Jew (Rom 1:16; 1:18-2:29), including the civilized and uncivilized (1:14). This multicultural variety was a reason why Paul wanted to connect with the church of Rome (1:13). The phenomenon inspired Paul to expound the notion that the Lord is the God of the nations, which the Spirit reinforced by the apostle's involvement in mission as recorded in Acts.[408]

---

[406] See David Bosch. *Transforming Mission: Paradigm Shifts in Theology of Mission.* Maryknoll, NY: Orbis Books, 1991, 175-176 and Saddington, *op. cit.*, 217-22.

[407] Paul's first link with Rome came through the expulsion of the Jewish people from the city during the reign of Claudius, which forced Aquila and Pricilla, two Jewish Christians, to leave Italy and flee to Corinth (49 CE; Acts 18:1-2). As fellow leather workers, Paul worked with the married couple around 50 CE. Because of his influence, they became trusted pastoral ministers, even adjusting the theology of Apollos (a leading Christian apologist; Acts 18:24-28) and overseeing the church in Ephesus with Timothy (Acts 18:18-19a; cf. Rom 16:3-5). A number of years after meeting Priscilla and Aquila, Paul, moved by the Spirit, yearns to see Rome (Acts 19:21; cf. 23:11). For the case of Priscilla and Aquila demonstrating the close intertwining of mission and migration, see vănThanh Nguyễn. "Migrants as Missionaries: The Case of Priscilla and Aquila." In vănThanh Nguyễn and John M. Prior, eds. *God's People on the Move: Biblical and Global Perspectives on Migration and Mission*, Eugene, OR: Pickwick Pubs., 2014, 62-75.

[408] See Romans 2:1-16; 15:7-13; 16:26; Acts 13:1-4; 16:6-7; 19:21; 20:23; 21:11. For an overview of Paul's mission in Acts, see Robert L. Gallagher. "From Pentecost to Protestantism: A World Perspective." In Nathan Bettcher, Robert L. Gallagher, and Bill Vasilakis, eds., *Changing Worlds: Our Part in God's Plan* Adelaide, SA: CRC Churches International, 2005, 87-106; and Robert L. Gallagher. "Missionary Methods: St. Paul's, St. Roland's, or Ours?" In Craig Ott and J.D. Payne, eds., *Missionary Methods: Research, Reflection, and Realities*, Evangelical Missiological Society Series, No. 21. Pasadena, CA: William Carey Library, 2013, 3-22.

Paul's Journey to Rome

Acts chronicles Paul's apostolic journey from Jerusalem, the capital of Judaism, to Rome, the capital of the Gentile Empire. When the Holy Spirit came upon the believers at Pentecost they continued the ministry of Christ by witnessing to his resurrection, first in Jerusalem, then in Judea, Samaria, and Galilee, and to the ends of the earth, which the writer considered was the city of Rome (Acts 1:8; 6:7; 9:31). During the final phase of Paul's journey, believers in Rome heard that he was coming, and met him at the Forum of Appius, a marketplace on the Appian Way (40 miles southeast of Rome), and escorted him to the first city (Acts 28:15). The journey serves as a resolution culminating in Paul's preaching of the gospel to the non-Jewish people (Acts 28:25-31). Rome, the control center of the wolf, is the appropriate finale of the proclamation of Christ's kingdom to the entire Gentile world.[409]

Paul's Relationships in Rome

To help prepare the way for Paul's visit to Rome, he wrote a letter to the church, most likely from Corinth around 57 CE (cf. Rom 15:25-26 with I Cor 16:1-7). The epistle reveals that the city church was the recipient of Paul's most developed theological treatise, composed of both Gentile and Jewish believers, and the hopeful launching pad of the apostle's mission to Spain (1:13-17; 15:24, 28). The central issue is the tension between Jewish and Gentile Christians concerning the non-Jewish adherence to the Mosaic Law regarding circumcision, Sabbath observance, and food laws.[410] Paul argues that the gospel of salvation is through faith in Jesus and the gift of the Holy Spirit, and not by obeying the law (1:16-17; cf. Gal 3:1-5; Acts 15:6-11).[411]

---

[409] Apparently, Paul was freed after his first trial even in the midst of Nero's destabilizing imperial government, and possibly visited Spain as he had hoped (Rom 15:24, 28). Tradition says that the Roman authorities again imprisoned Paul who eventually they beheaded along the Ostian Way between 64-67 CE, about the same time Peter died in Rome, for his Christian faith.

[410] See Romans 2:25-3:1; 4:9-12; 14:1-23; cf. Galatians 4:8-11; Acts 15:23-29.

[411] Asceticism was another feature of the 1st-century church in Rome. This is in accordance with Paul's letter (14:1-3, 21). Some of the church members used ascetic practices to measure the spiritually strong in comparison with the weak. Paul encourages the mature Christians to consider the weaker ascetic believers (14:13-17; 15:1-3). Others emphasized the mind-body dualism of asceticism (1:24; 6:19; 7:23-24; 12:1-2).

Paul developed a number of close relationships with women and men in Rome. In Romans 16, Paul names a contingent of associates who have been living in Rome for many years, including Christians known in other places. Paul had met many of these people while planting churches throughout the Aegean region (15:20, 22-23). In addition, Paul was associated with Christians who knew other believers in Rome (16:21-23). Beyond the doctrinal features, the occasional nature of the letter is evident since Paul knew many people within the city's churches and desired to strengthen his relationships with them. In Romans 16:1, he introduces Phoebe as a newcomer. He mentions some as being his colleagues with whom he had worked in the past (16:3, 9). He called others his relatives (16:7). The basis of Paul's association with the church in Rome was probably his close connection with five households (16: 5, 10, 11, 14, 15).

Paul describes his relationship with ten women leaders of the church in chapter 16.[412] His appreciation for them and their roles differ in several ways.[413] For instance, Priscilla was a home-church leader in Corinth, Ephesus, and Rome,[414] and a "coworker" with Paul in the empire's capital (16:3-5).[415] Mary (16:6) "worked very hard," as did Tryphaena, Tryphosa, and Persis who also "work hard in the Lord" (16:12).[416] Furthermore, Paul calls Phoebe a

---

[412] In the New Testament, there are 14 women mentioned who are associated with Paul: 13 in his letters and one in Acts, compared to 54 men named. The Pauline women, other than those in Romans 16 are, Lydia in Philippi (Acts 16:14-15, 40), Chloe in Corinth (I Cor 1:11), Nympha in Laodicea (Col 4:15), and Apphia in Colossae (Phm 2).

[413] The ten women of Rome are Phoebe, Priscilla, Mary, Junia, Tryphaena, Tryphosa, Persis, Rufus' mother (cf. Mk 15:21), Julia, and Nereus' sister (see Rom 16:1, 3, 6, 7, 12, 13, 15).

[414] See Acts 18:2, 18-19, 26; I Corinthians 16:19; and Romans 16:3-5.

[415] The use of *sunergoi* with respect to a fellow worker, occurs with Aquila (Rom 16:3-4), Urbanus (Rom 16:9), and Timothy (Rom 16:21) in the letter to the church in Rome. In addition, the word also arises with Apollos and Paul (I Cor 3:9); Titus (II Cor 8:23); Epaphroditus (Phil 2:25); Clement (Phil 4:3); Philemon (Phm 1); Demas (Phm 24); Luke (Phm 24); and others (Col 4:11). Also, see Acts 18:2, 18, 26; I Corinthians 16:19; II Timothy 4:19.

[416] The meaning of *kopiao* is in regards to the work of leadership in the church (II Tim 2:6), and is also designated towards Paul (I Cor 4:12; Gal 4:11; Phil 2:16; cf. Acts 20:35); Euodia and Syntyche ("shared my struggle in the gospel;" Phil 4:2-3); Claudia (II Tim 4:21); and others (I Cor 16:15-16; I Thess 5:12; I Tim 5:17).

"servant" of the church in Cenchrea (16:1).[417] He also names her as "a great help to many people" (16:2).[418] Rufus' mother, Julia, and Nereus' sister have a warm relationship with the apostle. Last, Paul calls Junia a "fellow prisoner," and "outstanding among the apostles" (16:7).[419] When we compare these Pauline expressions of his women coworkers in Rome with the same phrases he uses to portray male leaders in his pastoral letters, it is clear that the apostle highly esteems the females who serve alongside him, and considers them equal with the men in ministry. How we understand Paul's relationship with the church in Rome before his visit affects our interpretation of Romans and how we view his missional journey to the city.

Babylon, the City of Rome

The last of my biblical perspectives of Rome incorporates the first letter of Peter and the Revelation of John by considering the designation of the city as "Babylon." The author of I Peter makes a cryptic mention of Rome using the term "Babylon" (I Pe 5:13), although why there would be such a need is unknown, and seemingly unwarranted at that time. Both Jews and Christians referred to Babylon (Rome) as a place of exile. Writing from Rome around 64-65 CE, Peter warns the Christians of Asia Minor of impending persecution, probably at the end of Nero's reign,[420]even though some new

---

[417] The use of *diakonos* as a servant is also found in the office (Phil 1:1; I Tim 3:8, 12) and the ministry of Christ (Rom 15:8); Apollos (I Cor 3:5); Epaphras (Col 1:7); Timothy (I Tim 4:6); Tychicus (Eph 6:21; Col 4:7); and Paul (I Cor 3:5; Eph 3:7; Col 1:23, 25).

[418] The meaning of *prostatis* is patron in Romans 12:8, I Thessalonians 5:12, and I Timothy 3:4.

[419] The following males were "prisoners" of the Lord: Aristarchus (Col 4:10), Epaphras (Phm 23), and Paul (Eph 3:1; 4:1; II Tim 1:8; Phm 1, 9). Furthermore, the New Testament uses the term *apostolos* to refer to men in all other Pauline passages (e.g. I Cor 4:9; 9:5-6; 12:28-29; II Cor 11:5, 13; 12:11-12; cf. Acts 14:4, 14).

[420] In the first 300 years of Christianity, the church was an illegal and marginalized minority whom the Roman world persecuted. Persecutions were sporadic, however. Yet, some of the emperors were particularly violent against Christians such as Nero (c. 64 CE), Septimius Severus (203 CE), Decius (250-251 CE), Valerian (257-259 CE), Aurelian (274 CE), and Diocletian (c. 303 CE). For the causes and results of the persecutions, see Stephen B. Bevans and Roger P. Schroeder. *Constants in Context: A Theology of Mission for Today*. American Society of Missiology Series, No. 30. Maryknoll, NY: Orbis Books, 2004, 80-81; Jo-Marie Claassen. "Cornelius Fronto: A 'Libyan Monad' at Rome." In *Acta Classica* 52 (2009): 47-71; and John Mark Terry. "Missions in the Early Church." In John Mark Terry and Robert L. Gallagher, eds., *Encountering the History of Missions: From the Early Church to Today*, Grand Rapids, MI: Baker Academic, 2017, 1-22, esp. 2-6.

believers were already experiencing local persecution for their faith in Christ (2:2-3).

In Revelation, John also writes about the imperial city of Rome in negative terms. Depicted as a great megalopolis located on seven mountains, it rules over the kings of the world with a multitude of every nation and language under its jurisdiction (17:9, 15, 18).[421] The rulers and merchants of the earth have compromised their integrity by "living deliciously with her" (18:9), emphasizing the traffic of luxurious goods that have made them rich (18:3, 12-13), and the artistic splendor of the city (18:22). The sinister focus of John's concern is that Rome has drunk "the blood of the saints" of Jesus (17:6). Perhaps this is a reference to the death of Peter and Paul.

The tradition of the late 2nd century depicts Peter working and suffering martyrdom in Rome. In the 4th century comes the notion that he was the first bishop of the church in the metropolis, even though the letters of Paul make no mention of such a situation. The *First Epistle of Clement* claims that both Peter and Paul died in Rome, undoubtedly during the Nero massacres of 64 CE.[422] From the contemporary records, it seems that the Christian population was extensive and separate from the Jewish people, and much despised without any explanation. A century later, the tombs of Peter (Vatican Hill near the Circus of Nero) and Paul (on the road to Ostia between the Temple of Diana and the Appian Way to Puteoli) were recognized, and churches subsequently built on the sites of the graves.

Missiological Perspectives of Rome

Having considered some historical and biblical perspectives, what should be our missiological approach to Rome? This is a poignant question

---

[421] J. Julius Scott, Jr. *Customs and Controversies: Intertestamental Jewish Backgrounds of the New Testament.* Grand Rapids, MI: Baker Books, 1995, 190-91.

[422] *The First Epistle of Clement* is a letter addressed to the Christians in the city of Corinth. Pope Clement I (35-99 CE) composed the letter most likely around 96 CE. It ranks with the *Didache* (a short anonymous 1st-century early church treatise that deals with Christian ethics, rituals, and organization) as one of the earliest of the existing Christian documents outside the canonical New Testament. Also, see Tacitus, a senator and a historian of the Roman Empire (56-120 CE; *Annals* 15.44) and Suetonius, a Roman historian (c. 69-122 CE; *Nero* 16).

when the symbol of Rome for over 2,000 years is a wolf ready to devour anyone opposing its secular interests. The answer to these questions rests with Jesus Christ since he is the quintessential leader and pathfinder of our Christian faith.

Jesus the Leader

The gospels portray Jesus as fully God, and fully human. The Holy Spirit empowered Jesus to accomplish all that he taught and did. His miracles and revelation came by the Spirit dynamically and functionally united with him. The Lukan beginnings of the Lord's mission underscore this truth. At the baptism of Jesus, while he was praying, the Spirit came upon him, and he began his public ministry (Lk 3:21-23a).[423] Luke 4:1 uniquely accentuates that our Lord was full of the Spirit as the Spirit led him into the wilderness to face Satan's temptation. Jesus then returns to Galilee in the power of the Spirit to begin his declaration and expression of the kingdom of God (Lk 4:14).

In the Nazarene synagogue, Jesus declares Isaiah 61:1-2a as his mission statement to underscore his dependency on the Holy Spirit (Lk 4:18-19). The Spirit enabled Jesus to preach the good news to the poor. The Spirit anointed him to proclaim release to those imprisoned by the devil (Ac 10:38). The Spirit empowered the Messiah to bring healing to the blind, and release to those crushed by the brokenness of life. The Spirit of God prompted the Son to announce the coming of the year of Jubilee (Lk 4:19).[424] God fulfilled the messianic promises of the First Testament because he gave the Holy Spirit to Christ to announce and demonstrate the kingdom (Lk 4:43; 6:20; 8:1; 11:2). Jesus chose to function in his earthly responsibility dependent on the Spirit.[425]

---

[423] In the Father's commissioning of the Son, Luke uses the metaphor of a dove to highlight the humility of the Spirit of God.

[424] For an understanding of Jubilee, see Leviticus 25:8-55.

[425] For an expanded perception of the association between the Holy Spirit, Jesus Messiah, and mission, see Robert L. Gallagher. "Transformational Teaching: Engaging in Pneumatic Teaching Praxis." In Cheri L. Pierson and Will Bankston, eds., *Thinking Theologically about Language Teaching: Christian Perspectives on an Educational Calling*, Carlisle, UK: Langham Global Library, 2017, 135-62, esp. 138-47; and Robert L. Gallagher. "The Forgotten Factor: The Holy Spirit and Mission in Protestant Missiological Writings from 1945-95." In Charles Van Engen, Nancy Thomas, and

Even though Jesus is God, the gospels portray him as the model of leadership that his followers should copy. As Jesus says, "A student is not above his teacher, but everyone who is fully trained will be like his teacher" (Lk 6:40). If Jesus is our teacher, then he needs to fully train us, and thus replicate his person and mission (Acts 2:22; 10:38). At Pentecost, the Spirit remained upon the followers of Christ to witness to the ends of the earth.[426] Through the gift of the Holy Spirit, Jesus wants all believing generations to continue his mission (Acts 2:38-39): a mission of humility in love, acceptance, and forgiveness.

Jesus the Lamb

In startling contrast to Rome's metaphor of a wolf is the metaphor of Jesus the Messiah. John the Baptist squeezes Leviticus into his bellowing call, "Look, the Lamb of God, who takes away the sin of the world" (Jn 1:29).[427] On seeing Jesus the next day, the Baptist repeats the proclamation, "Look, the Lamb of God" (Jn 1:36). These pronouncements bear witness that Christ is the fulfillment of the Passover lamb in Israel's exodus from Egypt.[428] John the Baptist joins the liberation of the Israelite slaves together with the substitutionary death of Christ.[429] Jesus brings liberty to God's enslaved

---

Robert Gallagher, eds., *Footprints of God: A Narrative Theology of Mission*, 199-214. Eugene, OR: Wipf & Stock, [1999] 2011.

[426] See Luke 24:46-49; Acts 1:7-8; 2:1-4, 17-18, 21.

[427] For the scriptures that declare Jesus Messiah as the Lamb of God, see Isaiah 53:7; Acts 8:32, 35; Revelation 5:6, 8, 12-13; 6:1; 13:8. God has redeemed believers from their empty way of life with "the precious blood of Christ, a lamb without blemish or defect . . . chosen before the creation of the world" (I Pe 1:19-20a; cf. Heb 9:14). For scriptural references using the metaphor of lambs and sheep to represent God's people, see Matthew 7:15; 9:36; 10:6; 12:11-12; 15:24; 18:12-13; 25:32-33; 26:31; Mark 6:34; 14:27; Luke 15:4; 17:7; John 10:1-30; 21:15-17; Romans 8:36; Hebrews 13:20; I Peter 2:25.

[428] For the notion of Jesus as the Passover Lamb, see I Corinthians 5:7; Mark 14:12; Luke 22:7; Deuteronomy 16:1-8. Regarding support of the view that the Gospel of John uses paschal imagery, see Raymond E. Brown. *The Gospel According to John*. Vol. 1. London: Chapman, [1966] 1982, 58-62; Margaret Davies. "Rhetoric and Reference in the Fourth Gospel," *Journal for the Study of the New Testament Supplement* 69 (1992): 177-211; and Dorothy Lee. "Paschal Imagery in the Gospel of John: A Narrative and Symbolic Reading," *Pacifica* 24 (2011): 13-28.

[429] The Lamb is the crucified, resurrected, exalted, and victorious Christ (Rev 5:6, 8, 12-13; 6:1, 16). Dietrich Bonhoeffer affirms, "The figure of the Crucified invalidates all thoughts that take success for its standard" (*Ethics*. New York: Simon & Schuster, [1949] 1995, 78). In addition, the Chinese character for "righteousness" is pictorially composed of

people delivering them from the devil's chains of sin and death and leads them to the Promised Land of the abiding presence of the Holy Spirit.430

To enlighten the metaphor of Jesus the Lamb, consider William Blake's (1757-1827) portrayal in his poem, "The Lamb." In comparing Jesus to a lamb, the English poet in his second stanza ponders, "For he calls himself a Lamb: he is meek and he is mild."431 Jesus as a lamb has the characteristics of innocence, gentleness, quietness, obedience, and tenderness. Jesus himself declares, "I am gentle and humble in heart" (Mt 11:29).432 Similar to a lamb before its sacrifice, Christ was humble unto death and obedient to God's predetermined plan and purpose.433 Jesus additionally highlights the humility of a lamb by employing the metaphors of childlikeness and servanthood in his teaching and example of godly ministry.

Humility of a Child

In response to the disciples asking Jesus who is the greatest in the kingdom of heaven, he calls a child to stand in the middle of the audience.434

---

two words: a "lamb" that is positioned over "me." At the cross, Jesus the Lamb imputed his righteousness on me, and took upon himself my sin and shame.

430 John 8 continues the correlation between redemption from slavery and sin involving the devil (31-47). Hebrews 4:1-13 describes the Promised Land that the Christian community inherits through the death and resurrection of Jesus, as a land of Sabbath rest and peace where the believers dwell in the presence of God's Spirit.

431 David E. Erdman, ed. *The Complete Poetry and Prose of William Blake.* New York: Anchor Books, 1988.

432 The triumphal entry of Jesus into Jerusalem as recorded in the gospels (Mt 21:1-9; Mk 11:1-10; Lk 19:29-38; Jn 12:12-15) has only Matthew fully quoting Zechariah 9:9 (cf. Isa 62:11), which emphasizes the humility of King Jesus. "Say to the Daughter of Zion, 'See, your king comes to you, gentle [humble] and riding on a donkey, on a colt, the foal of a donkey'" (Mt 21:5).

433 See Luke 22:22; Acts 2:23; 3:18; 4:28; and I Peter 1:20; 2:21-25. The Spirit guided Philip to connect with the Ethiopian eunuch who was studying Isaiah 53:7-8. "He was led like a sheep to the slaughter and as a lamb before the shearer is silent, so he did not open his mouth. In his humiliation, he was deprived of justice. Who can speak of his descendants? For his life was taken from the earth." Then Philip began with the Isaianic passage being read by the treasury official, "and told him the good news about Jesus" (Acts 8:35).

434 For other passages where the disciples ask the question, "Who is the greatest?" see Matthew 18:1-5; Mark 9:33-40; and Luke 9:46-48. During the last supper in Luke 22:24-27, "A dispute also arose among them as to which of them was considered to be greatest. Jesus said to them, 'The kings of the Gentiles lord it over them; and those who exercise authority over them call themselves Benefactors. But you are not to be like that. Instead, the greatest among you should be like the youngest, and the one who rules like the one who serves. For who is greater, the one who is at the table or the one who serves? Is it not the one who is at the table? But I am among you as one who serves.'" Also, see Matthew 20:25-28 and Mark 10:42-45. For a demonstration of the

He then proclaims, "Unless you change and become like little children, you will never enter the kingdom of heaven. Therefore, whoever humbles himself like this child is the greatest in the kingdom of heaven" (Mt 18:3-4).[435] The focus of the disciples was on prominence and power, which they felt was legitimate since they were concerned for God's kingdom. Yet, Jesus reverses the direction of their thinking by pointing to the attitude and behavior of a child. How did the youngster humble herself? She listened, obeyed, and waited for Jesus to give further instruction. The child had no status or right in society. She did know, however, that Jesus was a person of authority, and worthy of obedience.[436]

Matthew 18 further underscores this teaching when Jesus centers on how an individual (1-14) and a community (15-35) should handle conflict.[437] To handle disagreement between individuals there is a need of humility. "See that you do not look down on one of these little ones" (10). Likewise, in the church, conflicts are resolved only when people are willing to listen (15-17). To listen you need to humble yourself. The consequences of not listening in humility and accordingly not forgiving people are felt in this life and the next (32-35; cf. Mt 6:14-15).

Humility of a Servant

Another metaphor Jesus uses to teach about headship is servanthood. In reply to the mother of the sons of Zebedee requesting kingdom privilege

---

disciples' racial prejudice against Samaritans, see Luke 9:51-56, which occurs immediately after they were disputing among themselves as to who is the greatest, and how to prevent a person ministering demon deliverance in the name of Jesus (Lk 9:46-50).

[435] The gospel writers repeat the narrative of Matthew 18:1-5 in Mark 9:33-37 and Luke 9:46-48.

[436] The authors of Matthew 19:13-15, Mark 10:13-16, and Luke 18:15-17 document Jesus' metaphor of children as examples of godly leadership. Also, see Matthew 18:1-6.

[437] The preceding narrative of chapters 14-17 confirms how Jesus handled conflict with the political and religious leaders, demonic powers, and even the disciples who were opposing the Lord's purposes. In accordance with Matthew's structural pattern, he follows the narrative with a dialogue, which teaches on the same topic, and forms a progressive story from Jesus' birth to resurrection.

for her sons, James and John (the sons of thunder), Jesus uses the opportunity to reinforce his inside-out leadership style.[438]

> Jesus called them [the 12 disciples] together and said, "You know that the rulers of the Gentiles lord it over them, and their high officials exercise authority over them. Not so with you. Instead, whoever wants to become great among you must be your servant, and whoever wants to be first must be your slave, just as the Son of Man did not come to be served, but to serve, and to give his life as a ransom for many.[439]

Jesus contrasts the secular authorities with that of his kingdom. His followers are not to follow the way of the world. The disciple of Jesus is to put on the hessian robe of a humble servant, which mirrors his sacrifice for the good of the many.[440] Jesus came to earth as a servant.[441] If the Son of Man came to serve, then how much more should his followers walk the same path?[442] As Jesus testifies, "No servant is greater than his master, nor is a messenger greater than the one who sent him. Now that you know these things, you will be blessed if you do them" (Jn 13:16-17).[443]

The last of the five teaching dialogues in Matthew 23-25 emphasizes Jesus' instruction regarding the importance of humility in mission by highlighting the inadequacy of the scribes and Pharisees (23:1-12). The

---

[438] Mark also mentions in his gospel (10:35-45) the episode of Matthew 20:20-28. For references to James and John, see Matthew 4:21; 10:2; and Mark 3:17. For a perspective on the inside-out leadership style of Jesus, see Robert L. Gallagher. "Mission from the Inside Out: An Integrated Analysis of Selected Latin American Protestant 'Writings' in Spirituality and Mission." In *Missiology: An International Review* 40:1 (January 2012): 9-22.

[439] Matthew 20:25-28. See Mark 10:42-45 and Luke 22:25-27 for a parallel rendering. In the passage, Jesus plays on the concept of the price paid to redeem a slave. The Lord paid the price by his death on the cross as a slave to buy humanity from the slavery of sin and death. Hence, his followers are to obey his teaching and example, and become community slaves of God.

[440] For other scriptures on the servanthood of Jesus, see Isaiah 42:1; Luke 12:37; 22:27; John 13:13-16; II Corinthians 8:9; and Philippians 2:7.

[441] For the suffering servant passage, see Isaiah 52:13-53:12. Also, see John 11:47-53; 18:14; Galatians 1:4; 2:20; Romans 4:25; I Corinthians 15:3; Hebrews 5:1, 3; I Timothy 2:6; and I Peter 2:24.

[442] In Daniel 7:13-14, the phrase "the Son of Man," is a messianic title, which is reinforced by the juxtaposition of Peter's use of "Christ" in Mark 8:29, together with two verses later when Jesus calls himself the "Son of Man" (Mk 8:31).

[443] Jesus states in Matthew 10:24-25, "A student is not above his teacher, nor a servant above his master. It is enough for the student to be like his teacher, and the servant like his master." Also, see John 15:20; cf. Luke 17:7-10.

teaching block follows a narrative section underscoring the God-given authority of the Messiah (Mt 19-22). Jesus' warning of seeking titles of recognition independent of God's authority is trinitarian in arrangement. The Spirit is the One who teachers (8), there is only one Father in heaven (9), and Jesus is the Leader (10). The climax of the pericope: "The greatest among you will be your servant. All who exalt themselves will be humbled, and all who humble themselves will be exalted" (11-12; NRSV). Jesus embeds the exhortation of humble servanthood in a searchlight focused on the religious leadership. The gospel author immediately follows this episode by the seven funeral woes of Jesus aimed at the hypocritical control of the scribes and Pharisees (13-36).[444]

Humility of a Foot Washer

How then do we present God in such an environment among a people of power? At the last supper in John 13, verses 1 and 3 make it clear that the Messiah knew where he had come from, who he was, and where he was going. Coming from God, and having finished God's mission, Jesus was going back to the Father to receive total authority and power (Jn 17:4, 1-26). When the twelve disciples came into the upper room to celebrate the Jewish Passover, according to custom they found a basin full of water and a towel. However, there was no servant to wash their feet. Everyone in the room knew the cultural norm. Before you eat, a servant washes your feet. No one moved. All knew the truth, but not one disciple was willing to humble himself and wash each other's feet. Walking the dusty streets of 1st century Palestine inevitably

---

[444] For an example of mission humility responding to poverty and human need, see Jude Tiersma Watson. "Mother Teresa: To Suffer with Joy." In Charles Van Engen, Nancy Thomas, and Robert Gallagher, eds., *Footprints of God: A Narrative Theology of Mission*, Eugene, OR: Wipf & Stock, [1999] 2011, 114-23. For an illustration of ecclesiastical humility, see Robert L. Gallagher. "Martin of Tours." In George Thomas Kurian, ed., *The Encyclopedia of Christian Civilization*, Vol. 3, Chichester, UK: Wiley-Blackwell, 2012, 1428; and "Herman of Alaska." In George T. Kurian, ed., *Encyclopedia of Christian Civilization*, Vol. 2, Boston, MA: Blackwell Publishing, 2008, 1140-1141.

meant treading through piles of dung and garbage. This made it necessary to wash people's feet as they entered someone's home.[445]

As the Passover meal proceeded, Jesus arose from his reclining position, unfolded his outer garment, picked up the basin of water and a towel, and began to move from one man to another. Jesus made his way around his reclining followers stopping at each one. Kneeling, he spent loving time pouring water on the grime of their toes, and holding their calloused legs, scrubbed the dirt away, drying each pair of gnarled feet. The Creator of all things lowered himself by dirtying his hands in humility. When Jesus completed the task, he once again put on his outer garment and reclined at the dining table before he spoke.

> Do you understand what I have done for you? he asked them. You call me Teacher and Lord, and rightly so, for that is who I am. Now that I, your Lord and Teacher, have washed your feet, you also should wash one another's feet. I have set you an example that you should do as I have done for you. I tell you the truth, no servant is greater than his master, nor is a messenger greater than the one *who sent him. Now that you know these things, you will be blessed if you do them.*[446]

Jesus gives us an example of what we should do: wash one another's feet. By doing this, we are following the new commandment to love another. If we love one another, then people will know that we belong to the Lord (13:34-35). This example of humble service is additionally underscored when the gospel writer bookends the foot-washing ceremony with a portrait of Judas, the son of Simon Iscariot (13:2, 18-30). Jesus ate the Passover meal with Judas, the man he knew was a thief (Jn 12:4-6). Jesus bathed the feet of Judas by kneeling before the man he knew would betray him (cf. Jn 6:70-71).

---

[445] For a Christian understanding of the essence of humility, see Bernard of Clairvaux. *The Steps of Humility*. Cambridge: Cambridge University Press, 1940; Michael W. Austin. *Humility and Human Flourishing: A Study of Analytic Moral Theology*. New York: Oxford University Press, 2018; and "Humility, Pride, and the Presidency of Donald Trump." In Ronald J. Sider, ed., *The Spiritual Danger of Donald Trump: 30 Evangelical Christians on Justice, Truth, and Moral Integrity*, Eugene, OR: Cascade Books, 2020, 42-46.

[446] John 13:12b-17.

The gentle obedience of the Savior surrendered in love to Judas, the ravenous wolf whose only thought was to devour the Lamb. Is the Lord challenging his lambs to eat with and wash the feet of those wolves who desire to persecute them?[447]

What does Jesus mean when he says that his followers need to wash one another's feet? We could comprehend what Jesus is teaching either literally or figuratively. That is, we understand the Lord's instructions by washing one another's feet with a basin, towel, and water. Alternatively, it could mean that the foot washing is emblematic, and we do it in a way other than through a physical action. As an example of a literal approach, Pope Francis[448] during Maundy Thursday in 2013 at a prison outside Rome washed the feet of 12 inmates, including a Muslim woman. The pope laid aside his papal garments of power and girded himself with the humility of Jesus. Solanus Casey[449] serves as an illustration of the symbolic approach. Relegated as a door attendant and porter at the Saint Bonaventure Monastery in Detroit, Father Casey became God's prophet of divine healing and intercessory prayer among the sick and poor touching countless lives with Christian hope. In 1957, more than 20,000 people attended the funeral of this humble foot washer.

Conclusion

The editing of this volume took place during the summer of 2020, during the Covid-19 pandemic, and after the reckoning of systemic racism that followed the killing of George Floyd in Minneapolis and the prolonged demonstrations throughout the US. This particular point in time causes us to reflect more deeply and globally about the role of God's people at this critical and complicated time.

Is there redemption and hope for the wolves? We have the promise in scripture of the wolves sitting and eating with the lambs. Thus, there must be

---

447 Cf. Jesus' instructions to his followers in the Sermon on the Mount about the kingdom of God that he has brought to earth: "Love your enemies; pray for those who persecute you" (Mt 5:44).
448 Pope Francis I (1936-present; p. 2013-present).
449 Solanus Casey (1870-1957) was a member of the Order of Friars Minor Capuchin.

a massive transformation among the wolves for this to take place. Some might prefer to see the wolves thrown into eternal fire. But God has another intent, that the lamb will be the instrument of transformation of the wolf. The Empire of Rome persecuted Christians mercilessly, but it did not take long before Rome fell. The empire could not stand in the face of radical godly love. Dear reader, in your city, have you ever seen this kind of radical love? What might this look like in your context?

What happens when Christians are the ones in power, when they are the wolves, so to speak? Paul wrote the book of Romans when Christians were the minority with no power in society. What happens when God's people hold considerable power? How can they avoid being co-opted by the systems of power? The Church of the Lamb must refuse to be co-opted by systems that abuse power. So, then, what does it mean to be a follower of the Lamb of God in the midst of contexts of injustice? Christians in Rome had little opportunity to stand up for a more just society. What does this look like in your context? How might God want God's people to use their power to impact the unjust structures of society? As Cornel West has said, justice is what love looks like in the public sphere.

Chapter 11: Jerusalem

by David P. Leong[450]

God's Mission of Longing for the City of God

Throughout the biblical depictions of God's Holy City in Isaiah, Jeremiah, Mark, and Revelation, I explore the arc of God's mission as it runs through Jerusalem: the city itself and the rich eschatological symbolism of the Temple Mount. In each narrative, an undercurrent of longing informs a missiological reading of Jerusalem. This longing takes many forms: a desire for God's truth to be lifted high among the nations, a lament over Israel's unfaithfulness and corruption, a hope for a place of worship for all people, and a tension of witnessing heaven on earth.

Psalm 137

> By the rivers of Babylon, there we sat down and there we
>
> > wept when we remembered Zion.
>
> On the willows there we hung up our harps.
>
> For there, our captors asked us for songs, and our
>
> > tormentors asked for mirth, saying, "Sing us one of the
>
> > songs of Zion!"

---

450 David P. Leong (Ph.D. in Intercultural Studies from Fuller Theological Seminary) is Associate Professor of Missiology at Seattle Pacific University and Seminary, where he directs a program in Global and Urban Ministry. David is the author of *Race and Place: How Urban Geography Shapes the Journey to Reconciliation* (InterVarsity Press, 2017) and *Street Signs: Toward a Missional Theology of Urban Cultural Engagement* (Pickwick, 2012). David and his family live in community in South Seattle and enjoy the diversity, vibrancy, and creativity of their neighborhood.

How could we sing the LORD's song in a foreign land?

If I forget you, O Jerusalem, let my right hand wither!

Let my tongue cling to the roof of my mouth, if I do not
remember you, if I do not set Jerusalem above my
highest joy.[451]

Introduction

Cities are richly layered cultural texts, always thick with meaning and memory just below the surface of their everyday physical features. Given the incredibly complex and contested history and geography of Jerusalem, it is especially the case that the city of Jerusalem is as much a symbolic idea as it is a particular geographic municipality. To capture the essence of this deep symbolism is no simple task of description or translation; rather, it is an interpretive work, an exegetical[452] process, with many different dimensions. What follows is an attempt at a deep reading of urban Jerusalem, one that

---

[451] Note by CVE: The process of editing this collection of chapters about the cities of the Bible has provided a number of surprises for us. One of those has come in this chapter on Jerusalem. In the political climate of today, the view of immigrants and immigration has taken on a whole new meaning. Scripture describes three different attitudes and responses on the part of the Israelites enslaved and taken into exile in Babylon. Psalm 137, cited above, expresses one response. A second response by the same people, experiencing the same suffering, in the same place, at the same time is articulated by the prophet Jeremiah. He tells the exiles, "Thus says the Lord of hosts to all the exiles whom I have sent into exile from Jerusalem to Babylon: Build houses and live in them; plant gardens and eat what they produce...seek the welfare of the city where I have sent you into exile and pray...on its behalf, for in its welfare you will find your welfare" (Jer 29:4-7 nrsv). A third response is recorded in the first chapter of Daniel. Daniel and his three friends found a way to contribute to their new context. "To these four young men God gave knowledge and skill in every aspect of literature and wisdom....They were stationed in the king's court. In every matter of wisdom and understanding concerning which the king inquired of them, he found them ten times better than all the magicians and enchanters in his whole kingdom. And Daniel continued there until the first year of King Cyrus" (Dan 1: 19-21 nrsv). For 64 years, Daniel served as a counselor to the kings of Babylon. Yet, at various times, we are told that all of them suffered greatly at the hands of their captors. The nearly contradictory responses to the city represented by these three passages give voice and vision to how immigrants today can respond to their difficult situations. We are called, even in exile, even as immigrants, to seek the welfare of the city. Together, we all long for the City of God.

[452] I have written about a method of "urban exegesis" elsewhere, the details of which will not be fully employed for this chapter. For a fuller exploration of the topic, see David Leong, *Street Signs: A Missional Theology of Urban Cultural Engagement*. Eugene, OR: Pickwick Publ., 2012, 97-114.

takes both past and present into account, as well as the worlds behind, of, and in front of the biblical text.[453] Throughout this reading, my emphasis will be missiological in terms of understanding the meaning of the city and the activity of the *missio Dei*, the Trinitarian God whose sending nature invites the People of God to participate in the work of reconciling all things.[454]

The tension relayed by the Psalmist in Babylonian exile is a multifaceted yearning. In Psalm 137's concise nine verses we experience the full range of emotion for those whose hearts are at home only in Zion. In this sense, Jerusalem is both the "highest joy" (v.6) of its people and yet the very source of their deep anguish. The displacement of God's People has forced them into more than geographic wandering or political uncertainty; to be apart from Zion is a collective crisis of identity. How could the chosen people of God, whose destiny was to be lifted among the nations, fulfill their calling in the real world of pagan pluralism while being removed from the place they saw as integral to that vocation? Further, how could the voice and goodness of God be trusted amid such apparent dissonance between who they were supposed to be and all the obstacles to that vision right in front of them?

This tension and yearning are both historical and contemporary. One way to read Jerusalem in this context is fundamentally as a city of longing. University of Cambridge's Simon Goldhill describes how "this is the memory of Jerusalem, a history of generations of longing: longing for a touch of the divine, longing for a better world, longing for a lost home, longing to find an answer, here in this place, only here."[455] A longing that evokes both joy and pain characterizes much of the biblical witness about Jerusalem. As one of the central locations – both literal and figurative – of God's activity in the world, Jerusalem holds all the hope of the Divine Presence in the Most Holy Place

---

453 This "deep reading" is also delimited and may not seem comprehensive enough for historical or biblical scholars of Jerusalem; my interpretation here is narrow in scope and missiological in focus.

454 Colossians 1:16-20. See also Craig Van Gelder and Dwight J. Zscheile, *Participating in God's Mission: A Theological Missiology for the Church in America*. Grand Rapids: Eerdmans, 2018, 275-286.

455 Simon Goldhill, *Jerusalem: City of Longing,* Cambridge, MA: Harvard University Press, 2008, 6.

and all the despair of seeing God's city destroyed at the hands of foreign powers who would desecrate Zion's beauty as a result of Yahweh's judgment.

Across this range of history, and the weight of its collective hope and lament, there is no way to offer a comprehensive reading that does justice to what Jerusalem means in all its richly textured biblical context. Rather, in the selections of Scripture that follow, the arc of longing in God's story runs through Jerusalem at four critical junctures: Isaiah's New Jerusalem, Jeremiah's corrupt temple, Mark's temple cleansing, and Revelation's heavenly city. In each of these depictions of God's holy city, the reader witnesses the unfolding of God's mission to reveal through Zion the calling, forming, and sending of a particular people. The subsequent implications of this mission reach as far back as the Abrahamic covenant and as far forward as the ongoing crisis of Palestinian occupation and oppression. May the Spirit of God, who illumines the hearts and minds of people of faith, guide this reading for the sake of God's world.

Isaiah's New Jerusalem

Throughout the book of Isaiah, a recurring theme "focuses on the life, the shortcomings, the fate, and the destiny of the city of Jerusalem, in a fashion unequaled in Scripture."[456] After the opening chapter recounts the sins of God's People, who "have forsaken the Lord" and "despised the Holy One of Israel" (1:4), the second chapter casts a powerful eschatological vision of how "the mountain of the Lord's house shall be established as the highest of the mountains... all the nations shall stream to it. Many peoples shall come and say, 'Come, let us go up to the mountain of the Lord, to the house of the God of Jacob.' ... For out of Zion shall go forth instruction, and the word of the Lord from Jerusalem" (2:2-3).

Despite Israel's unfaithfulness and the empty religiosity that allowed injustice to run rampant through the city, the prophet Isaiah sees another

---

[456] John Goldingay, *New International Biblical Commentary: Isaiah,* Peabody, MA: Hendrickson Publishers, Inc., 2001, 7.

possibility: a renewed and restored Jerusalem that sets the house of the Lord high above the nations for both the glory of Yahweh and the flourishing of all peoples. As Isaiah lifts his eyes to the heavenly horizon, this New Jerusalem is a city on a hill, out of which God's peace and justice reigns. The many nations that flow to Zion "shall beat their swords into plowshares, and their spears into pruning hooks; nation shall not lift sword against nation, neither shall they learn war any more" (2:4). In contrast to the violence and struggle of warring nations, Yahweh the righteous judge establishes a central, pervasive *Shalom* for all. What a powerful and compelling image of the city of God! Yet this image must always be held in tension with not only the ancient conflicts over Jerusalem's rule and conquest but also the contemporary political struggles over land and power that continue to this day.

What does Isaiah's New Jerusalem mean for readers – past and present – who are longing to see the prophet's peaceful vision fulfilled in a time of strife? In the immediate context of Isaiah's original audience, the New Jerusalem is a symbol of God's intention to recreate the broken world and to place a particular community of people at its center. This centripetal trajectory of God's mission locates the Holy City as a focal point around which the nations move toward God's word of truth and the people formed by that truth. In the final chapters of Isaiah, the prophet then returns to this image as he sees Yahweh "create new heavens and a new earth. ... I am about to create Jerusalem as a joy, and its people as a delight. ... No more shall the sound of weeping be heard in it, or the cry of distress" (65:17-19).

This restorative vision of a gathered people in Zion who delight in the Lord, a people at peace with themselves and their neighbors, is what bookends the whole text of Isaiah with New Jerusalem language and symbolism. The key to making sense of this text today is to understand how this eschatological city is a liminal hope between *already* and *not yet*. The New Jerusalem is already a reality because Yahweh's justice radiates from God's being and communities covenanted to Yahweh. This centrifugal exuberance of the *missio Dei* is part and parcel of the Triune God's character and existence. Any place where God's People are caught up in this activity of the divine community is a realization of the heavenly city. At the same time, the New Jerusalem is not yet fully realized because the restorative work God is in the midst of is still playing out on this side of the broken creation.

Walter Brueggemann reminds us that Isaiah's "new infrastructure of the city will be marked by peace, justice, righteousness, and faithfulness. That is the long-term vision of the tradition of Isaiah. ...Such qualities are not simply theological ideas but conditions that prevail in actual social relationships."[457] In our urban world of social structures and institutional policies, the peace and justice of Yahweh is possible at moments, but also incredibly difficult to scale and maintain. While there is no quantifiable way to balance the already-not-yet aspects of the New Jerusalem, a liminal hope is still hope, however thin or in-between it may feel. For our purposes, Isaiah's vision sets the stage for the following readings of Jerusalem in Jeremiah, Mark, and Revelation. Hope is our starting point because as we will see in Jeremiah and Mark, no biblical depiction of Zion is complete without confronting the forces of darkness and deception at the heart of the city of God.

Jeremiah's Corrupt Temple

To move from Isaiah's New Jerusalem to the famous "Temple Sermon" of Jeremiah 7:1-15 is to transition from an eschatological hope to a sharp admonition about the dangers of self-deception and false worship located in the center of Jerusalem. The temple system consisted not only of its physical structure that represented the house of the Lord in its layout and architecture, but also the priestly class and religious elites who would facilitate the liturgies of Israel's worshipping community. Thus the Temple symbolizes both the geographic centralization of Jerusalem's seat of power and the particular place where God's presence dwells on earth. N.T. Wright

---

[457] Walter Brueggemann, *Isaiah 40-66: Westminster Bible Companion,* Louisville, KY: Westminster John Knox Press, 1998, 247.

describes the Temple as "umbilically linked"[458] to the heavens, the connection point where the People of God receive the life-giving goodness of Yahweh. The elaborate partitioning of the Second Temple – from its outer courts into the Most Holy Place – reflects the careful process by which people access God's *Shekinah,* the glory of the Divine Presence. Put simply, the integrity and righteousness of the temple system is critical to the identity of Jerusalem and all who gather there.

This context is what makes Jeremiah's confrontational sermon so striking. After being instructed to "proclaim the word of the Lord at the gate of the Jerusalem Temple as Judah gathers for worship,"[459] the prophet unleashes a clarion call to repentance. Jerusalem has become a place of hypocrisy and deception, a place where empty liturgical language repeatedly affirming the Temple of the Lord holds no real meaning because injustice goes unnoticed just beyond the temple walls. Rather than worshipping the God of Israel who delights in *hesed, mishpat,* and *tzedakah* ("steadfast love, justice, and righteousness"[460]), Judah's rituals of religiosity are blind to the oppression that characterizes their daily lives. Foreigners, orphans, and widows are suffering in the streets, but empty liturgies persist. How could a people covenanted to Yahweh be so deceived?

> Walter Brueggemann identifies this central flaw of Judah:
> They have no sense of shame at the distance between their liturgy and their ethics. ...The temple has become a place of refuge, hiding, and safety for those who violate torah through their life in the world. The torah violators attempt to hide in the sanctity of the ritual. The temple becomes a means of cover-up for the destructive way life is lived in the real world. This escapist use of liturgy is self-deceptive, for it will not protect Judah from the realities of the covenant.[461]

---

458 N.T. Wright and Michael F. Bird, *The New Testament in Its World,* Grand Rapids, MI: Zondervan Academic, 2019, 103-115.

459 John M. Bracke, *Jeremiah 1-29: Westminster Bible Companion,* Louisville, KY: Westminster John Knox Press, 2000, 75.

460 Jeremiah 9:24 groups this "holy triad" in a pattern that echoes throughout much of the Law and the Prophets.

461 Walter Brueggemann, *A Commentary on Jeremiah: Exile and Homecoming,* Grand Rapids, MI: Wm. B. Eerdmans Publishing Co., 1998, 79-80.

In a tragically common pattern in Jerusalem, recitations and proclamations of God's goodness are hollow refrains that serve to insulate the religious from the cries of the poor. Busy maintaining the appearance of piety, the people of Judah cannot hear the prophet's warnings and therefore cannot heed his instruction. Their insistence of self-righteousness is, in fact, in fact a deep, spiritual corruption made all the more pointed by the prophetic word of the Lord: "Has this house, which is called by my name, become a den of robbers in your sight? You know, I too am watching, says the Lord" (7:11).

The haunting nature of this question will be explored further in the following reading of Mark's gospel, but this prophetic reading of Jerusalem must first be connected to the broader mission of God. If "the temple sermon shows the prophet in profound conflict with the dominant temple ideology on which the state relied,"[462] then in what ways is Jeremiah's corrupt Temple instructive for communities seeking to participate with the *missio Dei* toward Isaiah's vision of the New Jerusalem? We must be able to connect the idolatry and hypocrisy of the temple system in Jeremiah with the myriad ways in which institutionalized religion facilitates the construction of systems of oppression in our cities today. It is important to note that the organizational structures that create religious institutions are not inherently problematic. However, as was the case with Jeremiah's Temple, concentrations of power and wealth that control a narrow theological narrative can easily deceive a people into believing their worship does not require justice or hospitality for those outside their community.

In a voice that echoes the prophetic refrain of Micah 6, Jeremiah reminds us to ask more honestly: what does the Lord require of us? And what does the city of God look like when the People of God faithfully worship the Lord who "has brought down the powerful from their thrones and lifted the lowly; he has filled the hungry with good things and sent the rich away empty" (Luke 1:52-53)? While Mark's gospel offers some clues, Jeremiah's temple

---

[462] Walter Brueggemann, *Jeremiah 1-25: To Pluck Up, to Tear Down.* Grand Rapids, MI: Wm. B. Eerdmans Publishing Co., 1988, 74.

invites us to lament and repent. "The object of lament is the city of Jerusalem.... The city is portrayed as abandoned by God and it is God who is the agent of the city's destruction."[463] A prophetic lament over Jerusalem recognizes the tragedy of false worship and grieves over a community that cannot move toward repentance until it first faces judgment.

In the chapter before Jeremiah's laying out God's judgment in the temple sermon, he offers a simple reminder for those with ears to hear. "Thus says the Lord: Stand at the crossroads, and look, and ask for the ancient paths, where the good way lies; and walk in it, and find rest for your souls" (6:16). Sadly, the people of Jerusalem were not willing to hear this prophetic word of the Lord, and the discipline of Yahweh's righteous anger would "be poured out on this place, on human beings and animals, on the trees of the field and the fruit of the ground; it will burn and not be quenched" (7:20). In the wake of such destruction, could a seed of hope for the city of God be present in the person of Jesus Christ as he entered Jerusalem many generations later?

Mark's Temple Cleansing

The intertestamental period between the prophets and the gospels could be characterized as a quiet longing, a long-suffering season of waiting on Yahweh for the promises of deliverance made so many generations before. Jerusalem was repeatedly the site of Israel's disappointment; their experiences of exile and homecoming had left many with a sense of loss over who they were in the face of foreign subjugation and occupation. Messianic hopes were not only core to Israel's cultural narratives and shared identity; they were increasingly a political necessity that would make Yahweh king over the seemingly undefeatable Roman Empire.

So when we arrive in Jerusalem with Jesus in Mark 11, at the "triumphal entry" that would precipitate his passion week and an inexorable march toward Golgotha, we must understand the prophetic nature of the

---

[463] Soong-Chan Rah, *Prophetic Lament: A Call for Justice in Troubled Times,* Downers Grove, IL: InterVarsity Press, 2015, 82.

temple cleansing as a fulfillment of God doing for Israel what they could not do for themselves. Once again, the temple in Jerusalem is at the center of God's agenda, and Jesus' confrontation with the temple system will harness the prophetic energy of both Jeremiah and Isaiah to accomplish Yahweh's restorative mission to "create new heavens and a new earth" (Isaiah 65:17).

On the way to Jerusalem, the temple cleansing narrative is sandwiched by what seems like an unusual textual pairing about a fig tree. Before Jesus enters the temple for a fateful encounter with the Jewish religious establishment, "he was hungry" (11:12). Longing for more than merely physical sustenance, Jesus was hungry for the fruit of righteousness that would come from faithful worship during the Passover. That was a sacred time when Israel would remember God's deliverance by reenacting a symbolic meal that was rich with the imagery of Yahweh's salvific and definitive action on their behalf. But as he approached the fig tree, instead of fruit, "he found nothing but leaves" (11:13). Tragically, it was a tree that at first appeared to be fruitful, but upon closer examination was barren. "The fig tree would indeed have been understood as a symbol for Israel meant to bear fruit at the eschaton. The point is that Jesus has come and is ready to gather in God's People, but they are bearing no fruit at all."[464] Jesus, therefore, curses the tree, and the scene cuts quickly to the temple.

While the temple cleansing narratives in other gospels provide more context and detail, Mark's account is concise and to the point. As soon as Jesus arrives in the temple courts, he begins driving people out, turning over tables, and generally making a provocative scene in what was surely a spectacle of confrontation in front of the Passover crowds. "The entire prophetic act is a current rebuke of the leadership's operation of the temple and the people who submit to it, an act they could hardly ignore. It is a prophetic indictment that explains why Jesus must face death."[465] Much like

---

[464] Ben Witherington III, *The Gospel of Mark: A Socio-Rhetorical Commentary,* Grand Rapids, MI: Wm. B. Eerdmans Publishing Co., 2001, 313.
[465] Darrell Bock, *Mark: New Cambridge Bible Commentary,* New York, NY: Cambridge University Press, 2015, 293.

the rationale behind Jeremiah's temple sermon, Jesus continues in the prophetic tradition by calling out the falsehood and hypocrisy of a temple system that appears to be one thing but is in actuality another.

The weight of Jesus' prophetic condemnation is anchored to two specific texts: "My house shall be called a house of prayer for all nations" from Isaiah 56:7 and "den of robbers" from Jeremiah 7:11. These contrasting images of the house of the Lord depict exactly how far the temple reality has drifted from its vocation to be a blessing to *panta ta ethne*. Isaiah 56 beautifully outlines the breadth of God's salvific plan, specifically including eunuchs and foreigners who were seen as unclean and outside of Yahweh's blessing and covenant. "These I will bring to my holy mountain and make them joyful in my house of prayer; their burnt offerings and their sacrifices will be accepted on my altar" (Isaiah 56:7). But rather than embracing Isaiah's wider vision of Jerusalem as a place where all people from every tribe, tongue, and nation could gather, the temple had become a narrow, myopic community of people who could not see beyond themselves and the crisis of their self-righteous religiosity.

Jesus longs for Isaiah's eschatological hope to be realized in the present, but in the same way that Jeremiah's Jerusalem could not embody obedience, neither could the temple that Jesus confronted receive his message. However, unlike Jeremiah's lament over an unrepentant city that would face Yahweh's wrath, Jesus' temple cleansing narrative concludes with a seed of hope in the form of a withered fig tree. Out of a fruitless tree, a little faith can put down miraculous roots for future generations. Facing the death threats of a corrupt temple system, Jesus tells his disciples to "Have faith in God. Truly I tell you, if you say to this mountain, 'Be taken up and thrown into the sea,' and if you do not doubt in your heart, but believe that what you say will come to pass, it will be done for you" (Mark 11:22-23).

Followers of Jesus who understood the significance of the Temple Mount and the destiny of the nation that was tied to Zion could not have imagined that a New Jerusalem would transcend its physical location. But this is precisely what Jesus invites people to see with the eyes of faith: a temple in the city of God that extends beyond its geography and a people constituted there whose social imagination makes another world possible. As we move toward our final Jerusalem text at the end of the book of Revelation, we will retrace the contours of Isaiah's restored city, Jeremiah's lament, and Mark's reimagined temple.

Revelation's Heavenly City

Beginning and ending with the New Jerusalem motif perhaps runs the risk of emphasizing the transcendent nature of God's mission over its more immanent implications for urban missiology, but only if we see the heavenly city as an either-or reality. A bifurcated framework of "earthly" and "heavenly" cities is a dangerous dichotomy that could be traced back to the kinds of dualism present in St. Augustine's classic philosophical treatise, *The City of God*. Though Augustine is understandably more concerned with existential and apologetic questions about the Christian faith in a post-Roman world than the details of urban politics, *The City of God* is not the only influential text that tends to position the mystical city of heaven in opposition to the material world of the earthly city. Western Christianity has inherited a largely dualistic spirituality that often does not quite know how to make sense of the heavenly realm in general, let alone the particularities of an apocalyptic text like John's Revelation. With that cautionary note in mind, because Revelation's heavenly city draws heavily on Isaiah's vision of the New Jerusalem, I will attempt a reading of Revelation 21 that is attentive to both the transcendent, immanent *missio Dei* and the already-not-yet reign of God that breaks into the present through a city where the One seated on the throne says "See, I am making all things new" (21:5).

Many of the difficulties in interpreting the book of Revelation have to do with its genre-blending as an epistle, prophetic text, and apocalyptic literature, but this multifaceted nature of the book is a big part of what makes its implications for understanding Jerusalem so relevant and impactful. As

John pulls back the curtain on another worldly realm of visions and creatures that stir the eschatological imagination, we must also remember the historic purposes of circulated letters that offered hope and encouragement to Christian communities who were experiencing violent persecution under Roman rule. The apocalyptic imagery of the New Jerusalem was not simply a distant hope of God's cosmic victory on the other side of earthly life; quite the contrary, the heavenly city was a near and present reality that the slain Lamb on the throne had already defeated death! When faced with oppression of the Evil One embodied by imperial violence, they "conquered him by the blood of the Lamb and by the word of their testimony, for they did not cling to life even in the face of death" (12:11). The courage early Christians summoned to bear witness to a God who was remaking the broken world did not come from a faint vision of a heavenly city in the clouds. Rather, "the holy city, the new Jerusalem, coming down out of heaven from God" (21:2) was an already realized fulfillment of Isaiah's new earth.

As "Isaiah and several others make plain, precisely because it is restored *Jerusalem*, it cannot be anywhere else but on earth....No one 'goes up' to heaven; rather, heaven is now seen as coming down to earth."[466] This characteristic of the New Jerusalem that is unique to the Revelation text highlights an important geographic shift: rather than the nations flowing to Zion (Isaiah 2:2), God has drawn near to the nations. In incarnational language, God has "moved into the neighborhood"[467] and made a dwelling, his tabernacle, among the people. "See, the home of God is among mortals. He will dwell with them; they will be his Peoples, and God himself will be with them" (21:3). Strikingly, this vision "saw no temple in the city, for its temple is the Lord God the Almighty and the Lamb" (21:22). The once irreplaceable

---

[466] Gordon D. Fee, *Revelation: A New Covenant Commentary,* Eugene, OR: Cascade Book, 2011, 292.

[467] This famous paraphrase of John 1:14 from Eugene Peterson's *The Message* remains a succinct incarnational metaphor for the God who "tabernacles" with us in the person of Jesus.

Temple, the center of Jerusalem's life and identity, as well as the site of Jerusalem's infidelity, has been transformed.

The Christological layers of this temple metaphor must not be missed. God makes a dwelling among the nations through the incarnate One. The New Jerusalem is a poignant reminder that the One who sits on the throne in the center of the city of God is Jesus Christ himself. No longer is a temple needed, for "the Most High does not dwell in houses made with human hands" (Acts 7:48). This recognition from the apostle Stephen comes from the conviction of the Holy Spirit who was loosed when the temple curtain was torn, then embodied in the lives of believers after Pentecost.

In its final chapter, Revelation describes a New Jerusalem that echoes all the hope of Isaiah's *shalom* and the completeness of the creation story from the Garden of Eden to the newly restored city.[468] In the heart of the city of God flows

> the river of the water of life, bright as crystal, flowing from the throne of God and of the Lamb through the middle of the street of the city. On either side of the river is the tree of life with its twelve kinds of fruit, producing its fruit each month; and the leaves of the tree are for the healing of the nations (22:1-2).

As we consider the mission of God in and through the cities of our world, the people who are called, formed, and sent for God's purposes must offer the wholeness and fruitfulness that comes from a community who inhabit the heavenly city for the healing it offers to others. But the question remains: what does this participation in God's mission look like in the cities of the world? Revelation reminds us that "John and many of his readers lived both geographically and symbolically between Jerusalem and Rome."[469] To discern the path of faithful discipleship today is in many ways the same

---

[468] In my most recent book, *Race and Place,* Downers Grove, IL: InterVarsity Press, 2017, I borrow Ray Bakke's language in the third chapter titled "From the Garden to the City" (59-81).
[469] Richard Bauckham. *The Theology of the Book of Revelation,* Cambridge, UK: Cambridge University Press, 1993, 126.

journey: to live in the light of the New Jerusalem while still recognizing the shadow of the Roman empire. Temptations to distort the heavenly city abound. There is detached mysticism, idealized activism, and religious isolationism. Faithful citizens of the New Jerusalem must resist these distortions with Spirit-empowered wisdom and community-centered praxis.

Conclusion

Moving from text to life in the city of Jerusalem is not a simple application of biblical principles to particular ethical dilemmas. Instead, to participate with God in the New Creation work of making the heavenly city an earthly reality is always a delicate tension of discerning kingdom citizenship that is faithful to the Holy Spirit while resisting the spirit of empire. This process of discernment in the current context of Jerusalem must be attentive to the reconciling nature of the Spirit that overcomes the politics of division and fear.

Put simply, "Jerusalem is a city bombarded by conflict....[It] is the poster child for the divided city. It is divided over religion and religiosity as well as by race, ethnicity, and class. The battle over who owns and controls Jerusalem is the focus of national, regional, and international attention."[470] How could the city that represents the uniquely shared Abrahamic roots of Judaism, Christianity, and Islam be so afflicted with long-standing struggles over land, boundaries, and power? Why is the fear and tribalism of these monotheistic faiths seemingly so destructive of the unity of affirming and worshipping the one, true God? These questions are not meant to diminish the obvious significance of these historic conflicts and the complexity of their cultural, religious, political, and geographic roots.

We need to understand that the City of God in the Scriptures is not a winner-takes-all competition in which Yahweh vanquishes Israel's foes and then lifts an ethnically homogeneous chosen people in the contested city we

---

[470] Anne B. Shlay and Gillad Rosen, *Jerusalem: The Spatial Politics of a Divided Metropolis,* Cambridge, UK: Polity Press, 2015, 6-7.

call Jerusalem. Instead, throughout this reading, we have seen a nuanced biblical narrative in which Jerusalem and its Temple is a physical site for something so much deeper. It is a sign that God is drawing all people to God's self. In this remaking of the broken creation, a peculiar people, unified in their diversity, are offering themselves on behalf of God's world. This strange community, reconciled to one another in Christ, is called to become a cross-shaped people because the One at the center of their heavenly city is the Lamb who was slain.

What might interfaith dialogue and interreligious cooperation look like between Jews, Christians, and Muslims if Christians embraced cruciformity[471] as their central political ethic? How might contested spaces for worship and prayer be reimagined if Christians understood their vocation not as dominating their religious rivals, but as serving their neighbors in loving friendship? This vision is the compelling peace of Isaiah's holy city where nations no longer study war, where there is radical hospitality of a "house of prayer for all nations," and where there is a prophetic hope of heaven coming to earth. To realize such a vision in the present may require the confrontation of Jesus who overturns our religious sentimentalisms and self-righteous deceptions, but this cleansing work is necessary when our cities resemble too much of the empires of this world, and not enough of God's upside-down kingdom.

Ultimately, none of this missiological reading of Jerusalem is possible without the wisdom, compassion, and activity of the Holy Spirit whose presence with God's People is the catalyst and fuel for the transformation of communities. Israeli-Palestinian conflict cannot be negotiated away with new policy proposals when hardened hearts over generational suffering have not been softened with empathy that is foundational to justice.[472] Islamophobic

---

[471] See Michael Gorman, *Inhabiting the Cruciform God: Kenosis, Justification, and Theosis in Paul's Narrative Soteriology,* Grand Rapids, MI: Wm. B. Eerdmans Publishing Co., 2009, 129-155.

[472] Though I cannot address this historic conflict with sufficient detail here, another role of the Spirit is the conviction that undergirds liberation from oppression. See Naim Stifan

prejudices in Western Christianity will not recede simply because Miroslav Volf describes "a common word"[473] between Muslims and Christians, helpful as his theological work may be in cultivating hospitable spaces of understanding. People in Jerusalem who have been repeatedly traumatized by violence cannot turn the other cheek when their pain and suffering has become an ingrained component of their identity. In each of these spaces characterized by conflict, the "imperial consciousness"[474] that divides and conquers the hearts and minds of people is a powerful enemy. Only the humility, gentleness, and "still small voice" (I Kings 19:11-13) of the Spirit can animate the ministry of reconciliation so desperately needed in places like Jerusalem.

Paying attention to the movement of the Holy Spirit in the city of God is an essential practice that people of faith must cultivate with their lives together. Participation in God's mission is always a Spirit-filled and communally discerned activity, in Jerusalem and to the ends of the earth. As the Spirit of God inhabits communities that are longing for God's peace and justice to spill over into the world, may the healing life of the New Jerusalem and the triumphant love of Lamb on the throne send the Church as a courageous people into our cities, streets, and neighborhoods.

Ateek, *A Palestinian Theology of Liberation: The Bible, Justice, and Palestine-Israel Conflict,* Maryknoll, NY: Orbis Books, 2017.

[473] Miroslav Volf, Ghazi bin Muhammad, and Melissa Yarrington, *A Common Word: Muslims and Christians on Loving God and Neighbor,* Grand Rapids, MI: Wm. B. Eerdmans Publishing Co., 2010, 18-29.

[474] Walter Brueggemann, *The Prophetic Imagination,* Minneapolis, MN: Fortress Press, 1978, 33-35.

Conclusion

by Charles E. Van Engen[475]

Preparing to write this Conclusion, I reviewed one more time the metaphors that have arisen in the reflections on God's mission in eleven cities mentioned in the Bible. Obviously, there are many other cities and towns such as Bethlehem, Bethany, Colossae, Thessalonica, and others that are also important to the biblical narrative. Just naming them brings to mind the different stories of God's mission that happened in different ways, in such a variety of places, each with its own emphasis. The cities we chose for this book are ones that arose naturally in our brainstorming together as editors and called for attention. The ones chosen are meant to be illustrative, not exhaustive. We leave it to the readers to explore other cities mentioned in the Bible, drawing out the metaphors of God's mission as depicted there.

The Use of Metaphor to Understand the City

As Jude pointed out in the Introduction, metaphors give us windows, lenses, paradigms for understanding the city. Metaphors help us to

---

[475] Charles (Chuck) E. Van Engen (PhD in Missiology from the Free University of Amsterdam) is the Arthur F. Glasser Senior Professor Emeritus of Biblical Theology of Mission in the School of Intercultural Studies at Fuller Theological Seminary, where he taught from 1988 to 2015. Chuck was born and raised in Chiapas, Mexico, of missionary parents. Author or editor of numerous books and articles, his recent publications include *The State of Missiology Today* (InterVarsity Press) and *Transforming Mission Theology* (William Carey Library). He is a founder of the Latin American Christian Ministries, which provides doctoral studies in theology for Latin American scholars.

comprehend the complex kaleidoscope of characteristics that make up a city. The city is extraordinarily complex and defies fragmented simplistic approaches. Urban theory has drawn from disciplines like history, sociology, geography, economics, politics, demographics, religious affiliation, ethnography, art, and so on. Too often the assumptions, research methodologies, and findings of these studies do not interact with each other. But the reality involves a simultaneous interfacing and intersecting of all of these. The city must be approached in a posture of humility because each of us only sees a part of the whole.

We might think of the city as a kind of kaleidoscope. A kaleidoscope is filled with many small pieces of glass, each a different color. Every piece is important. Each piece offers a different view specific to its color. But put them all together, shine a light through them, look through the kaleidoscope, and the pieces fall together into a pattern that no one piece can give. Turn the kaleidoscope and you will see another different pattern made up of the same pieces but now intersecting differently. So are the cities of our world. Each city is a different kaleidoscopic reality created by unique interconnections of all the various aspects of life in the city. How can we catch a glimpse of the big picture and not be blinded by the brilliance of one part?

Many folks dealing with the city have wrestled with this problem. An example is the work of urban architects and engineers. They have considered "The role of human metaphors on urban theories and practices."[476] For example, Omid Vernoos at the Institute for Urban and Regional Planning of the Technische Universität Berlin writes,

> Justifying the physical arrangement of the city by means of human analogy has been done by philosophers, architects, and urbanists, since the ancient Greeks. Through the development of science, especially the life sciences, this analogy has been broadened and the city has been metaphorically considered as a living and growing organism.

---

[476] Title of a digital article by urban sociologist, Omid Vernoos, "The role of human metaphors on urban theories and practices," 2018; accessed September 7, 2020 from https://www.semanticscholar.org/paper/The-role-of-human-metaphors-on-urban-theories-and-Vernoos/5bfc4b18072a7aa00a7eb37198e5029711bfa1d3?p2df

In this context, the metaphor has played a fundamental role as a cognitive device for transferring the human concepts to urban theories or vice versa. [477]

Metaphors help us to understand the city in at least three ways. First, they help us associate and integrate different perspectives of the city derived from numerous disciplines. Secondly, they help us contextualize our thinking about a specific city. Every city is unique with its own skyline, sounds, and smells. Metaphors help us recognize the unique features of a city. Thirdly, metaphors are open concepts; there is always room for additional data and deeper reflection. They help us incorporate new perceptions of a city that foster creativity.[478]

The use of metaphor in human rationality is not new. In the West, Enlightenment thinkers drew from the Greeks and Latins in deepening and broadening the use of propositions in human thought. This led to centuries of Western thought being heavily influenced by propositional thinking. Forgotten was metaphorical rationality, a mode of thinking common to great civilizations around the globe, from ancient times to the present. Metaphor is a commonly used form of rationality in Asia, Africa, Latin America, and the Pacific.

Metaphor is also used throughout the Bible. It might be thought of as visual theology. One of the greatest illustrations of metaphorical theology was

---

[477] *Ibid., Abstract.* A discussion as to how metaphor can assist in communication in civil engineering in urban construction projects has been offered by Ana Roldán-Riejos, "Types of metaphor in civil engineering communication." *Revista Española de Lingüística Aplicada*, 2013, 105-122.
https://www.google.com/search?q=Rold%C3%A1n-Riejos%2C+Ana.+(2013).+Types+of+metaphor+in+civil+engineering+communication.+Revista+Espanola+de+Linguistica+Aplicada.+105-122&rlz=1C1GCEA_enUS832US832&oq=Rold%C3%A1n-Riejos%2C+Ana.+(2013).+Types+of+metaphor+in+civil+engineering+communication.+Revista+Espanola+de+Linguistica+Aplicada.+105-122&aqs=chrome.69i57.2630j0j15&sourceid=chrome&ie=UTF-8. Accessed September 7, 2020.

[478] Two classic examples of the use of metaphor in theology have been used in ecclesiology. Sometimes they have been called "images," as in Paul S. Minear, *Images of the Church in the New Testament*, Philadelphia: Westminster, 1960. Other times they have been called "models," as in Avery Dulles, *Models of the Church in the New Testament*. N. Y.: Doubleday, 1974, 1978, 1991, 2002.

the tabernacle. Called the "tent of meeting" and the "tent of the covenant," the tabernacle of the wilderness in Exodus was a visual representation of the covenantal relationship of God with God's People. This visual or metaphorical theology was the foundational pattern for the construction of Solomon's temple – and subsequent temples – in Jerusalem. Much biblical theology is in fact metaphorical theology. Think, for example, of the Song of Solomon. Think of the prophets. In the New Testament, Jesus' parables are essentially metaphorical theology.

Paul's Use of Metaphor

For years we have read Paul through a lens of propositional rationality. We often think of Paul as a scholar, teacher, theologian, and missionary evangelist. But Paul was first and foremost a businessman, an urbanite who supported his mission by means of his craft (I Thess 2:9).[479] From the first day of the week (our Sunday) until mid-day on the sixth day of the week (our Friday), Paul plied his trade. Paul was a businessman writing to followers of Jesus in the cities of his world. And he thought and wrote metaphorically. The preponderance of Western biblical theologies and commentaries on the book of Romans that have been written from a mostly propositional approach has overshadowed for many of us the way Paul used metaphor in his theological reflection.[480] Though he extensively used propositional thinking in his theological method, the Apostle Paul also valued the use of metaphor.

---

[479] Many commentaries on Paul strikingly fail to take into consideration his urban lens.

[480] In Ephesians, for example, Paul uses at least fifteen different word pictures. The most important of these are saints (used nine times), body (used eight times), soldier with armor (used eight times), and wife (used seven times). A series of lesser images embellish the major conceptions: chosen people of God (used four times), children or family (used four times), workmanship, building, or temple (used three times), a song of praise or offering (used two times), a new humanity, or new self (used two times). Finally, a whole range of images flash once: the breadth, length, height and depth of God's love, imitators of God, kingdom of Christ, children of light, wise people, and ambassadors. These lucid metaphors are verbal photographs that help us understand the nature of the Church as Paul describes it in Ephesians. See Charles Van Engen. *God's Missionary People: Rethinking the Purpose of the Local Church*. G.R.: Baker, 1991, 48-49.

In his letters to the city churches most of which he himself had founded, Paul develops his understanding of mission around the ideas of faith, love, and hope.[481] As if it were a kind of signature, Paul salted his letters with references to that triad of missiological ideas. Mixing their order, and interweaving them with other contextual agendas, Paul gives us a glimpse of what might be called the "*habitus*," the glue that holds together his mission theology. In what follows, the order of love, faith, and hope gives a sense of movement on the road to God's future.[482]

Looking over the metaphors highlighted in the chapters of this book, I realized that a common thread is God's trinitarian mission that expresses this triad in the city. Love involves the present-oriented relationships that seek the welfare of the city. Faith draws from the past revelation and past formative experiences and has to do with new hearts and minds. Hope is the future direction of the city, with vision, purpose, and transformation that seeks to change the present reality toward a new future. Here is a summary outline of the triad in terms of God's mission in the city.

LOVE: God Loves the City[483]

In I Cor 13:13, Paul writes the church in Corinth, "And now faith, hope, and love abide, these three; and the greatest of these is love." (NRSV) We might echo Paul by saying that the greatest lived-out demonstration of God's mission in the city is *agape*, self-giving love of neighbor (Matt 19:19; 22:39; Mk 12:31; Rom 13:9; Gal 5:14; James 2:8). The psalmist says, "God is in the midst of the city: it shall not be moved" (Ps 46:5 NRSV).

---

[481] See, for example, Rom 5:1-5; Rom 12:9-13; I Cor 13:13; Gal 5:5-6; Eph 1:15; Phil 1:9-11; Col 1:3-6; 2:7; 1:23 coupled with 2:2, 2:7 and 3:14; I Thess 1:3, 5:8; II Thess 1:3 with 2:13-17; I Tim 4:9-12; II Tim 1:5, 13-14; Titus 1:2; Philemon 5-6; and -- however we deal with its authorship -- Hebrews 6:9-12, 18-20. The importance of this triad can be seen in the phenomenal influence that Augustine's *Enchiridian on Faith, Hope, and Love* has had on Christian thought down through the centuries.

[482] Taken from Charles Van Engen. *Transforming Mission Theology*. Pasadena: WCL, 2017, 292-293. For a summary description of a theology of mission flowing from this triad, see *Ibid., 291-302*. The three subsections below are adapted from this chapter.

[483] See, e.g., Charles Van Engen and Jude Tiersma, edits. *God So Loves the City: Seeking a Theology for Urban Mission*. Monrovia: MARC, 1994; reprinted by Wipf & Stock, Eugene, Oregon, 2009.

The biblical story begins in a garden. We know that God loves rural landscapes. But God also loves the city where the concentration of humans is to be found; and God does not wish that any of them should perish (II Peter 3:9). The Bible portrays God as constantly interacting with the city. In this volume, we have seen many different metaphors. Yet they all point us in one direction: God's profound desire for a close covenantal relationship with humans: "I will be their God and they will be my people" echoes loudly throughout the pages of Scripture. (See, e.g., Lev 26:12; II Cor 6:16; Jer 30:22; 31:33; Ezek 11:20; Zech 8:8.)

If we love the city, we will want to study the city and seek to understand the city. We will want to immerse ourselves in the storied history of our city. Metaphors help us do that. They help us embrace the full reality of our city. Our mission flows from God's heart for the city and our comprehension of God's commitment to the city.

FAITH: God's People are Sent to the City

God's People are given the opportunity to give concrete expression to the gospel of Jesus Christ, in word, deed, and presence. It is only possible to contextualize this gospel if we understand the city where the Good News of God's grace is being lived out. Too often we tend to consider the city as merely the place where we can achieve our personal goals. We tend to forget that we are sent to live our faith in the city. Rather than being a place where we consume, our city becomes the place where we grow in understanding of the gospel of God's grace in Jesus Christ, a gospel that calls us to give of ourselves for the wellbeing of others. Luke illustrates this commitment to the city in his summary statement at the end of the Book of Acts, by mentioning that Paul is in house arrest in Rome, announcing the coming of the kingdom of God in Jesus Christ (Acts 28:30-31).

It is not enough to know God's heart for the city. We must also understand both the gospel and the city. Mission from faith will mean a continued search for ways in which our faith may be public faith. This involves wrestling with the straitjacket of the Enlightenment that has forced the concept of faith into a private expression of individual taste, as Lesslie Newbigin has demonstrated.[484] Missionary faith inevitably, rightly, and powerfully must be a public faith.

Mission from faith through the Holy Spirit will occur when the fruit of the Holy Spirit emanates through the lives of the People of God (Gal 5:22-26). Down through the history of mission, one would wish that the motivations, means, and goals of Christian mission had been more thoroughly permeated with love, joy, peace, patience, kindness, goodness, faithfulness, gentleness, and self—control. For the Church to be credible, it will need to conduct its mission as an expression of the fruit of the Spirit, conscious of Christ's lordship lived out by God's People in the cities of our world.[485]

HOPE: God Dwells in the City, in the Power of the Holy Spirit

Hope is possibly the most explosive concept that the Christian church has to offer. There is hope in the city and for the city because God dwells there. In Acts 2, the coming of the Holy Spirit at Pentecost happens in the city of Jerusalem. The gospel of the kingdom is announced in the streets of that city.

Today we are a long way from the unbelievable optimism of a hundred years ago regarding Western civilization and technology. These proved themselves to be empty and misguided and should not blind us to the impact that hope can have on the way people participate in God's mission. During the exile, the Israelites seem to have wavered between hopelessness and hope and the difference entailed a distinct hermeneutic of God's mission and their role in it. On the one hand, they were prone to moan, "How can we sing a song in a foreign land?" (Ps 137:4). But others followed the lead of Daniel and Esther. Theirs was a hope-filled approach that even the weeping prophet Jeremiah called for. "Build houses and live in them; plant gardens and eat their produce. Take wives and have sons and daughters.... Multiply there, and do not decrease. But seek the welfare of the city where I have sent you into exile, and

---

[484] See Lesslie Newbigin, *Foolishness to the Greeks: The Gospel and Western Culture.* G.R.: Eerdmans, 1986 and Lesslie Newbigin, *The Gospel in a Pluralist Society.* G.R.: Eerdmans, 1989.
[485] Adapted from Charles Van Engen, 2017, *op cit,* 294-295.

pray to the Lord on its behalf, for in its welfare you will find your welfare" (Jer 29:6-7).

A missiology of hope means that Christians care so deeply about their city that they will risk hoping for something new. They dare hope because they know that in Christ's reign, God's grace through faith brings about a radical and total transformation. In the city of Corinth, the message went out: "Therefore, if anyone is in Christ, (that one) is a new creation; the old has gone, the new has come!" (II Cor 5:17). A missiology of hope means that Christians dare to believe that together they can change the world. This is at the heart of mission. This missiology of hope is deeply and creatively transformational, for it seeks to be a sign of the present and coming reign of God. Through it, we recognize our profound commitment to radical transformation when we pray, "Your Kingdom Come" (Matt 6: 10). This involves change in all dimensions: structures and communities as well as the persons who inhabit them.

One day we will together enter a new city, the New Jerusalem. We will stand before the throne of the Lamb of God (Rev 7:14) who takes away the sin of the world (John 1:29). The Lamb is seated on the throne in the City of God. "The city does not need the sun or the moon...for the glory of God gives it light, and the Lamb is its lamp" (Rev 21:23). "The glory and honor of the nations will be brought into" this city (Rev 21:26). And flowing from the throne of the Lamb, down the middle of the great street of this city is the river of the water of life (Rev 22: 1-2) "whose streams make glad the city of God" (Ps 46:4). On each side of the river, we see the tree of life whose leaves "are for the healing of the nations" (Rev 22:2). There is hope for the city – now and not yet.

Dear reader, as you have caught a glimpse of God's mission through the kaleidoscope of these chapters, our hope for you is two-fold. First, we hope that these and other metaphors will encourage you to seek to understand the city where you have been placed and desire to see the reign of God come to that place. Secondly, we hope that these metaphors will challenge you to seek the welfare of the city to which you have been sent (Jer 29: 7). Our prayer continues to be, "Your Kingdom come, your will be done" in the city. May it be so.

CPSIA information can be obtained
at www.ICGtesting.com
Printed in the USA
LVHW020426200423
744689LV00002B/212